LEADING FROM EVERYWHERE

THE PRINCIPLES & PRACTICES OF CHARACTER BASED LEADERSHIP

GREGORY G. CAMPEAU

 FriesenPress

Suite 300 - 990 Fort St
Victoria, BC, V8V 3K2
Canada

www.friesenpress.com

ISBN
978-1-5255-5144-4 (Hardcover)
978-1-5255-5145-1 (Paperback)
978-1-5255-5146-8 (eBook)

1. BUSINESS & ECONOMICS, MANAGEMENT SCIENCE

Distributed to the trade by The Ingram Book Company

CONTENTS

PART 1: Creating Context 1

1. Welcome to Our Whitewater World
2. The Future Ain't What It Used to Be
3. Retooling for the Age of Turbulence – The Leadership Imperative
4. An Introduction to the Four Dimensions of Leadership

PART 2: An Enquiry into Leadership 31

5. Defining Leadership is Like Trying to Nail Jell-O to the Wall
6. Dispelling the Most Common Leadership Myths
7. Piecing Together the Leadership Puzzle

PART 3: Foundations in Personal & Interpersonal Effectiveness 67

8. Neuroscience – The Biology of Behaviour
9. They Call It Human Nature for a Good Reason
10. Emotional Intelligence – The Myths & the Mastery

PART 4: Personal Leadership – Optimizing Potential & Productivity 113

11. Strategic Self-Development
12. Life Leadership – The Poor Sailor Blames the Wind
13. Getting Things Done – Optimizing Personal Productivity

PART 5: Interpersonal Leadership – People Skills 101 163

14. Negotiating – The Tactical Side of Leadership
15. The Natural Laws of Interpersonal Dynamics
16. Three Leadership Core Conversational Competencies

PART 6: Team Leadership – Leading a High-Performance Team 207

17. Teamworx – High Performance Team & Team Players
18. Seven Roles of a Highly Effective Team Leader
19. Coaching and Feedback

PART 7: Organizational Leadership – Leading a High-Performance Organization 257

20. The High-Performance Twenty-First-Century Organization
21. Creating a Customer-Focused Culture of Engagement

For my beautiful wife, Pamela, without whom
this book would never be possible

WHY THIS BOOK?

With just a little contemplation, the undeniable ultimate truth becomes evident – that everything rises and falls on leadership: families, teams, organizations, communities, civilizations and, ultimately, our lives. The most painful leadership paradox is that the need for leadership has never been greater, and yet it is becoming increasingly difficult to locate truly effective leaders. Across the board, from politics to education, entertainment and organizations, both private and public sectors, the critical question today is where have all the true leaders gone?

I believe there is a character crisis; our society is suffering from truth decay. As a result, I fear we are all in the fast lane on the road to ruin. The societal red lights are flashing, and the signs of deterioration are everywhere. I encounter far too many low-trust (and thus dysfunctional) organizations, teams and families. Broken people and relationships abound. The frequency of bullying, homelessness, depression and suicide are growing at an alarming rate as pharmaceutical companies reap ever-increasing profits from the sale of anti-depressant drugs. Many individuals (and organizations) are increasingly anxious and insecure as they find themselves unmoored in a whitewater world, forever doomed to be buffeted by the strong winds of fate and circumstance.

It was Stephen Covey who first opened my eyes to the concept of "character." In the introduction to the most influential personal-development book ever written, he explained that all wisdom or success literature focused on character development as the foundation of success up until the earlier part of the last century, when he noticed the focus shifted from the "character ethic" to the "personality ethic." Most personal-development literature written in the last hundred years has focused on technique-based, quick-fix suggestions and solutions such as power communication skills and how to feign interest in your boss's hobbies.

Some of the personality ethic techniques and strategies are not without value; however, if truncated from character development, they can only provide short-term success at best. The simple truth is that, whenever a group of people, whether an organization, team, association, civilization or family, becomes more focused on consumption (getting – rights and privileges) than contribution (giving – service, duty and responsibilities), it will inevitably be doomed. The need for leadership is growing daily, and yet the question remains: where have all the leaders gone?

The allure of short-term, quick-fix solutions is powerful indeed, and I fear we have become an infomercial society focused on immediate gratification, fascinated with wealth-without-work, and band-aid and aspirin solutions. The problem is that you can't cure a disease with painkillers. There are simply no shortcuts to achieving true leadership effectiveness. Superficial solutions simply no longer work for the changing challenges we all now face. To succeed in the twenty-first century requires a fundamentally new mindset, skillset and toolset, which can be captured in one word – leadership! I have learned that there can be no true, sustainable leadership success unless it is built upon the bedrock of character.

Since the 1970s, our educational system no longer focuses on character development. The well-intended shift toward building the student's self-esteem has proven to be fundamentally flawed, and the educational hens are now coming home to roost. Every, and I mean every, employer complains desperately that it is becoming increasingly difficult to recruit young people with a good work ethic who are willing to accept feedback and compete in the rough-and-tumble real world where people do keep score.

We are living in a time when our prospects for success are increasingly dependent upon our leadership abilities. In this book, I offer inspiration and practical guidance to effectively meet the unpredictable challenges, both personal and professional, that we are confronted with now.

The original title of the book was *Leading from Everywhere in the Organization*, but as I began to outline the book, I realized this was not expansive enough, and that it should be *Leading from Everywhere in Your Life*. So, for the sake of brevity and simplicity, I landed on the short version – *Leading from Everywhere*.

HOW THIS BOOK IS DIFFERENT

This book is ambitiously holistic as I attempt to take a sweeping, panoramic perspective on the broadest of topics. My hope is that it will serve as a catalyst for your leadership development by sparing you from doing further research on leadership competencies. The four interrelated principles that guided me in writing this book are simplicity, practicality, conciseness and readability.

Simplicity

I am big believer in the KISS principle; the trick is to keep things simple without being simplistic. Highly effective leaders do this by identifying and then focusing on the key few things (20%) that make the most difference (80%). In every endeavour, these few key things are called the fundamentals or basics.

Practicality

Leadership literature tends to be chock-a-block full of psychological mumbo-jumbo and the dried pabulum of academic theory, but in this book, I attempt to bridge the wide gap between the theoretical and the practical. My advice is competency-based and designed to achieve the results that define effective leadership, creating walk-away value for you, the reader, and allowing you to apply what you learn. This book teaches both the principles (the **why** to do) and practices (the **what** and **how** to do) of truly effective leadership.

The walk-away value is about learning the practices, so I kindly request you be patient, as you must first understand the principles before learning the practices. The true practical power in this book lies in your own self-discovery through the sometimes-painful process of objective self-assessment. Galileo said, "You cannot teach a person anything. You can only help them discover it within themselves." I encourage you to also see yourself as a teacher of this material. The research is very clear that people learn to the degree that they are motivated to learn. If you read this book assuming you will have the opportunity to teach it to other people, it will optimize your learning process.

LEADING FROM EVERYWHERE

THE PRINCIPLES & PRACTICES OF CHARACTER-BASED LEADERSHIP

PART 1: CREATING CONTEXT

1. Welcome to Our Whitewater World
2. The Future Ain't What It Used to Be
3. Retooling for the Age of Turbulence – The Leadership Imperative
4. An Introduction to the Four Dimensions of Leadership

CHAPTER 1: WELCOME TO OUR WHITEWATER WORLD

Many people feel there has been a premature arrival of the future, and they find themselves cut adrift without a rudder in a whitewater world. In this chapter, I will create a context or frame of reference for the book by explaining what changes are happening in our world and why.

Early in my leadership workshop, I ask participants to discuss in small groups the following question: is our world today more like a freeway system or a wilderness? Most people's initial reaction, given the speed we are expected to move at today, is that our world seems more like a freeway system. However, upon further consideration, most groups come to the conclusion that the world today is much more like the wilderness or jungle than a freeway system because of greater unpredictability. I think perhaps the industrial-age world was more like a freeway, and whatever age we are in now is much more like a jungle. The most creative groups realize our harsh reality is that we are in a highly unpredictable jungle, and to compound the challenge, we are simultaneously expected to move at freeway-like speeds.

I then ask them this: if the world is more like the freeway system, what tool would be a greater value to you, an accurate map of the freeway system or a compass? (I always have to remind my engineering clients in the audience not to say GPS.) Participants consistently agree that, if the world is more freeway-like, then the tool of choice would be an accurate map; however, if the world is more like a jungle or wilderness, then there is a consistently broad consensus that the compass holds the greater value, as maps quickly become obsolete. I then ask this: if the world today were more analogous to a freeway system, then what would be of greater value, management ability or leadership ability? It always amazes me how intuitively and quickly my audiences respond to the question, as if the answer is obvious. We all have a compass, as we will discuss in Part 4, but tragically, many people never even take it out of their pocket.

Make no mistake, we are in the midst of something really big. We are going through historic, seismic changes on a global level. And yet, from our day-to-day and week-to-week perspective, we don't fully appreciate the magnitude of the ground-shaking changes we are all now experiencing. The great Canadian social scientist Marshall McLuhan said, about a half-century ago, "I don't know who discovered water, but I'm almost positive it wasn't the fish." I think one interpretation of McLuhan's quote would be that, once we are too close to something or become immersed in it, we don't see or fully understand and thus appreciate what's happening in the moment. I don't think people were walking around during the Renaissance, a few centuries ago, asking each other, "How are you enjoying the Renaissance?" It is only in retrospect that we are able to gain a loftier perspective and understand with accuracy what was really happening in the broader context of history.

So please allow me to take the grandest historical perspective to assist us in understanding the historic significance of what we're going through by borrowing from a British author named Alvin Toffler, who wrote a trilogy of books a few decades back. I found Toffler's second book, *The Third Wave*, particularly useful in helping me understand and appreciate the causes and magnitude of the universal disruption we are all now experiencing.

In the largest-scale synthesis of human history, Toffler uses the wave metaphor to explain the evolution of civilization throughout the millennia. He suggests the first wave of human civilization began approximately 10,000 years ago all around the planet when our species began to move away from hunting and gathering and into what Toffler refers to as the "agrarian age," which involved the domestication of plants and animals. This wave of human civilization lasted for about 9,750 years, give or take fifty years, before the advent of the second wave, which Toffler called the "industrial age." In 1900, a full 50% of North Americans lived on farms; by 1950, it had dropped to 5% and today it is down to 3%. There are still some vestiges of the agrarian model of society left today; for example, school is still out in the summer so the children can help bring in the crops. I have three grown children, and for the life of me, I can't seem to recall much harvesting taking place in our household throughout their educational years.

Toffler suggested that the emergence of the third wave began in the 1950s when there were more white-collar than blue-collar workers in North America and Western Europe. The only label Toffler gave the third wave was the "post-smokestack era." He suggested there has been an acceleration of history, in that events that used to take decades, if not centuries, to unfold are now happening in months, weeks or even days. The waves keep coming faster. Whereas the agricultural ways lasted for approximately 10,000 years, the industrial age has spent most of its energy after only 300 years.

A number of waves have happened so rapidly, crashing upon us, that only in retrospect will we be able to label them. I am old enough to remember the '60s, when the first label of the third wave was applied; we were told we were in the "space age," and everybody was drinking Tang, just like the astronauts did. Since the '60s, there have been attempts to apply a label to the age we are in, such as the "post-industrial age," the "information age," the "microchip era," the "age of technology," the "age of turbulence," the "age of paradox," the "age of anxiety," the "digital age" and the latest one I've encountered – the "exponential age."

Perhaps we have catapulted through multiple ages in the last few decades that we don't yet fully recognize, but whatever you want to call the age we are now in, leadership is becoming more important by the day.

The expression "whitewater world" comes from a landmark book called *Blown to Bits*, which was written by Philip Evans and Thomas Wurster in 2000. In it, they attempted to explain the forces driving the explosive and accelerative change we are now experiencing. Here are the seven interrelated driving factors of change.

1) **The globalization of markets and technologies:** It is truly a borderless world as new technologies shatter traditional barriers, changing what were once local and regional marketplaces into global marketplaces.

2) **The emergence of universal connectivity:** The linear, hardwired and controlled communication channels of the industrial age have dissolved, becoming obsolete almost overnight.

3) **The democratization of information:** The old adage is true – information is power and can no longer be controlled. The sudden democratization of information has shifted traditional power structures around the world in all dimensions of society. The old expression "power to the people" is becoming more of a reality by the day as old power and authority structures melt away.

4) **An exponential increase in competition:** New technologies mean that in many sectors of the economy, anyone with a computer is a potential new competitor. Unforeseen and completely unpredictable new forms of competition can neutralize strategic competitive advantages almost immediately, wiping out companies and even entire industries in the blink of an eye.

5) **Movement of wealth creation from financial capital to human capital:** In the industrial age, the most important assets were capital assets in the form of plants and equipment. In the information age, the most important asset is people in the form of intellectual and social capital.

6) **Free agency:** As people become more aware of their options and alternatives than ever before, they are no longer looking for jobs for life, but rather see themselves as free-agent contractors or hired guns. Company loyalty is quickly dissolving, and it is estimated that people graduating high school between 2005 and 2015 will have somewhere between seven to eleven jobs in their careers.

7) **Permanent whitewater:** We are being thrust into an increasingly unpredictable future faster than any generation to previously walk this planet. We must accept the hard reality that we are now in a constantly changing, churning, choppy world of perpetual turbulence. A client CEO recently said that, if you think you know what's going on, it only means you're

really confused. She added that trying to manage a business today is like trying to play badminton in a hurricane. The rate of change is already at a neck-snapping, jaw-dropping speed, and if you think there was lot of change up until now, fasten your seatbelt and hold on tight because we are all in for a wild ride into the future.

Our parents and grandparents, in the predictable and relatively stagnant industrial age that we all left only a few short decades ago, could gain their personal security by looking downstream in their life and with a high degree of accuracy project what it would look like. Your professional life in the industrial age was largely about getting into a big company, keeping your nose clean and getting out in forty-two years with a gold watch, which is exactly what my father did. That world no longer exists, and that is rapidly becoming painfully evident to many people. The whitewater world of the twenty-first century has been a boon for the pharmaceutical industry, as many people are completely unprepared for the challenges we all now face. They are in a state Alvin Toffler referred to as "future shock," which means they are constantly overwhelmed from the unrelenting and increasing rate of change and are anxious about the uncertainty of the future.

Here in the "age of anxiety," we are all being consistently confronted with a couple of vitally important questions. First, if we can no longer derive our personal security by accurately predicting our future, then where do we acquire our personal security? Second, why is it that some people see the future coming at us faster than ever before in human history as an abundance of low-hanging fruit, while other people see it as an anxiety-producing, menacing threat? I will do my very best to answer these crucial and pressing questions.

CHAPTER 2: THE FUTURE AIN'T WHAT IT USED TO BE

It was the poet laureate of baseball, Yogi Berra, who once claimed, "The future ain't what it used to be." This illogical truth is much more relevant today than when he said it seventy years ago. In Chapter 1, I explained why we are experiencing accelerating rates of change. In Chapter 2, I'm going to help you understand how our world is changing and what all these changes mean to us.

How Customers Have Changed

Customers today are more knowledgeable, sophisticated, value-conscious and informed of their options, but most of all (my workshop participants all agree) more demanding. They seem to want things free, perfect and yesterday. Customer loyalty is dissolving. We are now in the "value era" – if you don't deliver the product or service customers want when they want it, how they want it, at the price they want it, they will simply vote with their feet and take their wallets with them. The reason they can behave in such a manner is that choice gives them more power, and they are ready, willing and able to use it. The key question now is what do these more-demanding customers mean to the organizations and people who deal with them?

How Competition Has Changed

Your grandparents competed with someone across the street, your parents competed with someone across the city, and now we are expected to compete (and be benchmarked against) competitors from around the world. According to *Ward's Automotive Journal* in 1950, 76% of all the cars in the world were manufactured in North America; by 2001, it had dropped to only 22%.

Sudden out-of-the-blue technological advances that are completely unpredictable can change the competitive dynamics overnight, and marketplace advantages can be gained or lost almost instantly. In 1998, Kodak had 170,000 employees worldwide and a dominant 85% of the massive global photo-paper market. By 2001, a short three years later, Kodak was bankrupt. New forms of Internet competition have been particularly brutal on the retail sector. By the year 2020, it is estimated that a full 25% of shopping malls in North America will be mothballed or utilized for civic activities, such as walking places for seniors. Industry after industry, from razor blades to mattresses, all brick-and-mortar retailers are fighting a very painful and losing battle against new low-cost, online competitors that are gobbling up market share once held by traditional retailers.

How Organizations Have Changed

There are only two types of organizations these days – those that are changing and those that are failing. Of all the changes organizations face, such as mergers, acquisitions, restructuring and decentralization, the two most significant in the last few decades are that they have been flattened by taking out layers of management, and downsizing has placed increased productivity pressure on all employees. It is now a stripped-down, every-job-counts workplace environment. It is not uncommon to find departments that had a dozen employees a few years ago now down to seven employees, and those seven employees are expected to produce the same amount as the twelve did. The common refrain in all organizations, both public and private sector, is "next year we're just going to have to learn to do more with less."

How the Nature of Work Has Changed

Work itself has changed. It's not about muscle anymore; it's about the mind. It's not about manual skills; it's about thinking skills. It's not about brawn-power; it's about brainpower. Just a few decades ago, job descriptions were clear, and roles were well-defined. I worked in a car factory through the summer months to pay for my schooling, and my job was to stamp and stack 110 manifolds in my seven-and-a-half-hour shift. I knew when my job started, and I knew when my work was done. The administrative people in the office would have a stack of paper in their in-basket that they would stamp and staple and put into the out-basket. Jobs in the industrial age were more structured and black-and-white. However, when it comes to knowledge work, the key questions become what is it that needs to be done? And once started, when is it done? The nature of knowledge work demands we change from an industrial age efficiency mindset to an information age effectiveness mindset, which we will explore in detail later in the book.

How the Workplace Has Changed

I believe the most significant change that has occurred between the workplace of the industrial age and the workplace of today is that the nature of knowledge work is far more complex, which has driven an ever-greater need for interdependence in the workplace. It is estimated that knowledge workers (a term coined by Peter Drucker) spend 70% to 80% of their waking hours in one of the four forms of communication – reading, writing, speaking or listening.

In response to the need for ever-greater interdependence, the physical nature of the workspace has also been changing as fewer people have an office and many people have been relegated to a cubicle. Many large organizations are now employing the "hotelling" workplace philosophy, which means there are no longer permanent workspaces. The idea of hotelling is that, when you arrive at work, you locate an empty cubicle to plug in and work for the day, and the next day you find a new place to locate. In the industrial age, prime office space would be reserved for executive offices, but today prime office space is dedicated for meeting space.

The Germans created the open-office concept in the 1950s to enhance teamwork and communication; to facilitate the changing office structure, an

American efficiency expert named Robert Propst invented the cubicle. Referred to as the "father of the cubicle," later in life, he regretted this invention. He had originally designed the cubicle to promote productivity and privacy and failed to foresee how organizations would turn them into cost-saving cubicle farms to maximize office space. Today, many people working in cubicles, who are under ever-increasing productivity pressure, complain that their entire day in the helter-skelter, free-for-all open office environment is just one big daylong interruption. A growing number of knowledge workers report that they have to come into the office extra early before the war starts and then end up staying late, when the office chaos subsides, so they can get some real work done.

The following comparison chart summarizes the dramatic changes to the workplace that have occurred over the last few decades.

INDUSTRIAL-AGE WORKPLACE	INFORMATION-AGE WORKPLACE
Clearly defined, fixed jobs	More ambiguous, constant job redefinition
Command and control hierarchy	Empowered cross-functional teams
Vertical silos	Horizontally fluid network
Limited, linear communication	Multidimensional communication
Managers did the thinking	Everyone responsible for thinking
Focus energy on the boss	Focus energy on the customer
Strict managerial supervision	Accountable independence
Focus on performing tasks	Focus on contribution, adding value
Information held by management	Information flow is everyone's job
Decisions made at top	Decisions made at front line
Low need to acquire knowledge and skills	High need to acquire knowledge and skills
The domain of **MANAGERS**	The domain of **LEADERS**

How Employees Have Changed

As discussed, employees today are simply less loyal (with good reason). I frequently ask my seminar participants how employees have changed. The one word that quickly, consistently and emphatically surfaces is "entitled." Managers and business owners are lamenting that many young people don't appear to have the same work ethic as previous generations and seem much more concerned with work–life balance. Unlike my generation, who it might be said *lived to work*, more recent generations have a new ethos: *work to live*. In my generation and that of my parents, work was an end itself, and our work defined who we were. The new generations tend to see work as a means to an end of the lifestyle they want to achieve.

Unlike in the past, employees today will no longer blindly follow orders from above. They want to be involved in decision making. They will overtly push back against anything they don't agree with or see value in doing and will ask why things have to be done in a certain way. They are more aware of their rights and will demand to be treated respectfully. They are also more aware of their options, and if they feel they are not treated fairly or properly, they will quickly leave.

How Management Philosophy Has Changed

As a result of all these changes, our paradigm of managing the human asset has had to change. Those organizations that have failed to evolve their management philosophy are gone or soon to be gone.

The industrial revolution had hit full stride in North America and Western Europe in the latter part of the nineteenth century. The problem was, at that point in history, we had no idea how to organize and coordinate people into a big building called a factory. The only two organizational models available to emulate a century ago were the military and the Catholic Church.

The very first book ever written on organizational or management theory was by Henri Fayol, who was a manager in the coal mines of Southern France. In 1908, he wrote a book called *The Principles of Administration*. The title is self-explanatory in that the leaders of the day would be those were best able to administer, which meant planning, organizing, delegating and controlling. One could argue that the most significant or influential book on management theory was *The Principles of Scientific Management*, written in 1911 by Sir Frederick Winslow Taylor.

Fayol and Taylor are widely considered the two fathers of modern management theory, and it was these two books that provided the theoretical underpinnings of the first management philosophy or paradigm. Since then, there has been a constant and increasingly rapid evolution of management philosophy over the last hundred years in the Western world. Those organizations that have failed to evolve their approach on how they manage the human asset simply cannot compete with organizations that have changed, and thus they are no longer with us.

Allow me to provide a brief historical perspective on how the approach or philosophy of managing people has morphed and is continuing to do so. I will borrow Toffler's metaphor of waves because it is appropriate to view each of the paradigms as growing out of or upon the previous waves. There are also traces of each wave still apparent today.

Scientific Management Wave (1870–1920s)

In 1900, only 10% of North Americans had graduated senior matriculation or what we now know as high school. The first wave of management philosophy saw people as machines. Job simplification and separation were order-of-the-day to allow unsophisticated people to perform basic, repetitive, mindless tasks; to this end, Henry Ford invented the assembly line. Organizations were highly hierarchical and governed with a command-and-control philosophy, where the managers did the thinking and the workers did the working. It was in those days when we first began to refer to people as superiors and subordinates. These titles leave little doubt as to the underpinning managerial philosophy. The bosses wanted to be called superior because they actually thought they were, and we called the lowly frontline workers subordinates because they were evidently sub-ordinary.

Human Relations Wave (1930s)

In a landmark study conducted by Albert Mayo at a General Electric manufacturing facility in Hawthorne, Indiana, about eighty years ago, he achieved an unintended and somewhat surprising conclusion – if you paid attention to people and treated them nicely, they would work harder and become more productive. So began the emergence of the second wave, and it was a kinder, gentler way to manage people. It was a form of benevolent authoritarianism; the decisions were still made at the top and then the foot soldiers were given strict, rigid guidelines as to how to implement the executive decisions. For the first time, personnel departments (which we ideally now referred to as "human resource management departments") began to appear. I find it somewhat ironic that the original human resources people reported up to accountants – it was the finance department that had the payroll data, so who else would take on this new responsibility?

Human Resource Wave (1960s)

Although the fathers of the TQM (or total quality management) movement were both Americans, named Deming and Durant, the TQM movement was first wholeheartedly embraced by Japanese industry shortly after the Second World War. It had been rejected by North American industries, which were fat and happy and saw no real need to change. The adoption of the TQM principles allowed Japan to become a dominant manufacturing force in almost every major industry, from automobiles to steel to electronics, for a few decades. The simple and central guiding principle of the TQM movement was that the people closest to the problem should be the ones solving it.

It wasn't until the 1960s that the very first trace of "participative management" (what we now call "empowerment") appeared. Executives, realizing that customers wanted faster answers, finally understood that there were many bright, eager and capable people lower down in the organization who actually knew what was really happening and that perhaps all the decisions should not be made in the ivory tower of the executive boardrooms. The human resource wave meant that, for the first time in the economic history of the Western world, the **intellectual** capacities of people were recognized as something to be developed and leveraged. Independent human resources departments emerged. Peter Drucker first introduced the concept of empowerment under the banner, MBO (management by objective). This first attempt to push decision-making authority down into the organization was largely unsuccessful, as it became apparent that people at all levels of the organization were simply not ready for this fundamental change. This wave also saw the creation of training and development departments, as organizations realized for the first time that, if they wanted their companies to grow, they first had to have their people grow.

Empowerment Wave (1980s)

It was in the '80s when the impact of globalization began to be felt in painful ways for many organizations. Whereas in the industrial age the most important assets were capital assets, it became increasingly apparent that the most important asset was now the human asset, and the only path to maintaining competitiveness in the now-global arena was to unleash the potential, creativity, energy and commitment that largely lay dormant within the human asset in many organizations. It became equally apparent that the only true pathway to achieving higher degrees of employee engagement was by empowering them. This wave recognized that people want to be involved in doing something meaningful. It was also becoming painfully evident that traditional management philosophies and strategies were dangerously obsolete, and the essential ingredient for empowerment to take root and bring forth its benefits was **leadership demonstrated by managers and supervisors.**

Entrepreneurial Wave (1990s)

This wave quickly followed and built upon the "empowerment wave." Empowerment is giving people freedom to make their own decisions on how to do a given task. Getting employees to act as entrepreneurs goes beyond giving freedom on how to do a task and expands to giving people the authority to determine what tasks to do and when. Incessant customer demands for ever-faster response times, the greater need for innovation and the need for speed to market driven by shorter product development cycles pushed many organizations beyond the empowerment philosophy, as they needed people to take full and immediate initiative and not wait for direction from above. It was obvious that the hierarchical organization was no longer viable in a marketplace that demands fast, flexible responses to changing customer needs and competitive pressures. The entrepreneurial philosophy requires that all employees essentially act as their own boss. This requires everyone to maintain a holistic, enterprise-wide perspective because the desired outcome of this philosophy is for employees to think, make decisions and behave as if they "own the company." The essential ingredient for empowerment to work is **leadership demonstrated by everyone, everywhere in the organization.**

Holocracy Wave (2000s)

The most recent managerial model represents the complete death of the hierarchy and job titles. Perhaps it is best described as the "no-boss" model of an organization. Companies such as Zappos, Whole Foods Market, Gore-Tex and MorningStar Farms have adopted this new approach. These highly progressive organizations are best described as a community, a web or a fluid network made up of self-forming and self-managing teams. I have one client who has adopted this model, and I question whether it will work as many employees find it chaotic and disorderly. I believe that, for this new approach to work, it will require a very high degree of **leadership and self-accountability demonstrated by all employees.**

*Side note – As a serious student of history, I am convinced that everything has changed throughout human history except for one thing: **human nature**, or the nature within us, which we will explore in Part 3 of the book.

The most important learning takeaway from this brief historical perspective on the evolution of management philosophy is that the **need for leadership to be demonstrated at all levels in the organization has become increasingly vital with each successive wave** and will continue into our ever-faster approaching future!

Now that we know how everything is changing, the key question to be answered in Chapter 3 is this: what do all these changes mean to you?

CHAPTER 3: RETOOLING FOR THE AGE OF TURBULENCE – THE LEADERSHIP IMPERATIVE

The great evolutionary scientist Charles Darwin hypothesized in his classic book *On the Origin of Species* that survival was not a matter of being the fastest, the strongest or even the smartest; it was adaptability.

The famous historian and anthropologist Arnold Toynbee said that all of human history could be summed up in one paradoxical phrase: "Nothing fails like success." I think Toynbee was trying to help us recognize and appreciate a potentially tragic quirk that is evidently hardwired into our species' chromosomal structure because it keeps reoccurring throughout human history. The destructive quirk is that, as soon as we see ourselves as successful, we have a dangerous tendency to rest upon our laurels. He explained history through what he called his "challenge and response" theory, writing that when the civilization's response to the current environmental challenges was sufficient, this equalled stability and success. However, when the environmental challenges changed and the civilization's response failed to change, this equalled decline and ultimately the destruction of the civilization.

Given that the environmental challenges are changing rapidly, the key question now becomes have we changed our mindset, our skillset and our toolset so we can successfully adapt to the challenges of our new reality?

Peter Drucker, the most important management theorist and visionary of the twenty-first century, suggested that the greatest challenge for knowledge workers would not be the adaptation to new technologies but rather the realization that for the first time in 250 years we are all responsible for ourselves again. This new reality demands personal leadership. Unlike in the industrial age, where the organization was largely responsible for your career path and development, in the new economy the responsibility for your career path and development is completely in your control.

The following jobs have one thing in common: buggy-whip maker, elevator person, candlestick maker, movie projectionist, TV and typewriter repairman, video-store clerk and bank teller. Obsolescence is an increasingly menacing threat as many careers are quickly following suit, such as the factory worker, grocery-store clerk (almost all retail jobs are now vulnerable to replacement), newspaper worker, restaurant server, postal worker and taxi driver. The list grows with each technological improvement.

In the 1930s, a Czechoslovakian economist named Joseph Schumpeter created a concept called "creative destruction" to explain why some industries decline and die out while others are created and grow; this is the economy's method of re-creating itself. It is truly a good news/bad news story. The bad news is that technological advancements render entire industries obsolete and old jobs fade away. The good news is that technological advancements simultaneously create new industries and new jobs are created. The chart below, provided by the US Bureau of the Census, is the best way to illustrate the process of "creative destruction." (X = less than 5,000)

DESTRUCTION	YEAR 2000	PAST
Railroad employees	231,000	2,076,000 (1920)
Carriage and harness makers	X	109,000 (1900)
Telegraph operators	8,000	75,000 (1920)
Boilermakers	X	74,000 (1920)
Cobblers	25,000	102,000 (1900)

DESTRUCTION	YEAR 2000	PAST
Blacksmiths	X	238,000 (1910)
Watchmakers	X	101,000 (1920)
Telephone switch-board operators	213,000	421,000 (1970)
Farm workers	851,000	11,533,000 (1910)

CREATION		
Airline pilots and mechanics	248,000	0 (1910)
Healthcare technicians	6,002,000	X (1910)
Engineers	2,506,000	38,000 (1900)
Computer programmers	2,620,000	X (1950)
Auto mechanics	588,000	0 (1900)
Truck, bus and taxi drivers	4,219,000	0 (1900)
Professional athletes and sports announcers	127,000	X (1920)
Electricians	528,000	51,000 (1910)
Optometrists	21,400	X (1910)

This endless cycle of creative destruction relentlessly moves forward, and the challenge now is that this process is accelerating. This means we have less reaction time to make decisions and recover. The bad news and the hard truth for the twenty-first century is that there is no job security. However, the good news is there is employment security. If you possess the right blend of technical abilities and leadership abilities outlined in this book, there will always be employment or earning opportunities for you.

What Competencies Information-Age Employers Most Value

By now we have established that the game has changed, and the question is have your skill sets changed? Because if they haven't, it's tantamount to trying to play tennis with a golf club. You can play tennis with a golf club but it's very difficult, and I suspect you will not win often.

So what are the new core competencies that are required to succeed in the information-age workplace? Some recent research can assist us in pinpointing the skills and abilities that are a prerequisite for success.

A recent study by the US Department of Labor surveyed a massive number of human resource managers with the goal of identifying (aside from the specific technical skills required) what portable skills they most looked for when recruiting new employees. The survey responses were as follows:

1. Interpersonal effectiveness – the ability to build constructive relationships, be an effective team player and resolve conflict in a constructive manner
2. Ability to learn on the job
3. Ability to respond creatively to obstacles and setbacks
4. Adaptability – comfort dealing with change and ambiguity
5. Good oral communication skills, especially listening skills
6. Capacity to take initiative
7. Good time- and stress-management skills

A few years back, Harvard asked prospective employers what competencies they most valued when recruiting Harvard MBA students. These were the four most desired capabilities:

- Communication skills
- Interpersonal skills
- Capacity to take initiative
- Humility

If one were to analyze the research and distill into one word the most valuable competency in the information-age workplace, there is absolutely no doubt it would be **leadership**.

In the command-and-control world of the industrial age, the managers could get things done using the carrot and stick that came with a position power or formal authority granted by royal decree called an organizational chart. In that environment, leadership abilities were a luxury to have; however, in the new information-age workplace, with the focus on responsiveness, engagement, teamwork, empowerment and customer relations, leadership abilities are no longer a luxury – they are an absolute success imperative!

CHAPTER 4: INTRODUCTION TO THE FOUR DIMENSIONS OF LEADERSHIP

My attempt to cover all four dimensions of leadership represents a real challenge to keeping this book concise and readable. I realize that my overarching strategy is a bold endeavour, indeed, as many books have been written on each of the four individual dimensions of leadership. Thus, I am taking more of a macro than a micro view of each dimension and presenting a condensed distillation of the foundational principles and best practices.

Allow me to explain the overall structure of the book. Albert Einstein once suggested that there was nothing quite as practical as a good theory. Consistent with this sentiment, I kindly ask you to allow me in the first three parts of the book to establish a theoretical foundation of knowledge upon which we build the balance of the book. In parts 1, 2 and 3, we examine the principles of leadership or the WHY and WHAT of leadership effectiveness. Once the conceptual framework is in place, we then proceed to the practicalities or the HOW of effective leadership in parts 4 through 7. As we examine each of the four leadership dimensions, we focus on the applied side of leadership by learning strategies, skills, tactics and techniques that drive success in each of dimensions.

Personal Leadership

The newspaper reported that the police detective said the recent bank robbery appears to be an "inside job." I don't mean to associate leadership with bank robbery, but it is a highly appropriate expression because, the truth is, leadership is an inside job. The true starting point of leadership is best explained by its primary paradox – before we can effectively lead others, we first must effectively manage ourselves.

As we left the industrial age a few decades ago, everyone was given a big promotion with the fancy new title, CLO (chief life officer); yet tragically, many people have failed to recognize and accept the responsibilities of their new job title. Personal leadership is far more important now. In the relatively stagnant, structured and predictable world of the last century, people's lives were mostly predetermined, options were limited, and fewer life and career choices had to be made. The concept of a job for life is quickly coming to an end.

In Part 4 of the book, you will learn the success principles and practices of personal leadership, which include the core competencies: life leadership, personal productivity, problem solving and decision making, and strategic self-development.

Interpersonal Leadership

Allow me to state very self-evident truth – if you want your life to work, then the critical mass of your key relationships has to be working. In Part 5, we explore the interpersonal dimension of leadership, which is essentially about how to your build your "power grid."

We redefine what "people skills" really means and how to truly measure a person's true interpersonal effectiveness. We further dismiss the myth of the charismatic leader through explaining why some of the most introverted people could very well have superior interpersonal skills and be highly effective leaders. The simple explanation is that there are only two fundamental or core interpersonal communication competencies required to maintain a productive and stable relationships, and neither have to do with introversion or extroversion.

As formal authority power is dissolving rapidly in the twenty-first-century workplace, effective leaders must develop their power to make things happen by building a network of productive, constructive and sustainable relationships. The current workplace demands that all people at all levels of the organization demonstrate interpersonal leadership. Perhaps the most significant change from the industrial age to the information-age workplace is that the ever-greater complexity is driving ever-greater interdependence. The reason forcing this need for collaboration and communication is best illustrated by the following statistics.

In 1985, approximately 75% of the information and knowledge required to complete your work was contained in your own brain; by the year 2005, the amount of information required had dropped to 25%. The most important implication of this increasing information flow and complexity is that, unlike the industrial age where people could sit quietly in their offices with their doors closed doing their own thing, you need other people to do your job. The bottom line is that teamwork, communication and collaboration are becoming more important by the day. Your ability to deal with people is your only real source of employment security.

In Part 5 of the book, you will learn the success principles and practices of interpersonal leadership, which include the core competencies – how to gain influence with people, how to be an effective team player, how to speak persuasively and win people over to your way of thinking, how to deliver feedback effectively, and how to deal with disagreement and resolve conflict.

Team Leadership

A British author named Charles Handy wrote a book a few decades back called *The Age of Paradox*. One twenty-first-century paradox is that, as the need for teams and teamwork is increasing, it is increasingly difficult to find truly high-performance teams. The sad truth is that of the many teams I have observed first-hand, most were dysfunctional. A probable reason is to be found in the EQ (or emotional quotient) research, where they find that IQ is slowly increasing across the western world, whereas EQ has been decreasing over the last few decades (which explains many of our societal problems). Part 6 is about team leadership, and you will learn how to create a highly engaged and collaborative group with ordinary people and have them produce extraordinary results.

The ultimate goal of any team is to produce what is known as "synergy." Synergy is more than just a biz-babble-buzzword; it is a very real force in nature that is not yet completely understood. One definition of synergy is that the whole is greater than the sum of the parts. Synergy is also when one plus one equals three or four or ten. We will attempt to demystify this seemingly mystical, magical, metaphysical force by defining in practical terms what it really means and, most importantly, how to develop it.

In Part 6, you will learn the success principles and practices of team leadership, which include the seven essential roles of the team leader, characteristics of high-performance teams, how to motivate and engage team members, how to delegate and empower team members, and how to make team meetings meaningful.

Organizational Leadership

Organizational leadership is the loftiest form of leadership. It could also be called strategic leadership, as it involves the knowledge, strategies and competencies required to run an entire organization. For that reason, this dimension of leadership perhaps holds a higher degree of relevance for senior executives or business owners than it does for middle managers or frontline staff. However, it certainly holds true relevance for everyone in the organization because it doesn't matter whether you work as an independent entrepreneur, in a two-person partnership, as an employee in a company of 25, 250, or 25,000 employees – we all must develop and maintain an enterprise-wide mindset so we are able to think, act and make decisions as if we owned the company.

In Part 7, we examine the principles and practices of creating a high-performance, information-age organization. This applies to running any and all types of organizations. Although the primary focus of Part 4 is on running a business organization, the same concepts directly apply to any group of people working together, whether it is an association, church, team, band, club or family.

We identify the five defining characteristics of highly successful information-age organizations. Any organization that hopes to survive, let alone thrive, in the turbulent world of the twenty-first century must constantly be in aggressive pursuit of achieving the five key success factors, which are very different than those in the industrial age.

The starting point of organizational success is to be truly customer focused, and the starting point of being customer focused is to see the organization through the eyes of the customer. I challenge you to examine your organization by taking an objective "outside-in" look (customer's perspective) and "inside-out" look (organization's perspective) with the purpose of identifying organizational strengths and opportunities for improvement.

The central focus of this chapter is on the culture of the organization, and we will attempt to define what culture really means. I will again challenge you to assess how healthy your organizational culture currently is by providing examples of healthy and sick organizational culture in real-world terms.

LEADING FROM EVERYWHERE

THE PRINCIPLES & PRACTICES OF CHARACTER-BASED LEADERSHIP

PART 2: AN ENQUIRY INTO LEADERSHIP

5. Defining Leadership is Like Trying to Nail Jell-O to the Wall
6. Dispelling the Most Common Leadership Myths
7. Piecing Together the Leadership Puzzle

CHAPTER 5: DEFINING LEADERSHIP IS LIKE TRYING TO NAIL JELL-O TO THE WALL

In the last few decades, the ever-increasing importance of leadership has caused an explosion of research on the subject. Clearly, leadership is one of the most studied of the social sciences and, yet, paradoxically, it remains one of the least understood. Despite the mountains of research and the stream of studies, there is still no widely agreed-upon, clear, unequivocal definition of this gelatin-like subject of leadership and no understanding as to what separates effective leaders from ineffective leaders. Even with the burst of books, articles and seminars, the subject of leadership is still replete with dangerously obsolete myths, misconceptions and mistaken beliefs.

Leadership books abound; however, approach with caution, because most tend to fall into one of two categories. First are the books written by motivational speakers, which tend to be gimmicky, touchy-feely, fluffy and flavour-of-the-day, full of psychobabble, platitudes and stories offering little meaningful content. Even more common are the books written by academics, which tend to be overly complex and conceptual and are chockfull of the dried pabulum of academic theoretical mumbo-jumbo that once again provides negligible practical, real-world content that can be applied.

Okay, I know what you're thinking – that perhaps my critique of contemporary leadership literature is a little harsh. Truth be told, leadership is a challenging subject to study, wrap your head around and teach, for some very legitimate reasons.

Our first challenge is the squishy Jell-O thing; leadership is the softest of the soft skills. It is difficult to learn let alone teach something when most people struggle to even define it. Words that best describe leadership are subjective, amorphous, deep, expansive, multidimensional, holistic, intangible and ambiguous. Leadership is truly important and yet defies any clear definition, measurement or quantification. In this regard, it is similar to wisdom, emotional intelligence, character or the culture of an organization. I like how Warren Bennis, a leadership guru from USC who claims to have accumulated more than 350 definitions of leadership, suggested that leadership was a lot like pornography in that it is nearly impossible to define but you know it when you see it.

I ask my seminar participants this: is leadership an art or science? In short order, my audiences always agree that leadership is much more of an art than a science. It is a highly appropriate metaphor to see leadership as an art. Celebrated art expert Georges Braque once said, "The only thing that matters in art is the part that cannot be explained." I believe if we were to change the word "art" to "leadership," this statement retains its validity.

I accept that leadership is much more of a soft art than a hard science; however, for the teaching purposes in this book, my approach is to turn it into a black-and-white science. By doing this, I run the risk of the over-simplification of a highly subjective subject, so I kindly ask you to indulge me in my attempts to crystallize the sum and substance of the subject of leadership.

Whenever I encounter highly effective leaders, I value the opportunity to conduct my own personal research. I ask the person how they became such an effective leader, and more often than not they struggle to offer any tangible explanations as to the HOW. An explanation for this is that they are in a state known as "unconscious competence." This term was coined by the renowned psychologist Abraham Maslow, and it means that people in this state achieve results, which defines them as competent, but they are unable to explain specifically how they got the results. The attitudes, thoughts and behaviours that drive their leadership effectiveness just seem to happen naturally, with no strategic thought or conscious effort. Sadly, many people exist in a state at the other end of the spectrum (as I did for years) Maslow called "unconscious incompetence," which is not a good place to be. What makes this state so dangerous is that you don't even know that you don't know. This all-too-common phenomena will be explained in Part 3, where you will learn that the attitudes and behaviours of highly effective leaders have much more to do with the subconscious brain than the conscious brain.

A Historical Perspective on Leadership

I believe that at the root of many misconceptions and misunderstanding around the subject of leadership is that leadership has changed throughout the ages. It has been and remains an evolving concept and thus a moving target to define. A good starting point to the demystification process is to gain a brief historical perspective on how leadership practices have evolved through the ages.

Throughout human history, leadership has always been defined as the capacity to achieve "followership." However, the practices, and thus the characteristics, capabilities and competencies, required to achieve followership have changed throughout the ages, consistent with the changing challenges of the times. For the vast majority of history, the ugly truth is that leadership has largely been about "forced followership" because the individuals and the greater masses had little or no choice about who they were going to follow. This book is based on the premise that the authoritarian or coercive style of leadership is simply no longer effective.

As we peer back into the mists of time, the original leadership concept from the dark ages might be best referred to as the "strong man" theory of leadership. In a primitive world, the natural leader of any group would have been the biggest, strongest, fastest and fiercest person who would be best able to protect the tribe from enemies and capture the most prey.

In the nineteenth century, Thomas Carlyle summarized the recurring ideas about leadership in his theory of the "great man." This hypothesis put forth that leaders were exceptional persons or heroes that were able to use their charisma, intelligence, wisdom and political skill to have power and control over other people. The premise was that leadership was a matter of birth and only certain people were genetically superior and endowed with the qualities required. This definition is consistent with the divine right of king's political philosophy of the Middle Ages. Military prowess as demonstrated by courage and valour on the battlefield remained a central pillar of power for the "great man" style of leadership.

Some academics promote a more situational explanation of leadership called the "big bang" hypothesis. This theory suggests that leadership is mostly a matter of context and circumstance, and significant events made great leaders. This theory is based on the idea that Churchill was just hanging around in the late-1930s and it was the forthcoming events that made him into a great leader. Evidently, Lincoln was just killing time looking for something to do and it was the coincidence of the Civil War that made him into a great leader. I do accept that different challenges require different styles of leadership; however, I think significant events or crises don't make a leader a leader, as much as they expose who the real leaders are and are not.

As the industrial age hit full stride, what it meant to be a leader was reconceived to what we might call "organization men." The leadership competencies most suited for the times were broadly described as managerial. In other words, those people who were good bureaucrats, adept at planning, controlling, administrating and organizing, were best suited to be in charge. Leaders of the day were industry giants such as Frederick Taylor, Max Weber, Alfred Sloan, Henry Ford and Thomas Kettering. The ability to play politics and feign interest in your bosses became essential career skills to successfully navigate and climb the hierarchal corporate ladder in the commonplace "kiss-up and kick-down" cultures of industrial-age organizations.

As we rapidly morphed from the industrial-age economy to the post-industrial age, more service-based and economy-driven by the technology and financial sectors, what it took to be a leader began to change once again. Mostly in the last half of the last century, three new types of leaders with new knowledge and skillsets ascended to take centre stage and began to reinvent what leadership in the information-age looks like.

The first of the new type included high-profile people such as Bill Gates, Steve Jobs and, more recently, Mark Zuckerberg, Jeff Bezos, Elon Musk and Richard Branson. The new or post-industrial economy has created leaders we could refer to as "technical" or "risk-taker" leaders.

The second type of leader to simultaneously arise in the new economy is largely from the world of high finance. They are the wizards of Wall Street, the hedge-fund managers, investment bankers and wheeler-dealers skilled at mergers and acquisitions, leveraged buyouts and corporate takeovers. Let's agree to call this relatively new type of corporate chieftain "financial" or "leech" leaders. If you feel this label carries a negative connotation, that was my intention. This type of leadership does not create real value for anyone (except the executives and shareholders in the short term) and is largely driven by greed and self-interest. I have witnessed firsthand the incredibly destructive impact mergers and acquisitions often have on the culture of once-healthy organizations and the lives of the people that work there.

Make no mistake, I fully in the free-enterprise system; however, I also believe the impact of these leech leaders and corporate chieftains, with their mindless pursuit of short-term, bottom-line profits and ludicrously rich executive compensation packages, is causing the free-enterprise capitalistic economic system to run amuck. This new form is having a hugely destructive impact on many organizations and ultimately our society.

At the very heart of this book is the third emerging style of leadership: the "facilitative leader." These leaders have no need to use position, power, formal authority or control; rather, they rely on interpersonal effectiveness to build influence with people so people choose to listen and follow them. They motivate people by empowering and supporting them to achieve meaningful results on their own.

In summary, defining leadership is both a crucial starting point and an intimidating task because it is not a subject that fits neatly into any one box; rather, it is a gelatin-like, squishy subject, and it is almost impossible to nail down clear, specific, unambiguous terms.

CHAPTER 6: DISPELLING THE MOST COMMON LEADERSHIP MYTHS

Given the evolving nature of leadership, many people still, understandably, buy into myths that are deeply rooted and stuck in traditional beliefs that were at one time valid, and it is difficult to dislodge these dangerous, self-sabotaging beliefs. Before we attempt to define and understand what leadership really is, a good starting point is to clear away some widely held, perilous misconceptions and establish greater clarity as to what leadership is not.

Here are the four interrelated leadership myths I have most commonly encountered in almost three decades of studying and teaching leadership.

MYTH #1 – Leaders are Found at the Top of the Organization

This myth is particularly difficult to dismiss because in the very recent past, it was absolutely true. It was just a few short decades ago when people at the top of the organization were expected to act as leaders, and the very few people in executive roles and the vast balance of the rest of the people were expected to carry out the decisions and directions passed down to the hierarchical chain of command.

Tragically, this obsolete paradigm still exists today in far too many organizations and is a primary root cause of dysfunctional and toxic organizational cultures, resulting in predictably poor organizational performance as defined by all stakeholders. Old paradigms die hard, particularly when there are many people in the workforce who can still clearly remember when this model of management worked really well.

This book is designed to shatter that myth. The faster the rate of change, the greater the need for leadership to be demonstrated in every corner in the organization. You cannot possibly run an organization at world-class levels of speed and responsiveness with people waiting around for their orders from above and with internal communications having to go up one silo, across and then down another. To have any chance of surviving, let alone thriving, every organization must adopt a holistic leadership model where everyone has an enterprise-wide perspective and an entrepreneurial mindset, and where employees think, decide and behave as if they owned the company. The key strategic competitive damage of the twenty-first century in all industries and in all organizations is the development of leaders at all levels of the organization.

MYTH #2 - Leaders are Dynamic, Dominant and Charismatic

When it comes to identifying true leadership, the old expression that you can't tell a book by its cover is valid. Outward appearances and certain behaviours can be deceiving. We all demonstrate behaviours and abilities that are driven primarily by unconscious genetic predispositions that at first glance can easily give the appearance of effective leadership and generate short-term results though other people. In this book, the words "highly effective leader" refer specifically to the ability to generate lasting long-term results through people. Effective leaders get results, whereas highly effective leaders expand the capacity to achieve results.

Just as in the case of Myth #1, this second falsehood is difficult to shake off because in the very recent past it was valid. Leadership in industrial-age organizations was about being dominant, decisive and controlling. The prototypical manager of the industrial age was the take-charge Type-A personality, which again explains the pervasive and persistent nature of this myth.

A large part of human behaviour can be explained through the four genetic temperaments we will delve into in Part 3. Some people tend to be naturally more assertive (Type-A personalities), while others tend to be more naturally passive (Type-B personalities). Type-A people demonstrate behaviours such as decisiveness and a bias towards action and taking initiative that many people could perceive as leadership. However, employees today demand involvement and meaningful participation, which renders the traditional command-and-control managerial approach desperately inadequate for the modern workplace. I believe it's the more facilitative and inclusive management style that the Type-B temperament naturally demonstrates that is and will be the order of the day for the information-age workplace.

Some eyebrow-raising research that strongly validates this belief was recently conducted in a survey by Gallup, the global analytics and advice firm. The purpose of the research was to identify the competencies that created the very best managers. The research involved over 70,000 surveys in North America and Western Europe, and the findings were reported in a book called *First, Break All the Rules* by Marcus Buckingham. The peculiar title of this book was meant to signify the counterintuitive results of the research. The "rules" referred to the well-established norms and long-held practices of the industrial-age management paradigm.

One outcome of the Gallup research that held particular fascination for me was that over half the distilled group of the very best managers reported getting so nervous and anxious before having to deliver corrective feedback to someone that they had to go to the bathroom for fear of being physically sick. My immediate deduction was that these must have been Type-B managers, who are predictably strongly averse to any form of adversarial conversation with a possibility of conflict.

The second dimension of the temperament model refers to introversion (task orientation) and extroversion (people orientation). Many people tend to mistakenly associate leadership with behaviours exhibited by extroverted people who tend to be more outgoing, talkative and possess better "people skills." Research proves otherwise. Some highly effective leaders are more extroverted and charismatic, but most are not. I'm not saying it's bad to be charismatic, but charisma is not integral to effective leadership. Charisma might be figuratively considered to be the icing on the cake, but it's not the cake. Truly successful, sustainable leadership can only be built on the permanent bedrock of character and not on the fickleness of a sociable, likable personality.

In his best-selling book, *Built to Last*, co-written with Jerry Porras, Jim Collins makes a convincing case of the dangers of the charismatic leader, suggesting that they are actually counterproductive to the organization in the long run. The metaphor he used was that the high-profile, charismatic leaders that achieved short-term results were "time tellers," as the organizations struggled when they left. In contrast, the leaders who achieved sustainable long-term results were "clock builders," as they left thriving organizations in their wake as a result of effective leadership development. As a result of broad leadership development, after charismatic leaders leave, the organization struggles because of the vacuum left behind by the absence of a strong leader to take charge and start making decisions.

There is little argument that the most influential book on leadership of the first two decades of the new millennium is Collins's second book, *Good to Great*. Early on, Collins drives a long and convincing stake into the heart of the myth of the dynamic, charismatic leader. Based on extensive research, he proves that most effective leaders are quiet, shy, introverted and humble, and they have a genuine concern for the welfare of the organization over self.

MYTH #3 - Leaders are Highly Intelligent

To dismiss this myth, we have to circle back to one of the most persistent and perplexing questions in the study of leadership – are leaders born or made? My first response is "both," depending on the particular dimension of leadership. I will do my best to provide an answer to this long-debated question in the remainder of this book.

A first step in putting this widely held myth to rest is for people to realize there are varying dimensions and degrees of leadership effectiveness. Leadership is similar to other endeavours in that there are many average athletes, performers, artists and leaders, but truly great ones are rare. Don't make the mistake of buying into the common myth that being a lofty intellect is a prerequisite for leadership effectiveness, because the truth is, to succeed everyone must demonstrate leadership.

Through my observations over three decades, I'm absolutely convinced this belief is mostly false. I have encountered many people of average IQ, who have proven to be highly effective leaders, and even more frequently I come across people with high IQs loaded with academic credentials that turn out to be highly ineffective leaders in real-world practice.

Although IQ scores did correlate to higher grades in school, once people left school, the social scientists could find no correlation between IQ and career success. In fact, they frequently discovered a negative correlation between IQ and career success. By the mid- to late-twentieth century, the head-scratching question for social scientists around the world became this: "If it's not IQ that predicts or explains who will succeed, then what are the variables that do predict who will succeed?" The attempt to answer this crucial question spawned a new field of study known as "emotional intelligence." I suspect many readers are familiar with the term, which shows up as one of two short-form banners: EQ or EI. We now know with crystal clarity that leadership effectiveness has much more to do with EQ then IQ. We will examine this in greater detail in Chapter 10.

I do not want to leave the impression that IQ is unimportant, because it is a more significant success factor at the higher levels of leadership. To achieve success at an organizational or strategic leadership level, there are essential intellectual capacities required for success that go beyond the cognitive-thinking abilities of most people. These include:

- Ability to process large amounts of complex information
- Capacity to see the big picture and connect the dots
- Capacity for strategic, analytical and conceptual thinking
- Financial acumen

The myth of the highly intelligent leader that is most disturbing and depressing infers that leadership cannot be learned. If this were true, it would mean that my life's purpose and how I earn a living (teaching leadership) would be irrelevant. The truth is that not everyone has the natural ability or capacity to become a great leader, but everyone can enhance their leadership effectiveness and fulfill their own potential.

MYTH #4 - Demonstrating Leadership is Reserved for Your Professional Life

While this book is largely framed in the context of leadership in professional life, leadership competencies, strategies and techniques are likewise relevant and equally applicable in personal life. Many workshop participants throughout the years have reported back that what they learned had a greater benefit in their personal life than in their professional life. I believe that whatever success you achieve in your professional life will never make up for failure in your personal life. Gandhi said that life is one indivisible whole; one cannot do right in one area of life while attempting to do wrong in another.

These two lives are more interrelated than in the industrial age. The advent of dual-income families, telecommuting, home-based entrepreneurs and 24/7 communication has contributed to blurring the lines, making it increasingly difficult for many people to separate their personal and professional lives.

As you gain a deeper and clearer understanding of what leadership really is, it will become increasingly evident that leadership is a universal competency that must be demonstrated to achieve success in all dimensions of your life.

The primary reason for this is that, first, foremost and fundamentally, leadership is about relationships – all relationships. All of life occurs in relationships. We have three distinctly separate lives. The first is our public life, which consists of relationships with acquaintances, coworkers and neighbours. The second is our private life, which consists of relationships with family and friends. The third is our private life, which is the relationship we have with ourselves. Leadership is the cornerstone of success in all relationships.

Making a marriage work requires effective personal and interpersonal leadership demonstrated by both partners if the marriage has a chance of surviving, let alone thriving. The statistics that indicate between 40% and 50% of marriages today fail to survive provide very hard, tangible evidence of the dearth of leadership in society today.

Parenting is perhaps one of the purest examples or framework for effective leadership. As the old adage suggests, highly effective parents provide their children with both "roots" and "wings." Leadership development has two distinct components: character and competence. Roots refers to the child possessing a sense of internal personal security as a result of character development; wings refers to what psychologists call self-efficacy, which means the children believe they are capable and competent to solve life problems on their own.

Make no mistake – parenting is pure endeavour in leadership! Successful parenting outcomes are much more likely to occur if the parents have achieved influence with their children so they will listen and heed the advice and guidance they want to provide. Advice is only a value if the child accepts it. Many parents, with the best of intentions, end up extremely frustrated in their attempts to force their advice, ideas and promptings on their children. Tragically, the parents' efforts are counterproductive; I have often observed families where the parents have reached a state of counter-influence, which results in their children making critical, pivotal early-adult life decisions out of subconscious spite for their well-intended parents.

What makes these myths so deadly dangerous is that they undermine the very starting point of becoming a leader, which is to realize that you are a leader. These days, everyone must become a leader, and the vital first step is to see oneself as a leader.

Now that we have gained a historical perspective and shattered the most commonly held debilitating misconceptions, we've achieved a better understanding of what leadership is *not*. Let's proceed to Chapter 7 and attempt to get a handle on what leadership really is.

CHAPTER 7: PIECING TOGETHER THE LEADERSHIP PUZZLE

This chapter will provide you with five pieces of the leadership puzzle. The pieces are in the form of various perspectives, definitions and descriptions of leadership, which I believe are all valid, but each puzzle piece on its own is incomplete. Once the pieces are properly positioned, they will create a holistic montage or mosaic that gives a comprehensive understanding of what leadership really means in the most tangible and practical terms.

Five pieces of the leadership puzzle:

1. Seven seemingly subtle word differences that highly effective leaders seem to understand
2. Leadership and management – the essential differences
3. A collection of leadership definitions distilled down to one word
4. The Greeks got it right – the head is on the far side of the heart!
5. Twenty characteristics, capabilities and competencies of highly effective leaders

Seven Seemingly Subtle Word Differences that Highly Effective Leaders Seem to Understand

I believe that teaching leadership is much more of an art than a science, which means there's always room for skill enhancement. After nearly three decades of teaching and training, I am still trying to become a "Socratic" facilitator. Socrates realized that the most powerful method of learning is through self-discovery and thus the most powerful teaching (and coaching) technique is asking questions as opposed to providing answers. This works because people don't argue, disagree with or easily forget the conclusions, solutions and ideas they come up with themselves. Galileo expressed a similar sentiment when he said, "You cannot teach a person anything; you can only help them learn it for themselves."

So, allow me to begin with a series of questions. The first of the five puzzle pieces is simply a challenge to you to explain the differences between the following seven sets of words. My purpose is to "prime the pump," to stimulate thinking and add an element of intrigue.

Most people are careless with their use of our language; these seven word sets, which people interchange as if they were synonyms, provide excellent evidence of this careless language use. Some people can quickly and easily explain how the meaning of these words is different, but the majority of people struggle to explain what these words really mean. Upon further consideration, people realize the differences are not very subtle at all.

I suggest, to my accounting participants, that if we can reconcile these seemingly subtle word differences, there is tremendous intellectual value to be gained. We must learn to use our language with greater precision, and highly effective leaders somehow seem to understand the differences.

1) Simple and Easy

I watched a video of Steve Jobs giving a presentation, and as he held up his new invention, the iPhone, he suggested that he had created something "simple on the far side of complexity." I strongly suspect that he was borrowing part of an old quote from the American philosopher Oliver Wendell Holmes, who once said, "I would not give you a fig for simplicity on this side of complexity, but I give you my right arm for simplicity on the far side complexity."

I think Albert Einstein was trying to say the same thing when he said, "Simplicity is the pinnacle of sophistication." I have learned that keeping things simple without being simplistic is a hallmark of great leadership.

Simplicity is also fundamental to learning. However, I must beg your indulgence, as occasionally in this book, we must delve into the bowels of complexity, remembering that our ultimate objective is to arrive at eloquent simplicity on the far side of complexity. Being an effective leader, as in most endeavours in life, is really quite simple. However, I am not saying that becoming a highly effective leader is easy.

Perhaps I can provide clues to clarify the difference between the words "simple" and "easy" by recounting a story of a young man who came up to me after a multi-day course and said I had motivated him to set some goals. I said goals are a very good thing to have because trying to live your life without them is like trying to come back to some place you've never been. I then asked the young man if he had his goals with him, and sure enough he pulled out his list. His first goal was to run a marathon. I congratulated him on his admirable and lofty objective. He then went on to explain how he had just bought new running shoes and was super excited about running a marathon, and he said the only problem he was encountering was that he was finding all the running involved to be a real hassle and it was really getting him down.

2] Wisdom and Intelligence

My leadership workshop participants consistently quickly agree that these two words are not synonyms. I provoke the participants to think through this crucial difference by asking a series of questions.

- *Which is more important in becoming a highly effective leader?* This is the primary and central question. I then prompt people by asking, "When dealing with people, which is usually more important? When dealing with things, which is usually more important?"

- *Can a person be intelligent and not very wise?* I always get an immediate affirmative answer on this question. I ask my participants if they know anyone who is technically proficient, perhaps even brilliant, at what they do and yet should have never ever been made a manager of people. The response is always a resounding yes.

- *Can a person be wise and not very intelligent?* This question is one people struggle with. Perhaps an engineer in my audience said it best through the words of Forrest Gump: "Stupid is as stupid does."

- *How do you measure how intelligent a person is?* The answer is IQ testing, which measures two intelligences. First, the "mathematical/logical," based on how fast you can solve math problems, and second, "verbal," based on the size of your linguistic memory bank or how many words you knows at age seven.

- *Can you become more intelligent?* The answer is we don't think so. The most recent research suggests that IQ is largely a function of genetics and slightly malleable up to about age fifteen, after which it is essentially fixed. I ask what the difference is between a talent and a skill. The answer is that a talent is an innate natural ability that you either have or don't have. A good example of natural talent is hand-eye coordination, which my middle child, Tim, possesses. No matter the sport, within a short period of time, Tim looks like he has played his whole life. The great basketball coach John Wooden said, "You can't coach tall." IQ is much more of a talent.

- *How do you measure how wise a person is?* This question is consistently a real head-scratcher for people. Even my most sophisticated audiences end up giving me blank looks, with absolutely no idea how to answer this self-evident question.

- *Can you gain wisdom?* People always answer, "Of course!" I follow up with "Is wisdom literature new or old?" The immediate response is "old." I then suggest that is why they call this body of knowledge "wisdom" and not psychology, and ask why wisdom literature stood the test of time.

3] Character and Personality

The confusion between these two words, and people's inability to explain the difference between them, makes them perhaps the most tragic of all word sets. The near-universal lack of understanding of what character is and its vital importance is a very sad commentary on our educational system and explains many of the societal problems we are currently experiencing.

I was first introduced to the concept of character some twenty-five years ago when I was reading Stephen Covey's landmark personal development book *The Seven Habits of Highly Effective People*. The essential relationship between leadership and character quickly became crystal clear to me, and I immediately integrated the concept of character development into my material. Covey's book had such a huge impact on me, and there was a time when I struggled with tremendous guilt for stealing Covey's material. After a few years had transpired, in preparation for a workshop on presentation skills, I stumbled across *Rhetoric*, the original book on how to give a presentation, written by Aristotle. I will expand on the valuable lessons I learned from this book later in this chapter. Reading it alleviated the guilt I was experiencing for stealing Covey's content. It became evident that character was the very cornerstone of Greek philosophy, as Aristotle saw character as foundational to success in life, and it dawned on me where Covey got his material from. I was no longer racked with guilt.

The key question becomes which is more important to truly effective leadership? To a degree, this word difference has already been clarified in Chapter 6 when we effectively shattered the myth of the charismatic leader.

I ask my audiences two questions: In short-term relationships, which is more important to success, personality or character? In long-term relationships, which is more important to success? People seem to intuitively be able to answer these questions but are seldom able to explain why character is so fundamentally important. A clue to assist clarification is understanding that the root word of "personality" is the Latin word *persona*, which means "the actor's mask."

Understanding the difference between character and personality pretty much explains the counterintuitive truth that some of the most introverted and even shy people could very well possess the best interpersonal skills.

4) Reacting and Responding

This set of words is perhaps the easiest to reconcile, and most people are able to do so relatively rapidly. A reaction takes one of two forms: flying fists (fight) or fleet feet (flight). A reaction is emotional and in communication terms shows up as either verbal violence (yelling and screaming) or verbal silence (run to the bathroom, lock the door and don't come out for three hours). A life lesson it took me far too long to comprehend is that out-of-control emotions make smart people really stupid.

The key question becomes this: when the conversation gets tough and there's a lot at stake, can you respond and stay calm and reasonable? The nineteenth-century British author Rudyard Kipling asked the vital question: "Can you keep your head about you when all others lose theirs?" Learning to choose a response and not react to difficult situations or people is fundamental to becoming a highly effective leader.

5) Responsibility and Accountability

These two words are perhaps the most used and abused of all seven word sets. Most people use them interchangeably, but they do not mean the same thing. They are highly interrelated, which could be the root cause of this costly confusion.

The muddled meaning of these two words is a primary cause of lack of accountability, which is a major driver of organizational dysfunction and poor performance, and the Achilles heel of many organizations. Accountability is to organizational success as carbon is to steel. It is one of the very few denominators in all successful organizations. In any situation where people are working together, whether it be an organization (public or private sector), association, team, church, club or family, accountability is crucial for success of the group.

A common and damaging misconception is that people tend to associate the word "accountability" with dealing with poor performers. One of the many crucial lessons that took me far too long to learn when I managed people in my corporate life is that it is vital to hold your worst people, mediocre people and best people accountable; it is not an option.

Hint #1 – If you can understand the difference between reacting and responding, this will provide helpful insight into understanding the true meaning of the word responsibility.

Hint #2 – I tell my accounting friends that they are the ones best positioned to explain what accountability really means.

6) Values and Principles

These two words are used far too often as though they were synonyms when they are not. One of the challenges of clarifying the difference is that in an ideal situation, they are synonymous.

At first, this conversation might seem to be lofty, academic and reserved for only the intellectually elite. But this vital difference is intuitively understood because it is pure common sense. What first appears to be mysterious and deeply theoretical turns out, with a little contemplation, to be self-evident and providing highly practical value.

Chapter 10 is dedicated to clarifying the vital difference between values and principles. You will discover that it is timeless, changeless principles that govern success or failure in the short time one is on this planet, whether you are aware of them or not. Gaining clarity of principles leads us to an understanding of wisdom.

7) Self-esteem and Ego

The confusion surrounding these two words has pushed our educational system down the wrong path. For the last few decades well-intended educators have mistakenly shifted their focus to giving students self-esteem as opposed to facilitating student achievement.

Good intentions never make up for bad judgment. I think the root cause of this misdirection is that educators are confused about the causal factors of true self-esteem. The truth is, you cannot give a person self-esteem as much as you can help them earn it.

Not only are these two words not synonyms, they are mutually exclusive in that one has an ego to the degree one does not possess true self-esteem, or as the leadership guru Warren Bennis called it, positive self-regard.

A convincing argument can be made that if the greatest leaders in history have all been "servant" leaders, then it follows logically that ego is the exact opposite of highly effective leadership.

When you mention the word self-esteem, many people fear we're entering touchy-feely psychobabble conversation. But self-esteem to leadership is as carbon is to steel. People with healthy self-esteem demonstrate leadership behaviours naturally, with no conscious thought or effort.

When people ask if it's possible to have too much self-esteem, I respond by asking, "Is it possible to have too much physical health?" The illogical truth is that one of the most predictable manifestations of true self-esteem is humility.

To conclude this word-clarification challenge, allow me to re-emphasize the real practical learning value in this exercise. If you achieve clarity on these vital differences, that alone could be worth your investment of time and money in this book. Throughout the rest of the book, I will introduce a number of other word sets that provide further evidence of how carelessly we use our language and the value of having the words clarified.

Leadership & Management – The Essential Differences

A good place to start in the process of clarifying what leadership really means is to gain clarity on how it is different than management. Leadership and management are fundamentally important and fundamentally different. Most people really struggle when I ask them to explain this vital difference, but the confusion can be readily explained.

First, in the very recent past, leadership and management were considered to be synonymous. The sad truth is that there are far too many people who have been given managerial positions and titles that are highly ineffective leaders. The good news is that there are many people who do not have a position or title that are highly effective leaders.

Secondly, much of the confusion was spread by the management literature of the last thirty years. Many of the management books written since about 1980 have suggested that managers are bad and leaders are good, that you can't be a manager, you have to become a leader, and that managers tell and leaders sell. This left people with a negative impression of the words "management" and "manager."

Thirdly, what leadership and management really mean is easily confused because they are so highly interrelated and interdependent. If leadership is the yin, then management is the yang.

The Latin root word for leadership means "to go and to guide." The Latin root word for management means "to bring about" or "to make happen." The following chart contrasts the essential differences:

LEADERSHIP	MANAGEMENT
People/influence	**Things/control**
ENDS – purpose and results	MEANS – methods, processes
Challenges reality	Deals with reality
Answers why and what	Answers how and when
Direction	Speed
Long-range macro view	Short-range micro view
Develops	Maintains
Effectiveness focus	Efficiency focus
Innovates	Replicates
Top-line revenue (customer opinion)	Bottom-line profit (cost control)
Right brain	Left brain

LEADERSHIP	MANAGEMENT
Context, big picture	Content, details
Working ON things (production capacity)	Working IN things (producing results)
Defining what problems to solve	Solving problems
Vision/strategy and culture/values	Structure, systems and processes

It is obvious that leadership and management are both important; however, once again there is an essential sequence, and leadership must precede management because direction must precede speed.

Allow me to twist an old axiom: "Old paradigms never die; they just fade away." The problem is, the more successful the paradigm, the longer it takes to fade away. Sadly, today, many organizations are still over-managed and under-led. This tragic truth is a destructive vestige of the industrial-age management paradigm of command and control. It is not hard to imagine how the management-centric or control-based paradigm was perfectly appropriate for the relatively stagnant and largely predictable world of the last century. In the industrial age, it was more important to organizational success to have good management practices, but in our whitewater world today, it is ever more important to have effective leadership demonstrated at all levels of the organization.

A Collection of Leadership Definitions Distilled Down to One Word

Throughout nearly three decades of research on leadership, I have come across certain definitions that struck me as valid yet incomplete, so allow me to use a scattergun approach and present an assortment of definitions. As you read them, I challenge you to identify a central core theme, or if possible, pick the *one word* that best defines the distilled essence of leadership.

- "Leadership is not the ability to wield formal authority or to assert position power, but rather it is the ability to get people to listen and follow." – Robert B. Reich

- "Leadership is the art of getting someone else to do something that you want done because *they want to do it*." – Dwight D. Eisenhower

- "Leadership is getting people to follow you because they *want* to, not because they *have* to!" – Larry Wilson

- "Leadership is the qualities of moral character that enable a person to inspire and *influence* a group of people successfully!" – US Marine Corps

- "Leadership is the process of social *influence* in which one person can enlist the aid and support of others in the accomplishment of a common task." – Martin Chemers

- "Leadership is the process of moving a group in a direction through mostly non-coercive means." – John Kotter

- "Leadership is the process (act) of influencing the activities of an organized group in its efforts toward goal setting and goal achievement." – Ralph Stogdill

- "Leadership is the capacity to create a compelling vision and to translate vision into organizational realities; in short, leadership is the capacity to translate vision into reality." – Warren Bennis

- "A leader shapes and shares a vision, which gives point to the work of others." – Charles Handy

- "Leaders are individuals who establish direction for a group of individuals and who gain commitment from the group to this direction and then motivate members to achieve the outcomes." – Jay A. Conger

- "The only definition of a leader is someone that has followers."
  – Peter Drucker

My most complete definition to date, which has evolved over the last three decades, is: "Leadership is the *power* of *influence* with people gained through the *relationship* that *brings out the best* in people while achieving our desired long-term *results*." I remain a student of leadership today, as I have a sneaking suspicion my definition is also somehow incomplete.

Were you able to identify the central theme or, even better, the one word? If you study hard and long enough and peel enough layers of the leadership onion, at its very core is the one word: *influence*. At first glance, you may think this is an oversimplification, but this is a great example of identifying simplicity on the far side of complexity. John C. Maxwell convinced me of this twenty-five years ago in his book *Developing the Leader Within You*.

The ability to gain influence with people, to win people over to your way of thinking and get them to buy your ideas is the capstone or the crowning achievement; the highest form of interpersonal effectiveness. Influence (leadership) is also universal in that it applies in all dimensions of your life.

The ability to gain influence with people is becoming more important by the day, as we have already established that the traditional, control-based management paradigm is obsolete. The very best that traditional command-and-control management techniques can achieve with people is compliance, but there is no way one can engage people and unleash their energy, talent, commitment and creativity by using traditional formal authority. You can buy hands, you can buy brains, you can buy backs, but you cannot buy hearts. Commitment must be volunteered. To drive my point home, I asked my workshop participants the pointed question: "If your people have a vote, would you still be the boss?"

The Greeks Got it Right – The Head is on the Far Side of the Heart!

Aristotle broke the code on the subject of motivation. He realized there was a sequence in the process of motivating people to action that cannot be violated; as he stated, "a person's head is on the far side of their heart." To motivate a person, you must first appeal to their emotions before actively attempting to convince them using logic and reason. This ancient wisdom has recently been completely validated by cutting-edge neuroscience, as we will discuss in Chapter 8.

To clarify the difference between influence and persuasion, it is best to put both into the broader context of motivation. The motivation equation is:

$$Influence + Persuasion = Motivation$$

Motivation is basically the process of giving somebody a motive for action. The word "emotion" and the word "motivation" have the same Latin root word, *motere*, which means "to move."

Let's also make clear the difference between motivation and manipulation. The end result is the same – getting people to do your bidding. Manipulation is when you get somebody to do something for your own reasons. Motivation is when you get somebody to do something for their reasons.

Aristotle explained the essential sequence of motivating people to action through his ethos–pathos–logos model. Each dimension consists of two components.

Ethos

Ethos is the Greek root of the word "ethics." The two components of ethos are character and competence. Character is the source of trustworthiness. Competence is the source of credibility. Ethos could be defined as modelling or walking the talk, which is the source of moral authority.

This model explains the subtitle of the book: "character-based leadership." I have learned that character is the cornerstone foundation of leadership because trust is the essential ingredient in all interpersonal activities, and it can only come from people who are trustworthy. Authors James Kouzes and Barry Pozner, in their landmark book *Credibility*, validated this concept. The research was extensive and the findings were conclusive – what people valued first and foremost in their leaders was trustworthiness.

Ultimately, ethos is about what the audience believes about the speaker's motives and capabilities.

Pathos

Pathos is the Greek root of the word "empathy" and has two components: empathy and passion. Empathy is your capacity to understand others. Pathos is the essential emotional bond based on the speaker's ability to demonstrate empathy and the capacity to speak in an authentic and believable manner. The word "passion" means speaking from your heart and being sincere and genuine so you connect with people at an emotional level when speaking, which we cover in Chapter 16. Ultimately, pathos is about the audience and how they *feel* about the speaker, which is rooted in the belief that one cares. The best way to prove that you have a person's best interests at heart is to prove that you understand them.

Logos

Logos is the Greek root of the word "logic." The two components of logos are ends (what outcomes we are aiming for) and means (methods as to how we achieve outcomes).

Logos is about actively persuading people to change their thinking using logic and reason, employing such tools as cost-benefit analysis and return-on-investment calculations. The key to persuasion is in the end or outcome and what it will mean to the person to achieve it. Ultimately, logos is about getting people to **think** about the message and convincing them that it makes good sense.

Reading Greek philosophy was a real eye-opener for me, and in particular learning about the **ethos–pathos–logos** model. It was valuable as it helped me understand a number of things far beyond Aristotle's original intent of how to gain influence with your audience as a public speaker.

This model helped me understand where Stephen Covey obtained his material for his landmark book *The 7 Habits of Highly Effective People*. It explains the basic sequential structure of the book and why Covey used numbers and not bullets for each of the seven habits. Ethos is essentially habits 1, 2 and 3. Pathos is habits 4, 5 and 6. Logos is habit 7, in which he discusses how to enhance your capacity to think, use logic and reason, and expand your knowledge base.

Aristotle also helped me understand that the concept of motivation is sequential. You cannot permanently persuade people using logic and reason until you have first connected with them on an emotional level, which is largely achieved by identifying with the person and proving you care about and understand them. The primary paradox of gaining influence is that you cannot gain influence until you have been influenced by someone. A few years back, I was guilty of violating this principle with my youngest son, Jeff, who, much like his father, was never much of an academic, and after he graduated high school, I began pressuring him to go to post-secondary education.

A typical conversation sounded like this: "Get back to school, son; get back to school, son. Your brother and sister have degrees, so get back to school, son; it makes complete logical sense to get back to school."

My son would typically push back, saying, "I know, Dad, I know, but you just don't understand." I learned the hard way that the simple truth is you cannot attempt to persuade people using logic and reason until they first believe that you understand them. It's true in both medicine and when attempting to motivate people that "prescription before diagnosis is malpractice." I like the way St. Francis of Assisi put it about 800 years ago when he said, "Lord, first give me the strength to seek to understand then to be understood." I suspect it is this quote that was the source of Stephen Covey's most practical of his seven habits: "Seek first to understand, then to be understood."

This model explains the difference between influence (ethos and pathos) and persuasion (logos) and their consecutive and complementary natures. Influence is passive, whereas persuasion is active. Influence is about how people feel, whereas persuasion is about how people think. Influence is about emotion, whereas persuasion is about logic. Influence is constant (it is always being gained or lost) and has much more to do with the subconscious (emotional) brain, whereas persuasion has more to do with the conscious (logical) brain. As we will learn in Chapter 8 when we study a little neuroscience, the latest research validates what Aristotle said: the head is indeed on the far side of the heart.

Character development and leadership development are synonymous, which is excellent news because anyone can develop their character and thus enhance their leadership effectiveness. The good news is that it is really quite simple; the bad news is that it's not easy.

Twenty Characteristics, Capacities & Competencies of Highly Effective Leaders

The following twenty descriptors of highly effective leaders explain what leadership looks like in a practical, real-world, ground-level manner. My challenge to you is to assess yourself from 1 to 5 on each of the descriptors. A score of 5 means "very true" and a score of 1 means "not true." There is a total possible score of 100.

1. Highly effective leaders have high EQ because they possess healthy, internally driven self-esteem or unconditional positive self-regard.

2. Highly effective leaders naturally make people feel valued and important, which is the root source of their influence power with people.

3. Highly effective leaders possess a primarily positive outlook – they are fundamentally optimistic. They bring positive energy and improve almost any situation or circumstance.

4. Highly effective leaders make things happen! Leaders are proactive; they act on things as opposed to being acted upon. They are not risk averse; they take the initiative and have a "bias towards action."

5. Highly effective leaders are future-focused. They realize there are no rear-view mirrors on airplanes and that you cannot change the past. They think about the future, and plan and create a sense of movement by driving conversation to future mode. A very successful CEO of one of my clients once told me that whenever there is a problem, he applies the "three what" model: What happened? So what? Now what? Highly effective leaders quickly focus on the third "what," moving the conversation to solution mode.

6. Highly effective leaders are productive. They get things done and achieve results, which is a taproot of their self-esteem and their credibility with others.

7. Highly effective leaders have their ego in check and are truly service-oriented. The greatest leaders in human history were servant leaders, which means they were genuinely out to serve others.

8. Highly effective leaders are excellent listeners and are completely present with others; they seem to savour people's words when they are listening. Even in a crowded room, when they are conversing with you, they make you feel like you are the only person in the room.

9. Highly effective leaders are the first to step up and accept responsibility when things go wrong and the first to give away credit and share the accolades when things go right.

10. Highly effective leaders are resilient because they see success on the far side of failure. In other words, they don't see difficulties as failures; they call them glitches, setbacks, mistakes or errors and use them as feedback to determine what they should do next.

11. Highly effective leaders are humble, which means they are highly teachable; they welcome feedback because they are focused on learning. This deeply seated humility drives a hunger for learning as they take personal and professional development very seriously. Trying to separate learning from leadership is like trying to separate the sun from sunshine.

12. Highly effective leaders quickly admit mistakes, and when they are wrong, they genuinely apologize.

13. Highly effective leaders are assertive and honest communicators, as they demonstrate the courage to hold people accountable. They have a unique ability to tell people what they need to hear in a manner that they don't mind hearing it.

14. Highly effective leaders are authentic and open, with no hidden agendas; they are persuasive communicators who speak so people will listen, believe, understand and remember what they said.

15. Highly effective leaders play the long game as they maintain a sense of perspective and stay calm in problematic or crisis situations. They take a "long-term future view," realizing that life has up and downs, and they frequently use the old expression used in troubled times, "this too shall pass."

16. Highly effective leaders have a solution mindset; they focus on fixing problems, not fixing blame.

17. Highly effective leaders are modest in victory and gracious in defeat.

18. Highly effective leaders seem to have their life in balance. Aristotle called it the "golden mean," where there is nothing in excess and nothing in deficiency. There is balance in their professional and personal lives, between spending and saving, between reason and intuition, between empathy and assertiveness, between short-term pleasure and long-term happiness and so on. It is this innate sense of balance that provides them their sustainability.

19. Highly effective leaders are open-minded and tend not to think in either/or terms. F. Scott Fitzgerald once said that "the sign of a great mind is the ability to hold two opposing thoughts simultaneously and still function."

20. The most accurate measure of leadership effectiveness is to be found in the leader's wake. How many other leaders did they create? The great philosopher Goethe said, "Treat a person as they are, and they will remain as they are; treat a person as they could be, and they will become who they could be." Highly effective leaders are inclined to see the tallest oak tree in the smallest acorn. They naturally bring out the best in people because they perceive the best in people.

Dare I ask how your self-assessment went on the twenty defining descriptors of highly effective leaders? This is not meant to be a scientific assessment tool but rather a framework to help you identify your strengths and your greatest opportunities for improvement. An ideal score would be between 60 to 80 points. The good news about a score lower than 60 is that it indicates a high degree of honesty; the bad news is that it indicates there is some serious leadership development work to be done. The good news about a score higher than 80 points is that you are already a highly effective leader; the bad news is that you might just be delusional and completely out of touch with reality!

Now that you have the five puzzle pieces in place, hopefully you have a much clearer, comprehensive and complete understanding of what leadership really means and looks like in real-world terms. With that better understanding, let's now proceed to Part 3 to learn the principles behind leadership, or in other words the WHY leaders do what they do.

LEADING
FROM
EVERYWHERE

THE PRINCIPLES & PRACTICES OF CHARACTER-BASED LEADERSHIP

PART 3: FOUNDATIONS IN PERSONAL & INTERPERSONAL EFFECTIVENESS

8. Neuroscience – The Biology of Behaviour
9. They Call It Human Nature for a Good Reason
10. Emotional Intelligence – The Myths & the Mastery

CHAPTER 8: NEUROSCIENCE – THE BIOLOGY OF BEHAVIOUR

Many years ago, I was preparing for a course called *Training Skills for Trainers* in which I would teach people how to teach and train. A sweet side benefit of my preparation was that I learned how to better learn for myself. Rapid change requires rapid learning, and we will cover how to improve your learning capacity in Chapter 13.

A concept I became particularly fascinated with is called "accelerated learning" or "whole-brain learning." The father of this new teaching philosophy was a Bulgarian neurologist and psychiatrist named Georgi Lozanov, and it has proven to be remarkably effective in driving retention and transfer (from classroom to action) of training content. Accelerated learning strategies and techniques are now being used throughout the educational world.

The two basic principles underpinning accelerated learning are student relaxation and integration of the right brain. Lozanov found the more relaxed the student, the greater the retention, confirming that anxiety severely cripples the learning centre of the brain. Lozanov also discovered that words activated the left side of the brain, and if the teacher could use techniques that activated the right side of the brain, retention would increase dramatically.

To more fully comprehend the concept of accelerated learning, we must first understand a little bit about the brain. Many people are now familiar with the fact that we have a left brain and a right brain, but some remain unaware. The study of the human brain is called neuroscience and has expanded and intensified all around the globe over the last few decades. The bright light of research was magnified through the technological breakthrough called "magnetic resonance," which has allowed scientists to map the neural pathways of the brain with much greater accuracy than in the past.

As much as our knowledge and understanding of the human brain has grown dramatically over the last few decades, scientists still admit they know very little about the *mind*, and how it functions still remains a mystery. The human brain is the most complicated object scientists have ever encountered. It is a miraculous bio-computer that may never be fully understood. Although my research has been thorough, I do not pretend to be a scientist.

To begin our brief lesson in neuroscience, I kindly request that you make a fist with one hand and then wrap your other hand around the fist. What we have is a model of the human brain that is remarkably similar to the real thing. The fist represents the lower brain and the hand wrapped overtop represents the upper brain.

Recognizing that any attempt to divide and subdivide the brain by using semantics is doomed imprecision, allow me to introduce the latest widely accepted theory called the "triune brain" (triune means three-in-one). We have three brains that are highly interconnected: the first is the brain stem, called the reptilian brain or the "instinctive brain," which is unconscious. The second is the mammalian brain for the limbic system, which is subconscious. The third is the neocortex or the "thinking brain" (which splits into two sides about age seven), which is our conscious brain and performs the functions that make us uniquely human.

Because the first two brains are so highly interrelated and work so closely in harmony, they are considered to be one brain and technically called the reptilian/mammalian brain. This brain has been given different labels by various authors: lizard brain, first brain, dinosaur brain, monkey brain and horse brain. Throughout this book, I will refer to it as the lower brain.

The study of the human brain is a dynamic and rapidly enlarging area of research that is difficult to keep pace with, as there are constant new research findings that add to or replace existing theories. Let me emphasize that the following information is not psychobabble or merely a conceptual framework but rather biological realities based on the most recent scientific research.

Understanding the left and right brains is highly relevant because I believe you lead from the right brain and you *manage from the left brain*. So, let's first consider what we know about the left and right sides of the upper conscious brain:

LEFT BRAIN

Deductive thinking
(breaking things down)

Scientist

Analysis

Numbers, math

Language

Linear thinking

Content (trees)

RIGHT BRAIN

Inductive thinking
(building things up)

Artist

Creativity

Imagination

Music, rhythm

Spatial, holistic thinking

Context (forest)

Just as left-handed people use the right arm and right-handed people use the left arm, it is important to understand we all use both sides of the brain; however, one side becomes dominant. I had a workshop participant once say that he would get his right arm to be ambidextrous. Most people tend to have a left-brain or right-brain dominance to varying degrees, and it has a significant effect upon their consciousness and behaviours.

Key behavioural insights are to be found in understanding the left and right brains, but further research helped me understand that it is far more important to understand the relationship between the upper-conscious and the lower-subconscious brain.

Who people really are is essentially their lower brain; we just carry around a couple of upper-brain mind muscles (creative and analytical) that we occasionally engage when needed. Human behaviour, and thus leadership, has far more to do with the lower brain than the upper brain. When you're dealing with people, for all intents and purposes, you are dealing with their lower brain. To understand leadership is to understand people, and to understand people is to understand (to the degree that we do) how the lower-subconscious brain operates.

Ten Things to Understand about the Lower Brain to Successfully Manage It

1) The lower brain has only one purpose – *survival.*

The lower brain is basically a safety mechanism. It does almost everything with one single end-game purpose, which is to keep you safe and alive on this planet.

The lower brain governs the vast majority of your behaviour, and the scary thing is that it operates below conscious awareness. Just as you are not aware of your pancreas, liver and kidneys operating, you are not aware of the lower brain, but to be sure they are always operating.

Scientist think the lower brain is really old – 300 to 500 million years in evolutionary terms – whereas the upper brain is relatively new in evolutionary terms at only 3 to 4 million years old.

The subconscious lower brain is weirdly both very primitive and incredibly powerful in that it determines behaviours. The mind still remains a mystery, and scientists agree that we are just beginning to fully appreciate the power and full potential of the subconscious brain.

2) The lower brain is responsible for all *perception.*

One of the few areas of complete neuroscience certainty is that all the neural pathways that connect us to our world (sensory input) go directly to the lower brain, which explains why people frequently refer to the lower brain as the "first brain" because it receives information first. The lower brain uses the five senses to be aware of the environment, scanning for potential threats and dangers. A great example of the power of the lower brain is that scientists now estimate it takes in information 30,000 times faster than the upper-conscious brain. As you look back into the mists of human history, we have a word for the Homo sapiens–like creatures that were not aware of their environment, and the word is "dead."

Perception is a very odd process, and perhaps the best illustration is to be found in romantic relationships. Have you ever known someone, like a friend or sibling, who is dating or getting involved with a loser? Try as you may, but they just don't see this person as the true loser they are because the old adage is so true – love is blind. It is fundamental when dealing with people to understand that our perception is NOT reality. It is just the best our five feeble senses can do in attempting to define reality.

3) The lower brain is *instinctive*.

Upon perception of danger, the lower brain's fight-or-flight instinct reaction kicks in and commandeers our consciousness. If you are naturally a fighter, the blood flows instantly to your arms so you can pick up a rock or stick to bludgeon the saber-toothed tiger to death, or if you are naturally a flighter, the blood races to your buttocks and thigh muscles, enabling you to run thirty miles an hour and climb a tree.

A paradoxical aspect of the lower brain is that it is all-powerful in many ways, but it cannot tell the difference between something real and imagined. I ask people if they have ever woken up in the middle of the night with their heart pounding after a bad dream. Another example would be if you ever had to write a difficult exam; even if you knew your stuff, upon seeing the exam you might not be able to recall the information. The reason is that the all-powerful lower brain cannot tell the difference between a saber-toothed tiger and the exam, evoking the same physiological fight-or-flight reaction and shutting down your access to the part of the brain where the information resides; until you calm down and allow the blood to go back to the upper-conscious brain, you can't answer the question.

In 1850, Ralph Waldo Emerson said, "When you're angry, count to ten, and when really angry count to a hundred." Emerson had no clue about the science of the brain, but he did understand that when people count, they calm down. We now know why. When you have a fight-or-flight reaction, the lower brain has seized control of your consciousness. If the upper left-brain counts, you are literally shifting your consciousness back up into the rational upper brain.

In Chapter 7, I challenged you to explain the difference between reacting and responding. Understanding the upper and lower brain dynamics fully explains this vital difference. The lower brain can only react. I always ask my students how many species have the capacity to choose the response to a given environmental stimuli, such as an adversarial coworker, a highly aggressive customer or an obstinate teenager. An engineer once responded with the number three. I am still trying to figure out what the other two species are. I believe we are the only species on the planet that has the capacity to choose a response and not react. However, there is a catch – the only people who can *choose* a response as opposed to *reacting* are those who have developed their character to the point they are "response-able." This capacity has long been called maturity, whereas most recently academics want to label this capacity as EQ (emotional intelligence). We will explore this concept in detail in Chapter 10.

4) The lower brain is the wellspring of all ***emotion.***

For thousands of years, philosophers have deliberated about head and heart, intellect and emotion, sense and sensibilities. In the last few decades, science has validated that your upper brain is your head and your lower brain is your heart. When I say the word "emotion," this includes all moods, feelings, attitudes, intuitions and, most importantly for this book, motivations. Emotion and motivation have the same Latin root word, *motere* ("to move"). Whether people are happy or sad, and whether your employees are motivated or unmotivated has little or nothing to do with the upper brain and everything to do with the lower brain. If leadership is fundamentally about motivation (and it is), then leadership is really about the lower brain.

The lower emotional brain is also the seat of your values and beliefs. You think with your upper brain, but your beliefs are held in the lower brain, and if I mess with your belief system, I'm playing with nitroglycerin. If you ask people to articulate their values and beliefs off the top of their head, they will almost always struggle because their values and beliefs are not in the top their head; rather, they are held deeply within the recesses of the lower subconscious brain. If I were to observe you for a week and watch where you spend your time and money, I could probably assess your values accurately.

This explains why your parents told you to never discuss politics or religion in public. Earlier in this chapter, I spoke about how old the lower brain is in evolutionary terms. The risk I run by speaking as if evolutionary theory is scientific fact is that if you believe in creation, then the lower brain will reject that fact and I would lose significant credibility. A few years back when discussing the different ages of the brains, I was asked a question that I still struggle to answer today: "If we have evolved from monkeys, then how come there are still monkeys?"

It is vital to understand the purpose emotions are designed to serve. Basically, emotions are nature's feedback mechanism, signalling to you with positive or negative feelings and telling when you are on track or off. In Chapter 10, we will explore the subject of EQ and the role of emotions in much greater detail.

Scientists are ever more certain that the lower brain, specifically the limbic system, is the mind–body connection, which controls both your emotions and your immune system. Scientists believe that the vast majority of illnesses are psychosomatic, meaning psychological illnesses will inevitably manifest in some sort of physical illness, because *psycho*, "the mind," makes *soma*, "the body," sick.

5) The lower brain wants *immediate gratification.*

Clearly the lower brain does not understand the difference between pleasure and happiness. This is another set of words people confuse. When I ask my students to explain the difference between pleasure and happiness, I usually just get blank stares, but there was one young lady who answered the question almost immediately. She said it was obvious to her that pleasure was a temporal, visceral sensation, whereas happiness is a state of being. I replied, "Exactly," and when I went home to look those words up, I realized how accurate the young lady was.

The lower brain is forever in constant pursuit of pleasure, as it has a very short time horizon and does not anticipate consequences well. The lower brain is the impulse centre of the brain, whereas the upper brain is the impulse-*control* centre of the brain. The reason teenagers tend to take such crazy risks is that the upper impulse-control brain does not fully mature until age twenty-one to twenty-three.

To understand procrastination is to understand the power of the lower brain. Your upper brain is usually aware of the right task to be doing at the moment, but the lower brain's inner self talk is likely to suggest that you are not really in the mood or you just don't feel like it right now. A grad student once lamented in a time-management workshop that the only time she ever cleans her fridge is when she has an exam to study for. To the lower brain, suddenly cleaning the fridge becomes absolutely fascinating relative to studying, because the childlike lower brain is instinctively programmed to always take the path of least resistance and risk.

The ability to control the lower brain and delay gratification is foundational to psychological health. The ability to say no to something you want right now for something more in the future is absolutely fundamental to living a successful life. This self-control dimension of character is universal to all wisdom literature.

6) The lower brain is largely *visually driven.*

Confucius said a picture is worth a thousand words. Although he obviously knew nothing about the brain, we can now explain the potency of pictures with our species because our subconscious brain is almost exclusively visually driven. The lower brain is the emotional brain and it largely thinks in pictures, which explains why they call great leaders visionaries. Understanding the visual nature of the lower brain helps illuminate why top-performing athletes and performers prepare through a process called "visualization"; it's how you train the lower brain.

Have you created a vision for your team or organization? Have you created a vision for your life? Beware, be very careful, what you picture and imagine because the lower brain is specifically designed to bring whatever you imagine into reality with no conscious effort or strategic thought.

7) The lower brain is the ***creative brain***.

Some people might argue that creativity comes from the right brain or the upper brain; however, I believe the true source of creativity is the lower brain, and then the creative idea manifests into our consciousness through the right brain.

The old adage that your best ideas don't come at the office is true; they tend to come to you on the walk, the bike, the treadmill, or when you're cleaning the garage. The reason is in the irony that the lower brain takes in information incredibly fast, yet its creative operational system is much slower and only works in a relaxed state or when you're doing a basic task or activity that does not require a lot of upper-brain intellectual horsepower.

8) The lower brain is an *outcome-activated* mechanism.

An engineer once suggested to me that the lower brain is a teleological mechanism. I could not even find the word in the dictionary. The word *teleo* in Latin means "the end point," which serves as the prefix for words such as telegraph, telephone, television and telescope. What it means in plain talk is that the lower brain is a result-based apparatus.

Beginning a task or project without clarity of the desired outcome is a sure-fire recipe for procrastination because the lower brain will not be motivated to do the task or able to unleash its unlimited creative power unless it has a clear target or goal. The good news is that the lower brain cannot resist a question regarding a target or goal. So, to overcome procrastination the best technique is to clarify the desired results or outcomes and visualize your goal.

9) The lower brain is the ***habit*** brain.

The lower brain desperately wants to keep your behaviour the same today as it was yesterday for the simple reason that you survived yesterday. It does not like the unknown. When you examine why people resist change, you will find that like almost all other human behaviours it's rooted in the lower brain. To the lower brain, change means the unknown, unknown means risk,

risk means danger and danger means certain painful, inevitable death, so the lower brain spends a lot of energy keeping you safe within your "comfort zone." The lower brain basically wants to take all risk out of your life. The problem is it is unaware that the greatest risk of all is the risk of riskless living. No risk, no reward. If you take all risk out of life, you are simultaneously removing any chance for true achievement and success. Helen Keller said, "Life is either an exciting adventure or nothing at all."

The habit memory is technically referred to as the non-declarative or procedural memory. What this means is that anything you do consistently for a relatively short period of time automatically gets relegated from the upper conscious brain to the lower subconscious brain, and you have yourself a new habit. About 120 years ago, William James suggested it took twenty-one to thirty days to form a new habit. More recent research from Oxford University in England suggests that true habit formation takes closer to sixty to sixty-five days to become permanent.

As an example, if I move my wastepaper basket from one side of my desk to the other, I am most likely throwing paper on the floor for about three weeks until it becomes second nature or habit. Or, when you're driving your car and it begins to rain, you don't need ask yourself, "Now where are those windshield wipers?" (Unless it's a rental car.) Rather, you just turn them on and don't even remember doing it because it is subconscious second nature.

A wise person once said good habits are hard to form and easy to live with, whereas bad habits are easy to form and hard to live with. We either have success habits or failure habits, but the vast majority of our behaviour is driven habitually. I've learned that to change behaviour means to change habits, and we will discuss this in Chapter 13

10) The lower brain has its own language.

Throughout the balance of this book, I will discuss how to best manage your lower brain and the lower brain in others, so it is fundamental to understand that the lower subconscious brain has its own language operational system. The upper brain speaks the language of logic whereas the lower brain speaks the language of emotion based on the *meaning* of the incoming information, called the "meta message."

The language of the lower brain or its operational system is based on it asking two perpetual questions to identify the speaker's *intentions* and the *meaning* of the message.

Intention

The upper brain governs the *content* of what you say, whereas the lower brain deals with the intent of what you say. The first questions the lower brain is always asking are "Safe or not safe? Trust or don't trust?" It is asking, "Are we having this conversation for my benefit or for your benefit?" You do not hear this question being asked because it is subconscious, but make no mistake, it's always asking this question. The starting point of success with people in any situation is having their lower brain believe that you have their best interest at heart.

Meaning

We have already established that the lower brain is an incredibly powerful bio-computer, and yet the operational system of the lower brain is very basic, as it is simply based on one thing: *meaning*. The lower brain is always asking, "What does this *mean* to me?" There are electrical currents within the brain that are charging neurons with either positive or negative meaning. The potency of the meaning can be massive or marginal, but there are no neutral meanings. The lower brain automatically develops a positive or negative association to all things and people.

Key Learning Points

Understanding the dynamics of the upper and lower brain completely validates what Aristotle said about the head being on the far side of the heart, as the latest brain research validates that the head is indeed on the far side of the heart. It further explains the difference between influence and persuasion and why, bio-logically, I cannot possibly persuade the upper brain using logic and reason until the lower brain gatekeeper has first granted permission by gaining influence with the person.

Understanding the lower brain also explains the 360°-perception gap. Thankfully the days of the traditional performance appraisal are coming to an end and the idea of the manager being judge and jury are over. The future will be a form of multiple-source feedback. Almost all executives are now being evaluated by what they refer to as 360° feedback. It is also referred to as "multiple-source" feedback or "peer review" feedback. In organizations with the most progressive human resources practices, in particular the high-tech sector, all employees are being evaluated by multiple sources. There is always a difference or gap between how we perceive ourselves and how we are perceived by others; it is only a matter of degree as to how wide the gap this. Understanding the upper and lower brain fully explains the reason for the gap. The subconscious brain (which we are not aware of) fully controls the four big behaviour drivers: perception, instinct, emotion and habit.

Closing the perception gap between self-perception and how others perceive you is fundamental to becoming a highly effective leader. The sooner in your career you receive multiple-source feedback, the better off you'll be. Helping you close your perception gap is a central objective of this book.

The lower brain can be both your best friend and your worst enemy. It can be the source of positive energy, motivation, intuition and unlimited creativity. Or, once the lower brain takes charge, the predictable outcomes are procrastination, negative energy and a trail of broken relationships down the roadway of life. It's all a matter of control. Are you in control of your lower brain or is it in control of you?

Understanding that the vast majority of human behaviour is driven subconsciously further explains why people frequently cannot describe how they achieved their leadership success because it just seems to happen naturally or subconsciously.

The only thing in human history that has never changed and will never change is human nature. The lower brain is the nature within us and, thus, as with all of nature, it is regulated by natural laws. This will be discussed in the next chapter.

CHAPTER 9: THEY CALL IT HUMAN NATURE FOR A GOOD REASON

They call it human nature for the simple reason that we are governed by natural laws or principles. These laws operate regardless of if we are aware of them, understand them, accept them or agree with them; it does not matter. It is vitally important for leaders to understand these laws or principles given that they explain the cause-and-effect dynamics of life's success or failure in the short time that one is on this planet.

At first glance, the concept of natural laws may appear for many to be mysterious, philosophical and reserved for the intellectually elite. Yet with just a little consideration, these principles become self-evident. While at first it may seem theoretical, it will soon provide enormous practical application value. I believe the reason many people suggest common sense is not so common anymore is that society has somehow lost touch with these eternal truths.

It was Stephen Covey who first introduced me to the notion of natural laws. This was a real "aha" moment for me, and I was motivated to learn more. As I began to study philosophy, I quickly realized that natural laws have been the subject of philosophical debate and discussion for thousands of years. Natural laws are also referred to as "universal laws," "eternal laws" or "principles." For my left-brain, scientific-type reader, Sir Isaac Newton referred to the ironclad law of the universe as the "law of cause and effect."

Natural laws are different than what philosophers call "positive laws," which are created by humans. These laws or principles are truly universal in that they apply to all human beings and are not unique to any civilization, religion or ethnicity.

In Chapter 7, I challenged you to explain the difference between values and principles. Far too often, people toss these two words around as if they were synonymous, and this confusion based on the lack of knowledge of principles will almost always lead to tragedy. One of the challenges in attempting to clarify the difference is that, in an ideal situation, they are in fact one and the same, as wise people have aligned their values with correct timeless principles resulting in true security and sustainable success.

Values largely govern our behaviour and are held subconsciously, and they exist at many levels. There are societal values, which sociologists call "norms and mores." There are organizational values, which we refer to as the "culture" of the organization. We have family values, and perhaps most importantly we all possess personal values. Values are subjective, internal and constantly changing, whereas principles are self-evident, objective, external, timeless, changeless and bedrock truths that are unarguable because they are self-validating.

To paraphrase Marshall McLuhan's quote from Chapter 1, "Fish discover water last"; I suspect he was referring to natural laws. A paradox of the twenty-first century is that many people are unhappy and wondering why their lives are not working. They are endlessly searching for answers in the form of some new-age, high-tech, complicated or psychological solution, and yet these painfully obvious success principles are right in front of their noses the entire time. Tangible evidence of natural laws or principles is to be found all around us. Here are some examples:

The Farm

In 1900, a full 50% of North Americans lived on a farm; by 1950, it dropped 5% I believe when we left the farm as a society, we somehow drifted from correct principles, and the predictable bitter harvests are manifested broadly in family breakdown, bullying, increasing lack of civility and soaring rates of depression and suicide.

A classic text written by James Allen in 1903 called *As a Man Thinketh* suggested that your mind, your relationships and ultimately your life are like a garden or plot of land that must and will bring forth. The metaphor of your life as a garden can help us understand the difference between values and principles. Let's assume the farmer plants seeds in the spring, but his values change over the summer months. Instead of tending the plot of land consistently with correct gardening principles such as cultivating, watering and weeding, the farmer spends his summer months golfing, playing tennis and suntanning. It is vital to remember that Allen emphasized that the garden must and will bring forth. As the fall harvest season approaches, that plot of land (your life) will either create a bountiful harvest or it will be full of weeds. If you plant lentils, you will harvest lentils, and if you plant corn, you will harvest corn. Alan suggested it follows that good thoughts never produce bad results, and bad thoughts never produce good results. You can't fool Mother Nature.

Economics

They don't call them guidelines of economics or suggestions of economics; they call them laws of economics, and they do this for a very specific reason – you can't break principles. You can only break yourself, your family, your team, your organization or your civilization against them. A couple of well-known economic laws are "supply and demand" and "risk and reward." You can violate principles for a period of time, but many individuals, organizations and governments have found out the hard way that, in the long run, the laws of economics reign supreme and painful consequences will be realized directly proportionate to the degree of violation of the law.

Science & Mathematics

It is my understanding that the study of science is the pursuit to identify the laws or principles that explain our physical world. After the apple dropped on his head, Sir Isaac Newton identified and labelled the causal law as the "attraction of the masses," which you know as the law of gravity. Whether I am aware of this law, understand this law, like this law or agree with this law is utterly irrelevant because principles operate regardless.

The compass is a great example of how principles govern our physical world because the compass always points to true north. To illustrate the difference between values and principles, I ask participants in my leadership workshops to close their eyes and on the count of three to point north. Inevitably I have participants pointing in different directions. I then choose a participant to convince the group which way they believe north is by using oratory and persuasive skills. I soon suggest we could apply the democratic process and have the group vote to determine which way north is. The group quickly agrees the process of debate or democracy won't solve the problem. I ask, "If we did use debate or democracy to determine the direction you think north is, what would the people outside the room be likely to call those of you agreeing to this?" The answer is that they would call the group wrong and also very soon to be lost. True north is true north and is not subject to debate or democracy because it is a changeless principle.

Personal Dimension

All four components of self: physical, emotional, mental and spiritual are governed by natural laws or principles. However, only one of the four dimensions is where natural laws are readily perceptible and measurable, providing us with one of the most palpable and frequently painful examples of how natural laws govern.

It is our physical selves that provide the obvious proof of the power of principles. When it comes to cardiovascular conditioning, I can offer a 100% good-faith guarantee that, when you commit to working out, in a relatively short period there is a physical principle that will lower your blood pressure and heart rate. A person asked me why this happens, and I responded I didn't know because I'm not that bright; I just know that as sure as water flows downhill, it always happens, because it's a principle.

The weight-loss industry is littered with promises of solutions that may deliver short-term results, but the truth remains that weight-loss endeavours are governed by a very basic principle. If you consume more calories than you expend, your weight will increase, and if you expend more calories than you consume, you will lose weight. I realize that various combinations of proteins, fats and carbs can make a weight-loss difference; however, when all is said and done, the truth remains that a simple principle will determine success or failure.

Interpersonal Dimension

When you really think about it, every family, team, organization, association and eventually all civilizations are really just series of intertwined and overlapping relationships. Two truths are that life occurs in relationships, and all relationships are governed by natural laws or principles.

The great anthropologist Arnold Toynbee concluded after his life's work of studying ancient civilizations that every time a civilization had their norms and mores in alignment with correct principles, this resulted in stability, growth and success. He emphasized that every time (not most of the time) a society had their value systems stray from correct principles, this resulted in decline, destruction and eventually complete disintegration. A cursory review of human history would lead anyone to the exact same conclusion. A civilization is just a series of interpersonal relationships, as is an organization, team or family, and we have a relationship within ourselves.

Timeless Life Success Principles

Here is a list of some of the key life-success principles.

Personal Principles:

- *Responsibility*
- *Integrity*
- *Self-discipline/temperance*
- *Humility*
- *Courage*
- *Patience*
- *Industry/perseverance*
- *Modesty*

- *Cleanliness*
- *Excellence/quality*
- *Growth (personal and professional development)*

Inter-personal Principles:

- *Service*
- *Empathy/compassion*
- *Respect*
- *Dignity*
- *Politeness*
- *Honesty/truthfulness*
- *Justice/fairness*
- *Kindness*
- *Generosity*
- *Forgiveness*
- *Loyalty*

Key Learning Points

Gaining clarity about how principles are different than values leads us to an understanding of wisdom. Character could be defined as the capacity to align your values (thoughts and behaviours) with correct timeless principles. The basic truth is that, to the degree that you align your values and behaviours in harmony with these principles, you will experience success, and to the degree you do not live in harmony with these principles, you will experience failure.

Many people have the mistaken belief that the study of wisdom is a deeply profound, mysterious and secretive body of knowledge held in reserve only for the academic elite or those deeply philosophical people who sit on mountain-tops in loincloths chanting mantras. The truth is that wisdom is simple and straightforward, and has a lot of common sense. Wisdom is basically a body of literature that is an equation, formula or recipe as to how to live a success-ful life. So, to measure how wise a person is, the simple question is how well is their life working? Wisdom literature is very old, and that's why they don't call it psychology. So why did wisdom literature stand the test of time? Perhaps Churchill provided the answer when he said, "The truth is incontrovertible. Malice may attack, ignorance may deride, but in the end there is." Principles are the truth.

The reason you already intuitively know these principles are true and correct is because principles are embodied within all humankind. The repository of these timeless truths is our conscience. Our conscience is one of the four unique human endowments that explain why we have dominion on this planet, which we will explore in greater depth in Chapter 12.

It is vital to learn that we can choose our actions, but we cannot control the consequences of our actions because consequences are governed by principles. For example, you can choose to jump off a ten-storey building, but I don't suspect you'll have much success changing your mind as you pass the second floor. You can choose to eat whatever you want, exercise as little as you choose and chant positive affirmations that you will not gain weight, but whether you gain or lose weight is determined by principles.

We've established that it is not wise to be building houses on the beach because the only things in the human dimension that will stand the test of time are those built on the bedrock foundation of correct principles. In Jim Collins's book, *Built to Last*, he outlined his research findings, which identified why some companies were successful over time while others achieved short-term success and then vanished. His central conclusion was the companies that did achieve sustainable success adapted and changed their practices based on customer demands and competitive pressures. However, he identified that the secret of their success was based on the fact that they never changed or deviated from their core principles, which he referred as their "core philosophy." In all cases, the philosophy was specifically designed to nurture ongoing trust with all stakeholders.

Technically, principles are the manifestation of natural laws, so I refer to these laws as principles. It is vital that you understand the power of principles, as the understanding of natural laws is fundamental to the balance of the book.

CHAPTER 10: EMOTIONAL INTELLIGENCE - THE MYTHS AND THE MASTERY

Effective leadership behaviours flow naturally, with no conscious upper-brain thought or effort required, from people with high EQ, or emotional intelligence. The basic equation is:

EQ = Effective Leadership Behaviours

A word of warning: I have a love–hate relationship with the EQ literature. I very much value the deep and extensive research conducted over the last few decades, although the findings are more validating than eye-opening. The pre-eminent author Daniel Goleman, who I consider to be the godfather of this subject, nutshelled the research eloquently and concisely by saying, "We now have hard data on the soft stuff."

However, as much as experts in this field want to position the subject as scientific and objective, it is not. EQ at its core is still fundamentally subjective, with many authors and researchers holding very different ideas as to what it really is. There is a particular lack of consensus as to the strategies on how to develop it. I will be briefly pointing out the specific concerns I have with this supposedly new field of study. My opinions will likely be considered controversial and not be fully accepted by many in the psychological community. Many would consider my opinions provocative, as they are mainly inconsistent or even contrary to current pop psychology.

The first IQ test was developed in 1904 by the French psychologist Alfred Binet in response to requests from the French school system to help identify students who were at risk of falling behind and the French military, who were trying to decide which recruits were best suited for officer school and which should be sent to the front lines. The research around IQ conducted by social scientists over the last century was longitudinal and global, which lends to high degrees of validity. For example, they would test the IQ of the graduating university class in 1928, and as these people would retire forty years downstream, the research would compare career success relative to IQ. The outcomes were remarkably consistent.

As mentioned in Chapter 6, IQ scores do correlate to higher grades in school; however, once people left school, the social scientists could find no correlation between IQ and career success. In fact, frequently they discovered a negative correlation between IQ and career success.

From a personal perspective, all of us know people who succeed in school but fail in life, and vice versa. From a research perspective, the jury is in, the conclusions are crystal clear and the case is closed – EQ is a significantly more important success factor than IQ. The famed Harvard psychology professor David McClelland summed it up very nicely when he proclaimed, "The world is run by C+ students!"

When students ask what books to read on EQ, my first recommendation is Daniel Goleman's second book, *Working with Emotional Intelligence,* in which he focuses on the applied side of EQ. To validate the supremacy of EQ as a predictor of success, here are some of his research findings:

✓ *1975 Harvard study of law, medicine and business graduates found that IQ scores had no negative correlation to career success*

✓ *1994 study involving 121 organizations' abilities contributing to outstanding job performance – 73% were function of EQ!*

✓ *Forty-year study of PhD scientists at University of California at Berkeley found that EQ was four times as important to career success as IQ*

✓ *1995 study of international companies (IBM, Volvo, Pepsi) discovered over 90% of the capacities contributed to leadership effectiveness were functions of EQ*

The fundamental and primary importance of EQ can no longer be disputed. It is foundational to all personal and professional success. The more the job involves dealing with people, the greater the importance of EQ as a success factor. While EQ alone does not do anything for you, you can't do anything without EQ. Figuratively, EQ is to leadership what cardiovascular fitness is to playing sports. A soccer player might possess tremendous natural talent and work hard to develop highly honed skills, but all is for naught if after a few minutes of playing the player is on their knees gasping for oxygen.

What do you call people who have high IQ *and* high EQ? The answer is "highly successful." I do not mean to completely undermine the importance of IQ, because IQ is a wonderful thing to have and so is hand–eye coordination or musical talent. The study of IQ and EQ is really a good news/bad news story. The bad news is that IQ is much more an innate or natural talent than a skill, which means it is only marginally malleable up to about age fifteen to seventeen and then it is fixed for life. The really good news is that the key to truly effective leadership is in your EQ, which can be developed.

Emotional Intelligence, a Historical Perspective

- 1920s – The renowned psychologist Edward Thorndike, who was an original and forceful proponent of IQ, did admit there was a capacity unrelated to IQ that could not be measured. He called it "social intelligence," which he described as the ability to understand others and act wisely in human relations.

- 1930s – Dale Carnegie in his classic 1936 book *How to Win Friends and Influence People*, suggested that people skills were far more important than technical skills in determining career success. He referred to this ability as "human engineering."

- 1950s – Abraham Maslow, who is considered to be the father of humanistic psychology, was the first psychologist to study psychologically healthy people. Maslow did seminal research in the area of study now called EQ long before it was labelled EQ. Although he did have a major influence on Stephen Covey's work, I feel Maslow does not get near the credit he deserves for the contributions he made. Maslow considered people who were truly psychologically healthy to be "self-actualized," which means they are largely free from negative energies, insecurities, anxiety, depression and other forms of what psychologists call neurosis. I was pleasantly surprised to find out that Maslow estimated a low percentage (I have read it is somewhere between only 1% to 3%) of the western world's population ever achieved this lofty status of psychological health, as it helped me realize I was not alone in my struggles and almost everyone is fighting their own unseen battles.

- 1980s – Howard Gardner's breakthrough book *Frames of Mind* effectively refuted the supremacy of IQ and suggested that there were "multiple intelligences." Gardner made a convincing case that IQ testing was dramatically incomplete in that it only measures two (linguistic and mathematical/logical) of the seven innate intelligences or aptitudes. The other five intelligences he proposed were musical, visual/spatial, kinesthetic, intra-personal skills (self-management) and interpersonal skills. The British author Charles Handy later added two more that he called mechanical and factual (the ability to recall facts and statistics).

- 1985 – An Israeli psychiatrist named Reuven Bar-On is credited with the original creation of the label "emotional quotient," which was a play on the label IQ, intelligence quotient.

- 1990 – Yale and Harvard professors named Peter Salovey and John Mayer, respectively, are credited with being the first to coin the label "emotional intelligence," although they refuse to accept credit for the naming.

- 1995 – Daniel Goleman published *Emotional Intelligence*, establishing the topic outside academia and creating a seismic reaction in the fields of education, human resource management and specifically leadership development. The instant and universal appeal of this book was because there was finally a scientific approach to what was previously considered by many to be soft, touchy-feely psychobabble.

Some Basic Things to Know about EQ

EQ transcends race, ethnicity and gender. There appear to be natural gender differences – for example, women are naturally more empathic than men and are slightly less prone to depression – but in totality there is no gender advantage. The research on age correlation to EQ suggests that EQ peaks in a person's late forties.

There are many different definitions and descriptions of EQ, but there is one commonality in that every EQ model is broken into two separate components:

1) *Intra*personal – The capacity to effectively *manage your own emotions*
2) *Inter*personal – The capacity to *evoke favourable emotional responses from others*

To help people understand what EQ is in a more concrete and complete manner, I have developed a holistic competency model that explains in specific terms what is involved in each of the interrelated competencies.

EQ: Intrapersonal Dimension – Competency Model

❑ Self-awareness

- Emotional literacy – ability to read your current emotional state (mood) and understand why
- Capacity to stand apart from yourself and gain accurate situational awareness
- More complete and accurate perception of reality thus more accurate future predictions
- Capacity to objectively self-analyze

❑ Self-understanding

- Accurate self-assessment of your natural strengths and non-strengths
- Strong "sense of identity" resulting from a well-developed and clear value system
- Healthy acceptance of your human frailties, absence of illegitimate guilt

❑ Self-regulation

- Capacity to choose a response as opposed to reacting
- Self-discipline to make and keep commitments
- Ability to control your emotions, particularly anger, and calm yourself
- Capacity to control impulses and delay gratification
- Capacity to concentrate and focus when need arises

❑ Self-motivation

- Strong "sense of purpose"
- Achievement drive, goal orientation
- Ability to take prudent risk and initiative
- Initiative and courage to act as opposed to being acted upon
- Persistence, stick-to-it-iveness

❏ Self-confidence

- Belief in your ability to solve life's problems
- Absence of self-doubt and negative self-talk in moments of action
- Willingness to accept feedback about how you are perceived by others
- Comfort in dealing with change and ambiguity; not threatened by the unknown

❏ Practical intuition

- Common sense
- Good judgment, ability to make good decisions
- Ability to connect cause and effect of your behaviour and resulting circumstances
- Ability to balance between intuition and reason when making decisions

❏ Positive mood predisposition

- Natural predisposition towards predominately positive emotions (happiness)
- Natural predisposition towards calmness as opposed to anxiety
- Absence of illegitimate negative emotions and thought (worry, guilt, envy)
- Optimistic versus pessimistic thinking bias
- Emotional resiliency – capacity to maintain perspective in difficult situations

EQ: <u>Interpersonal</u> Dimension – Competency Model

❑ Service orientation

- Absence of ego and self-interest; truly focused on helping followers
- Contribution versus consumption mindset
- Altruistic behaviours based on genuine desire to help the human race
- Capacity to subjugate personal interests to the interests of the group

❑ Empathy

- Capacity to understand how others feel and why
- Capacity to listen non-judgmentally
- Being truly "present" when listening, focusing energy on others as opposed to self
- Absence of a need to pre-judge others
- Capacity to read how your words are impacting others
- Ability to perceive others accurately and efficiently

❑ Assertion

- Ability to ensure that your needs are being met
- Capacity to stand up for your just and fair rights
- Capacity to communicate your thoughts, feelings and ideas honestly, clearly, tactfully and persuasively
- Capacity to hold others accountable to their commitments

❑ Authenticity

- Capacity to be your "natural self" when communicating
- Absence of projected artificialities
- Natural spontaneity in behaviour, absence of inhibitions
- Absence of self-consciousness

❑   Relationship efficacy

- Capacity to build long-term relationships through greater fusion and obliteration of ego boundaries
- Interdependence, ability to be an effective team player
- Capacity to demonstrate patience and forgiveness
- Ability to get other people's needs met as well as your own

❑   Conflict resolution

- Ability to stay calm and reasonable in moments of conflict (choose a response and not react)
- Ability to negotiate by collaborative problem solving, ensuring all parties feel good about the outcome
- Ability to deal effectively with difficult people
- Ability to disagree without being disagreeable

❑   Leadership

- Ability to gain influence with others and win people over to your way of thinking
- Ability to have people follow you willingly
- Natural pre-disposition to perceive the potential in people
- Capacity to get results through others

The above two competency models are my attempt to make this intangible subject more tangible by giving a real-world handle on what EQ looks like. A second, less-academic approach to assist in gaining a ground-level appreciation of EQ is to provide examples of what low EQ looks like in action. Below is a partial list of the highly predictable, even inevitable destructive behavioural manifestations of low EQ.

Predictable Attitudes & Behaviours of Low-EQ People (the Opposite of Effective Leadership)

- ☐ Defensive, hypersensitive, easily and often offended
- ☐ Pettiness, nitpicking
- ☐ Blows things out of proportion or minimizes things
- ☐ Doesn't take responsibility for their feelings
- ☐ Doesn't listen well, interrupts, is insensitive or dismissive of others' feelings
- ☐ Blames, criticizes others
- ☐ Tends to complain a lot (even about things they have no control over)
- ☐ Lacks "situational awareness" due to self-consciousness (preoccupied by fear of being judged)
- ☐ Gossips, put-down artists
- ☐ Difficulty building and maintaining productive relationships
- ☐ Adjusts their personality based on who they are with
- ☐ Has a pessimistic outlook, sees problems in every opportunity
- ☐ Carries grudges, incapable of forgiving or letting go
- ☐ Judges and labels people
- ☐ Projects negative energy, uncomfortable to be around
- ☐ Doesn't consider other's feelings before acting
- ☐ Cannot and will not admit mistakes
- ☐ Finds it almost impossible to apologize
- ☐ Perceives themselves as victims of an unfair world
- ☐ Often feels inadequate but are fearful of appearing so, rarely admit when they don't know something
- ☐ Resistant to change, rigidly cling to their beliefs
- ☐ Spends a lot of time and energy rationalizing and making excuses for their problems and errors
- ☐ Often feels disappointed and bitter
- ☐ Loves to hear about other people's problems
- ☐ Seeks status and authority, tends to be a name-dropper
- ☐ Focused on getting the credit when things go well
- ☐ Focused on allocating blame and pointing fingers when things go wrong

- ☐ Needs other people or situations to be happy
- ☐ Demonstrates "know-it-all attitude"
- ☐ Braggarts who tend to one-up people

Beware, because the more crucial the conversation and the more at stake, the more likely the lack of EQ will manifest in the above destructive and counter-productive attitudes and behaviours. A secondary use for these descriptors is to perform a self-assessment. Put a check in each of the boxes where you are guilty as charged.

How to Develop Your EQ – Principles

The good news is that anyone can become physically fit and anyone can become more emotionally or psychologically fit because both physical and psychological health are governed by natural laws or principles. There is even more good news – the process is really quite simple – but the problem is that it's not easy.

In Chapter 7, I challenged you to define the difference between "simple" and "easy." I suspect many of you have already clarified the often-misunderstood difference, but allow me to confirm that the word "simple" refers to the degree of *complexity* involved, whereas the word "easy" refers to the degree of *effort* and *sacrifice* required to achieve success. I fear far too many people do not understand this vital difference, and as a result, they spend their lives looking for quick fixes, wealth without work, get-rich-quick schemes and shortcuts to success. In natural systems, there are no shortcuts. There are no shortcuts to physical fitness, to psychological health or to building sustainable, productive relationships, and there are no shortcuts to becoming a highly effective leader.

I have learned that in almost all endeavours, there are only a few basic or fundamental competencies. We know this to be true because if there were a lot of competencies, we wouldn't call them the fundamentals. A convincing case could be made that achieving success in almost all activities in life is really quite simple because it only involves sustained and focused effort on mastering the few fundamentals involved. Therefore, I believe the true development of EQ has much more to do with earning than learning.

People demonstrate effective leadership behaviours naturally to the degree that they have good EQ. To peel one more layer of the EQ onion, the primary underpinning principle is that **people demonstrate high EQ behaviours naturally to the degree that they possess healthy self-esteem.**

EQ is an "effect," whereas self-esteem is the "cause." Therefore, to improve EQ, you must improve self-esteem. I believe there is tremendous confusion surrounding this all-important subject, which means we must first clarify what self-esteem is. Then we must strive to understand the principles governing the cause and effect of self-esteem dynamics.

When I mention self-esteem, I run the risk of people starting to think, *Oh no, here we go, more touchy-feely, group hugs and spontaneous renditions of Kumbaya.* Let me assure you that self-esteem is not psychobabble or pop-psychology; it is real and it happens to be the cornerstone of success in all dimensions of life.

Perhaps the notion of self-esteem has been tarnished in recent years by the increasingly evident failure of the so-called "self-esteem movement" in the US educational system over the last few decades. Well-intended educators have made a terrible mistake on the subject of student self-esteem because of confusion around the true cause-and-effect principles that govern real self-esteem. They appear to lack understanding of the fundamental truth that you cannot *give* people true self-esteem but rather you must provide the environment where the student can *earn* true self-esteem. The expanded equation is this:

$$Self\text{-}Esteem = EQ = Effective\ Leadership\ Behaviours$$

What Self-Esteem Really Is

Allow me to provide a simple, valid and practical definition: *Self-esteem is the quality of the relationship we have with self.* Or, in the most basic terms: *Self-esteem is how we feel about ourselves.*

How one feels about self is a function of what one believes about self. Thus, self-esteem is a function of one's "self-image," how we perceive ourselves or what we believe about ourselves at a lower-brain subconscious level. Recalling from Chapter 8 that the lower emotional brain operates on the basis of **meaning**, you could refine my definition of self-esteem as, "the meaning of the relationship you have with yourself." To the emotional brain, the meaning is either positive or negative, massively or marginally, but the lower brain has no neutral gear. A law of nature says the only emotions that can come from a negative meaning are negative, and the only emotions that could come a positive meaning are positive.

There are many different short-term pleasures that can create a temporary positive emotional state; however, when all is said and done, the single most important factor that governs your emotional life (how happy you are) in a first, foremost and fundamental manner is your self-image. A wise philosopher once explained it by saying, "No matter where you go, there you are." The only emotions (how you feel about yourself) that can possibly come from a positive self-image are positive, and the only emotions that can come from a negative self-image are negative. The full equation is as follows:

$$Self\text{-}Image = Self\text{-}Esteem = EQ = Effective\ Leadership\ Behaviours$$

The great news is anyone can enhance their self-image. It follows logically that self-esteem and thus EQ and leadership effectiveness can be grown and developed!

The Need for Self-Esteem

Abraham Maslow helped me understand that our species has a hierarchical set of physiological and psychological needs. It is the pursuit to fulfill the unmet needs that drives our behaviour. Although physiological needs (mostly conscious) precede psychological needs (mostly unconscious), the need for self-esteem in our species is just as real and powerful as our need for air, food and water. Once physiological needs are satisfied (as they largely are in the western world), it is the psychological needs that play a more dominant role in determining behaviour.

There are only two sources of this precious, priceless substance called self-esteem – the opinion you have of yourself and the opinion others have of you. The governing principle is the more you achieve self-esteem through your opinion of yourself, naturally the less you need acceptance, approval and validation from others. The subconscious need to go externally for self-esteem is called

ego, which to the Greek philosophers meant "I" or "self." Those people who do not meet their self-esteem needs through the opinion of themselves have a subconscious need to get their self-esteem from others, which drives (unknowingly) the exact opposite of effective leadership behaviours.

The English word "secure" is a derivative of two Latin words: *se*, which means "without," and *cure*, which means "fear." As mentioned earlier in this book, we are now in the age of anxiety due to the ever-increasing rate of change. This has created a whitewater world where we can no longer source our personal security by predicting our future as our parents and grandparents could in the relatively stationary and predictable world of the industrial age. If you need to source your self-esteem externally today, through your position, possessions and other people's opinions, you are at ever-greater risk because external sources are like quicksand, offering no long-term stability. The only source of true personal security is to have a changeless core within you by aligning your values with correct, changeless, rock-solid principles.

Principle – To the degree you need to go externally (other people's opinions) to satisfy self-esteem needs, you are insecure. To the degree you achieve self-esteem to the opinion of self, you are secure.

I believe the only real way to improve your self-image and thus self-esteem is to EARN it through the long, hard process of becoming a person who is honestly worthy of esteem in their own eyes, by becoming a person of ever-greater ***character, control, competency*** and ***compassion.***

The "4 C's" of Developing True (Internally Driven) Self-Esteem

These four strategies are sure-fire, 100% guaranteed to work because they are principles. The benefits of following these four strategies to your psychological health will be just as certain and real as the benefits you enjoy in your physical health from doing exercise.

I strongly suspect many people in the psychological community would not buy into my beliefs as to how to develop true self-esteem; these beliefs are much more based in wisdom than pop psychology. But the following list of strategies is absolutely valid, although possibly incomplete.

1] Character

The cornerstone foundation of life success, according to the Greek philosophers, was the development of one's character. Ancient wisdom provides us with a crystal-clear consensus – character is foundational to success in *all* relationships, including the relationship with self!

Greek philosophy was essentially the study of happiness. The original and central purpose of the philosophers was to ascertain how to be happy (without intoxicants) and live a successful life. The first five letters of the word for happiness in Greek is *chara* because the Greeks figured out that the only source of true happiness is happiness with oneself, which is achieved through the character development required to lead a virtuous life. Abraham Lincoln concurred with the Greek philosophers in the most succinct manner when he said, "When I do good, I feel good."

Character is about the only thing that really matters, because character is to leadership what carbon is to steel. Tragically, most people today are dangerously uninformed and even completely unfamiliar with this. Similar to leadership and most other truly important things, character is a difficult topic to define concretely. The most common definition I hear is "who you are when no one else is watching." Character might be defined as the ability to fulfill a commitment you made to yourself or to someone else long after the mood in which the commitment was born has left you. Maybe the best measure of a person's true character is in how they treat people who can do nothing to them or for them. Character is simply the truth about who you really are and not what you appear to be.

The truest test of character is your capacity to make and keep (honour) commitments and promises. This means having a nonexistent to **say/do gap**. The best metric of a person's character is their PKR (promise-keeping ratio). If I make a commitment to someone and break it, predictably there's a price to pay in that relationship as the person won't trust me because I have proven not to be trustworthy. If you were to make a commitment to self and break it, do you think there's a price to be paid in relationship with self as result? If you were to consume poison unknowingly, wouldn't it kill you nonetheless? The answer is yes, the price will be paid; if we break commitments to ourselves, we will inevitably feel less self-trust or less secure. The frightening part is that the price is subconscious and psychological, manifesting in chronic negative emotions.

The starting point of developing character is to understand you can never make a commitment to self and break it. This is not psychology; rather, it is ancient wisdom. As Polonius said in Shakespeare's *Hamlet*: "This above all: to thine own self be true."

Dale Wimbrow wrote a classic poem in 1934 called "The Person in the Mirror" (the real title of this poem is "The Man in the Glass" – I took the liberty of modernizing the title). When I read that poem many years ago, it really struck me, and as a result it has stuck with me. Permit me to share an abbreviated, modernized version:

When you get what you want in your struggle for self
and the world makes you royalty for a day
Just go to the mirror and look at yourself
and see what that person has to say

For it isn't your father, mother, husband or wife
whose judgment upon you must pass
The person whose verdict counts the most in your life
is the one staring back from the glass

You may fool the whole world down the pathway
of life and get pats on the back as you pass
But your final reward will be heartaches and
tears if you've cheated the person in the glass

Sadly, many people are taking heaping spoonful's of psychological toxins on a daily basis and suffer from anxiety and depression, not consciously aware they are the authors of their own misfortune. I wholly accept there are many physiological reasons that can cause psychological disturbances that are completely independent of character deficiencies. However, I also believe there are many people who suffer psychological problems because they are not very happy with themselves.

Life is hard and full of ups and downs. Character also includes a dimension of we might call "mental toughness" or emotional resilience. In the simplest terms, it is your capacity to pick yourself up after having been knocked down. This is an absolute certainty in everyone's life; the key is to understand that it's not how many times you get knocked down but rather how many times you pick yourself up.

2) Control

This capacity for self-control has been referred to as many things throughout the years – self-discipline, dominion over self, self-mastery or willpower. Self-control and character are the flipside of the same coin in that they are inextricably linked. Because the measure of your character is the capacity to fulfill commitments, self-control is central to your ability to keep promises.

Chinese philosopher Lao Tzu, in a book written about 2,800 years ago called *Tao Te Ching,* which translated means "the path to a virtuous [character-based] and successful life" said, "The only path to a successful life is to live in harmony with the *laws of nature* and take control of your life, and the only way to take control of your life is to take complete responsibility for your life."

Maturity is best defined by your capacity to look at yourself in the mirror and say, "My life is not working, and it's my fault. I am responsible." The bad news is that you are responsible for your current circumstance, but the good news is that, as soon as you accept this truth, what it means to the lower brain is that you are in control. A sense of control is one of the purest forms of psychological vitamins and the best driver of personal security. The hard truth is that until a person can say, "I am who I am and where I am because of choices *I* made," they cannot say, "I choose otherwise."

The opposite of taking responsibility and creating a sense of control in your life is called victimhood. Perceiving yourself as a victim is an incredibly dangerous psychological place to be in. Victim mentality is rooted in the belief that your current circumstances are because of what other people have done to you. This belief is fundamentally disempowering. Victims never change and grow – if you believe your current issue is not your fault, you will never be motivated to change. The feeling of powerlessness is perhaps the deadliest of all psychological toxins.

Self-control is a measure of your ability to choose an upper-brain **response** as opposed to a lower-brain "fight-or-flight" **reaction**. Only people who are *response-able* or mature can make this choice. Self-control could also be defined as your capacity to delay gratification.

One of the most famous psychological experiments was a test of children's impulse control. These experiments are frequently referred to as the "marshmallow kids." It has been duplicated and videoed many times; it's easy to find on the Internet and humorous to watch. The original experiment was conducted in the 1960s by Walter Mischel, who was a psychology professor at Stanford University. He evaluated 573 four-year-old children from the school's daycare facility to test their capacity to delay gratification. The challenge was simple – he would tell the child he had to go for a brief period of time, leaving the child alone. He offered a marshmallow for the child to eat immediately, or if the child waited until his return, he would give the child a second marshmallow. Mischel kept track of as many of the four-year-olds as possible in their late teens and the findings were quite remarkable. The psychological and social difference between the marshmallow-eating preschoolers and their gratification-delaying peers was dramatic. He found that the four-year-olds that demonstrated the patience and impulse control to wait for the second marshmallow were more socially competent, assertive, empathic, better under stress, more confident, trustworthy and dependable. They took more initiative in project starts and were more persistent in project completion. The most tangible measurement was that they scored on average 210 points higher on the SAT exam than the marshmallow-gobbling toddlers. I believe that, whereas those in the psychological community found these results to be astounding, those who are grounded in philosophical literature find the results to be validation of ancient wisdom.

Perhaps there is no psychological ability more fundamentally important then resisting impulse: the ability to say no to something you want right now for something more you want in the future. A serious problem that many people have is they don't know or have not clarified what they want in the future, which undermines their capacity to delay gratification in a significant manner. Mischel summarized his study by saying that goal-directed, self-imposed delay of gratification is foundational to success in all of life's endeavours. Just as it is true that every time you break a commitment to self you are unknowingly consuming psychological toxins, every time you demonstrate self-control or self-denial, or as Covey would put it, "victory over self," you are consuming psychological vitamins of the purest kind. The lower emotional brain needs a sense of self-control as much as roses need rain.

After years of studying why some people are successful while others fail, Albert E.N. Gray ultimately came to a conclusion and wrote an essay called "The Common Denominator of Success." He determined that the so-called secret of every person who has ever been successful came down to one basic truth – they had the self-control required to form habits for doing things that unsuccessful people did not like to do. It's just as true as it sounds, and it's just as simple as it seems.

Furthermore, self-control is fundamental to interpersonal success because if you are reacting (verbal violence or verbal silence) as opposed to responding in crucial conversations, that conversation is sure to fail, and if your key conversations are failing, your relationships will be failing. If a few relationships are failing, your life will be failing.

3] Competency

Human resources professionals now frequently talk about "competencies." They agree that competency is defined by the capacity to achieve desired results. A very rich source of self-esteem is **achievement**. An old English adage says, "Those who chop their own firewood are thrice warm." You can get warm working up a sweat chopping the wood and then sitting in front of the burning logs, but the most important and sustainable warmth comes from a sense of accomplishment. One of the most powerful and potent fuels in the furnace of self-esteem is achievement for the simple reason that ships were designed to sail, planes were designed to fly and Homo sapiens were designed for achievement.

An associated element of this taproot of self-esteem is what psychologists referred to as "self-efficacy," which means a subconscious belief that one is capable and competent to deal with life's inevitable problems. Every time well-intended parents step in to solve their child's problems, the unintended negative meta message to the child's lower brain is *You are not capable*. My mother often said to me that I got myself into the problem so it was up to me to get myself out. This tough-love approach to parenting sends the child's lower brain the vital message *I think you are capable*.

Fundamental to successful leadership is the development of credibility, and fundamental to the development of credibility is the capacity to get things done, or simply put, to achieve desired results. You would know this set of skills under the industrial-age banner of "time management." We will redefine this competency as "personal productivity skills" in Chapter 13. We have already established that character is the root of trust whereas competence is the taproot of credibility.

4) Compassion

All the truly great leaders in human history, as defined by those who would achieve sustainable and even growing influence throughout their life and long after they were gone, were all servant leaders. This means they were genuinely motivated to serve others as opposed to having ego-driven self-aggrandizement. Any cursory review of history will lead you to the conclusion that all leaders driven by self-interest came to an ugly end. The principle of compassion is simply this: every time you help or serve someone else with no intention of getting something in return, you have just consumed psychological vitamins as you enhance your self-image.

Perhaps the greatest of all American philosophers, Ralph Waldo Emerson, put it this way: "One of the most beautiful compensations in life is that no person can help another without helping him or herself." When Albert Einstein was asked what the purpose of life was, he instantly responded, "To serve others." The renowned clinical psychiatrist Karl Menninger was once asked by a young newspaper reporter as he was closing out a press conference, "If you had a patient call and say they were about to commit suicide, what advice would you give the person?" Without missing a beat, Menninger replied he would tell the patient to go to the worst part of town, find somebody who really needed help and help them.

In summary, anyone can become a more effective leader because everyone can improve their self-image, thus self-esteem, thus EQ and thus leadership effectiveness. The catch is that true self-esteem must be earned. But remember, the process of growing self-esteem is quite simple – all you have to do is become the person you would want your children to become.

The Problems I Have with the EQ Literature

1) Both the abbreviations EI and EQ are erroneousness.

My belief is that both EI (emotional intelligence) and EQ (emotional quotient) labels are misnomers. The dictionary definition of the word intelligence is "one's mental or intellectual capacity or ability to learn or understand and solve complex problems through analysis and reason." The word "intelligence" comes from the Latin word *intelligere*, "to understand." Intelligence is your ability to comprehend different degrees of complexity or abstraction. As we established in Chapter 10, IQ is widely considered to be much more of an innate talent than a skill that can be learned and developed. To label EQ as intelligence is quite depressing because that would mean EQ is something you either have or don't have. Perhaps the most appropriate and accurate label would be "EF" for "emotional fitness," inferring something anyone can attain through effort.

I also struggle with the EQ label because the word "quotient" infers a measurement. Despite the vast number of EQ assessment tools available, I believe there is no standard, objective, hard or precise measurement of this all-important soft capacity. Although I offer a twenty-question EQ inventory, I warn participants that even in their heart of hearts when they are attempting to be honest in answering the questions, given the fact that the vast majority of our behaviour is driven subconsciously, true objectivity and accuracy is impossible to achieve.

A down-and-dirty acid-test measurement of your EQ is in the answer to the following question: when you take a look at the 20% relationships with people that you spend 80% of your time with, are they working as evidenced by deep, spontaneous, open and honest communication? If the answer is that most of those relationships are working, then you have good EQ. If the truth is that the critical mass of those key relationships is broken, then you must accept the sad fact that there is a common denominator.

2) EQ is not a science.

As much as EQ is presented as a science, at its very core, EQ is highly subjective. In the 1900s, the formal scientific community rejected psychology and other social sciences as true sciences because you could not measure or quantify experimental results. It was the pursuit of measurement that was the genesis of the second school of psychology called behavioural psychology, which was essentially attempting to analyze and quantify the behaviours of dogs, rats and pigeons. Does the name Pavlov ring a bell?

The scientific aspect of the research was largely focused on the importance of EQ as a predictive success factor. However, defining the cause-and-effect of EQ is still very much open to debate. The questions as to why people have a high or low EQ and how to develop it are much more challenging to define through scientific experimentation. Social scientists (another misnomer) have been receiving somewhat depressing news of late because some recent research referred to as "meta research," which means research on an existing body of research, have identified a very basic problem. Most social science experiments do not generate the same results or outcomes in subsequent identical experiments when attempting to replicate and thus validate their original findings. I do not believe the social sciences will ever be fully accepted by the formal scientific community because of the predictable unpredictability of their ongoing research. As we established previously, EQ and leadership are both much more of an art than a science.

3) EQ is not new.

When I first read Goleman's breakthrough book *Emotional Intelligence* in 1995, I was fascinated with this newly discovered field of study. After doing wide-ranging research, it slowly dawned on me that there was nothing really new in the EQ literature at all, but rather the academics and social scientists had just formalized and put more sophisticated labels on ancient wisdom. My sentiments regarding this field of study are perfectly expressed by the old adage that EQ literature is "old wine in new bottles."

In *How to Win Friends and Influence People,* Dale Carnegie suggested that, based on his personal observations, only 15% of career success is based on technical ability and skills, whereas a full 85% is based on the ability to deal with people. The EQ research really only validated Carnegie's conception.

Furthermore, I fear that scientific researchers, with their new level of sophistication, have over-complicated with academic jargon what we have already proven to be quite simple. Daniel Goleman, in the introduction to his book, admitted that we used to call EQ "character" or "maturity." So, don't be bamboozled by intellectual psychobabble, because you already know what EQ is – common sense, street smarts, people skills, self-confidence, positive attitude and wisdom.

4) Essential sequence never recognized.

All the literature breaks EQ down into the intrapersonal and interpersonal dimensions. A fundamental flaw or shortcoming in the EQ literature is that there is never recognition of the essential inviolate sequence of intrapersonal success preceding interpersonal success. I have looked for evidence of recognition of the sequence without finding a trace. Nowhere in the EQ literature is the essential sequence that Covey identified in the *7 Habits* acknowledged. The reason Covey used numbers and not bullets to organize the habits is that there is an essential sequence that cannot be violated. There is no possible way to achieve sustainable success at the interpersonal level (habits 4, 5, 6) until you have had some degree of success at the personal level (habits 1, 2, 3).

Although there are many EQ assessment tools out there, I don't believe any of them can deliver hard, objective measurement of your EQ. My twenty-question inventory is found in the index of this book, and I would kindly request you complete it. The challenge is to achieve accuracy of measurement because even in your heart of hearts, if you attempt to answer honestly and given the vast majority of our behaviour is driven subconsciously, you would be unable to answer in a truly accurate manner.

LEADING FROM EVERYWHERE

THE PRINCIPLES & PRACTICES OF CHARACTER-BASED LEADERSHIP

PART 4: PERSONAL LEADERSHIP – OPTIMIZING POTENTIAL & PRODUCTIVITY

11. Strategic Self-Development
12. Life Leadership – The Poor Sailor Blames the Wind
13. Getting Things Done – Optimizing Personal Productivity

CHAPTER 11: STRATEGIC SELF-DEVELOPMENT

We are being thrust into the future faster than any generation previously to walk this planet. There has been an acceleration of history, and we are all now living in a highly unpredictable whitewater world at an ever-increasing rate of change. Why is it that some people are thriving in the turbulence while others are riddled with anxiety? The answer lays in your capacity to adapt, which is directly related to your capacity to learn. It is really quite simple – rapid change requires rapid learning, which means that the single most important personal success strategy now and into the future is to fully commit to lifelong learning and strategic self-development. In the industrial age, one had to learn how to do the job, but now learning *is* your job!

I used to proudly say that I had fifteen years of corporate experience, and then it hit me one day that perhaps I should be more precise. The sad truth is that it is more accurate to say what I had was more like one year of experience fifteen times. As I reflect upon my corporate life, I realize, with some regret, that I was guilty of being so busy chopping wood that I failed to take enough time out to sharpen my axe. Which leads to the rhetorical question "how long does it take to chop down a tree with a hammer?" Highly effective leaders recognize the difference between working IN things and working ON things. Working IN things means producing results, while working ON things means enhancing your capacity to produce results. Perhaps Abraham Lincoln said it best: "If someone gave me eight hours to chop all the wood I could, I would spend six of them sharpening my axe." In one of Aesop's fables, he used the metaphor of the goose and the golden eggs. We all must produce the golden egg results we are being compensated to produce, but the key to true sustainable success is to keep the goose healthy by ongoing, never-ending learning, which increase our capacity to produce results.

Highly effective leaders are always on the grow. Growth is to leadership as carbon is to steel. Leaders are learners; trying to separate leadership from learning is like trying to separate the sun from sunshine. Samuel Butler, an American poet, once said, "Happiness is not virtue nor is it vice; happiness is simply growth. We are happiest when we are growing." Abraham Maslow, the father of humanistic psychology, suggested that you are psychologically healthy to the degree that you are growing. The term he used to describe the pinnacle of psychological health was "self-actualization." Leadership is about the actualization of your full potential. The process of becoming an effective leader is essentially the same process as becoming a highly functional, psychologically healthy human being.

I believe the most valid measurement of leadership effectiveness is assessing the growth in development of the people around the leader. The truest test of leadership is in how many other leaders the person developed. The acid test of truly effective leadership is this: does this person bring out the best in others? The bad news is that you cannot possibly bring out the best in others until first bringing out the best in yourself! The good news is the more you bring out the best in yourself, the more you will naturally bring out the best in others.

In 1903, James Allen wrote his classic book *As a Man Thinketh*. The central message of this book is in this quote: "They themselves are the makers of themselves." Many people are anxious to change their conditions and circumstances in life but they're not willing to change themselves. George Bernard Shaw remarked, "Life isn't about finding yourself; life is about creating yourself."

Just a few short decades ago in the industrial age, it was the organization that was responsible for the training and development of their people. It was human resource management that claimed your career. However, now we all must take personal responsibility for our own careers and professional development. We must become our own coaches. If you are waiting around for someone else to come along and motivate you to get started, it might be time to ask yourself this: what if they don't show up? Today and into the fast-approaching future, we all must take full responsibility for our own learning and development, and the time for action is now.

First, we must identify all potential resources available, with the ultimate strategic goal being the full deployment of our resources. The fulfillment of potential can only be achieved through the utilization of the four unique human endowments, or birth gifts, that we all possess, and tragically many people never even open up.

Fulfillment of Potential through Deployment of the Four Unique Human Endowments

Have you ever wondered why it's our species that has dominion on the planet? Or why we are the only species that can save other species from extinction? Philosophers have debated these questions for thousands of years and have concluded that our species has four unique endowments or capacities that no other species has that make us uniquely human. We've already established that both leadership and psychological health are rooted in growth and fulfillment of potential, which can only be realized through the full utilization of our species' unique endowments. Allow me to offer a warning to the wise – the dangerous truth is that the older you get, the more unfilled potential becomes increasingly toxic to your psychological health. A frightening nightmare would be that you're lying on your deathbed and someone knocks on the door and enters the room and it's the person you could have become.

Allow me to describe each of the four endowments and explain what each one empowers us to do. As you become aware of them, I challenge you to assess how effectively or to what degree you are currently utilizing them.

Self-Awareness

We are the only species on the planet that can think about our thoughts. We are the only species that is aware that we are going to die someday. In other words, we are the only species that can stand apart from self and observe our thoughts, attitudes and behaviour patterns. One of the few commonalities throughout all EQ literature is that it always begins with self-awareness because the self-evident first step of controlling emotions is to be aware of the emotions you are experiencing and why.

The birth gift of self-awareness gives our species the capacity to take a third-party perspective on self and thus change, learn and become the person you need to become. Art historians agree that one of Michelangelo's greatest achievements is the statue of David. Evidently at the unveiling of his masterpiece, a reporter was amazed and incredulous and asked how he could have possibly created such a perfect likeness of a human being. Michelangelo responded that it was really quite simple; all he did was chip away everything that wasn't David.

We established in Chapter 10 that the cornerstone foundation of Greek philosophy was character. The keystone of Greek philosophy, engraved over the Oracle of Delphi, is "know thyself." Self-awareness gives you the ability to know yourself, which allows you to leverage your natural strengths and minimize or chip away at your natural weaknesses.

My father used to say, "Forget formal education and get into the school of hard knocks." The problem was that he failed to tell me the whole story. I found out the hard way that the issue with the school of hard knocks is that the exam always precedes the lesson. After a few years of attending the school, I asked my father, "Isn't going to the school of hard knocks kind of the same as the criminal who proclaimed 'this hanging will be a very good lesson for me'?" The most dangerous myths are those that are partially true. Far too many people mistakenly buy in to the old axiom that you learn from experience. The problem is that it is only partially true. The full truth is that the real learning is to be found in the deployment of the unique human endowment called self-awareness, which allows us to **reflect** on our experience. You don't learn through experience, albeit pain is a good teacher, nearly to the degree you learn from **reflecting** on the experience. If you fail to use self-awareness to reflect on your life and behaviour, you are fundamentally crippling your capacity to learn from experience and dooming yourself to make the same mistakes throughout your life.

One of the many new challenges the information age presents is in our sensory-overloading electronic world of rings, pings, dings and 24/7 unlimited and universal access to information, resulting in very few people now making or taking the time anymore to go into the silence and reflect. For all of human history, people had more than enough time to reflect as they hacked at the ground with crude wooden implements attempting to feed their families or performed basic, mindless and repetitive tasks. I fear that the multitudes of digital distractions now available at our fingertips can soon become addictions that dramatically stunt the growth of many people as they expend massive hours in virtual-reality games that provide the pleasure of short-term escape. Because of electronic obsessions, many people spend little or no time reflecting and thus never really understand who they are, which results in a condition that psychiatrists refer to as "self-alienation." Always remember, technology makes for a wonderful slave but a terrible master. The key question today is are you in control of technology or is technology in control of you?

Independent Will

The human endowment of independent will means that we have the **power to choose**. All other species' behaviour is governed by instinct and genetic code; we are the only species that gets to choose thoughts, attitudes, decisions, behaviours and ultimately our lives. This endowment is truly a good news/bad news story. The good news is that you are responsible for taking control of your life. The bad news is that you are responsible for taking control over your life. In other words, you have the power to take personal responsibility, but you will be held responsible for the consequences of your choices and decisions. Those who fail to take control of their life predictably will chronically feel that they are not in control and end up in a terrible place called "victimhood." This is a dangerous place because it means that, if your circumstances are not your fault, then you are not in control and thus why would you ever need to change? In the simplest terms, this endowment provides you with the power to take control of your life, and failing to do so inevitably results in psychologically damaging feelings of powerlessness.

Up until the time of the ancient Greek philosophers, it was a given that your life was governed and predetermined by fate, and you really had no choice as to how well your life was going to work. They called it predestination. It was Aristotle who first identified, later in his life, that the decisions he saw people make early in their lives had an impact on how successful their lives were. He was the first to realize that we are free to choose, that it is our decisions that govern success and failure, and that our lives are not predestined by the fickle finger of fate.

Taking personal responsibility for your life means that you believe you are the primary cause (in control) of your circumstances. The belief that you are in control creates a proactive, problem-solving mindset and not a defeatist victim mentality. In the final analysis, we get to choose whether to be part of the problem or part of the solution. A classic poem called "Invictus" was written by a British poet named William Ernest Henry in 1875, and the closing line eloquently explains this unique human endowment: "I am the master of my fate; I am the captain of my soul."

Creative Imagination

The endowment of creative imagination gives our species alone the power to create. Everything is created at least twice, and the first creation is always in your mind. The building you are currently sitting in was created a number of times. The first creation was when someone pictured the house in their mind. The second creation was the hiring of an architect to create a blueprint and model. The third creation was the hiring of a contractor to build the physical structure.

This unique human endowment gives our species the capacity to create our future and become the person we need to become. We are the only species who can set our own life sail and write our own life story, and sadly many people don't even pick up the pen.

In Chapter 8, we established the reason great leaders are often called visionaries – our all-powerful subconscious brain, which is the motivational brain, operates largely on a visual basis. We all possess the same power to create a clear vision of what our ideal self and ideal life look like. The operating principle is the greater the clarity of the vision you can achieve, the greater the power to the subconscious mind to manifest your thoughts and visions into reality.

Conscience

This unique human endowment provides us with an inner guidance mechanism designed to direct us down the pathway of life. This is the least understood and most controversial of the endowments and has been called many things throughout the ages. In Eastern religion, they call it the "observer self." In philosophical literature, Emerson called it the "still small voice within." In psychological literature, Sigmund Freud called it the "superego," and Carl Jung called it the "collective unconscious." In spiritual literature, it is referred to as the "conscience," and Walt Disney called it Jiminy Cricket. Rodney Dangerfield said, "Your conscience is the part of you that feels bad when the rest your body feels so good." He also suggested that a clear conscience is usually a sign of a bad memory.

The question as to where the conscience comes from is still a source of heated debate that rages on today. Some people believe it is simply the result of Darwinian natural-selection processes, whereas other people, including me, believe our conscience is the spark of divinity within us. A psychopath is defined as a person who has had this spark snuffed out, which means they are very dangerous people who have little if any capacity to demonstrate empathy and experience no guilt or remorse upon hurting others.

It is nature's feedback system, in that negative emotions are nature's way of signalling to you that you are off track. We have a physical feedback system we call "nerves." When the young child touches the hot stove, the physical feedback system says, "Don't do that again." When you are suffering chronic negative emotions and thoughts, it's nature's way of telling you, "Don't do that anymore."

I believe, unlike many in the psychological community, that when you violate your conscience, you are taking "psychological toxins." Although, negative emotions created by violating your conscience do paradoxically serve a positive purpose — the negative emotions of guilt and shame are nature's way of saying you've made a mistake. The negative emotion of boredom is nature's way of telling you, "Get off your butt and go do something."

When I'm reading good literature and my brain frequently goes "aha" or "click-click," I know deep down I've stumbled across the truth. Our conscience is the repository of the wisdom of timeless correct principles we discussed in Chapter 9

I had a lot of recruiting to do in my corporate life, and I always strived to hire people who were conscientious, or you could say those who lived in harmony with and were guided by their conscience. I suggest that you strive to listen to the voice of wisdom within you and, as Jiminy Cricket said, "Let your conscience be your guide."

In conclusion, true happiness and true life success can only be achieved through fulfillment of your potential. To fulfill your potential requires the fullest possible utilization of the four unique human endowments.

Competency-Based Learning

Peter Drucker suggested that the key success principle is to "play to your strengths and organize around your weaknesses." What this means is you should focus on doing what comes naturally and surround yourself with people who are naturally talented at what you are not. If you want to implement this success strategy of leveraging your natural strengths (talents) and minimize your weaknesses, then the self-evident starting point is to follow the advice of the Greek philosophers – "know thyself." The sooner you gain clarity about what your natural talents are and what your predictable weaknesses are, the better your life will work.

A note of caution when playing to your natural strengths – it is crucial to understand the paradoxical truth that a person's greatest strength can quickly become their greatest weakness. One example of a natural strength being over-extended to the point of becoming a weakness is that I frequently encounter people who are gifted with the ability to analyze, and predictably they frequently struggle to make decisions because they suffer from "analysis paralysis." Another common example is that often people who are naturally empathic and support-ive of others are "pleasers" and really struggle when it is time to assert themselves and say no.

A significant trend in human resource management is that many organiza-tions are no longer turning people into "fix-it projects" as we did in the industrial age. The most progressive organizations have fundamentally changed their train-ing and development philosophy by focusing on developing the unique talents they see in their employees as opposed to the past when we would focus training efforts on "areas for improvement."

I think the same philosophy should guide your self-development efforts, meaning the primary focus of your learning should be the development of your strengths and to a lesser degree the fixing of your weaknesses. It is very important to be aware of your weaknesses, though, and if you do not have the luxury of surrounding yourself with people who have talents in your weaknesses, then at least maintain a conscious awareness of your weaknesses so you can limit the damage they do in your life.

The difference between training and development is that training is about enhancing competencies to achieve better results in your current role, whereas development is about enhancing the competencies and getting you ready to move up to your next role. Strategic self-development means that when you are determining what you should focus your efforts on learning, metaphorically you should use a rifle and not a shotgun; in other words, your efforts are more effective if they are targeted and not random.

To help you pinpoint the specific skills and knowledge you could most benefit from developing is to "begin with the end in mind" and reverse-engineer the process as follows:

1. Break the job into **roles**. You may have two roles or twenty roles. If you have the type of job where you wear many hats and perform many rules, you may want to sit with your manager and clarify what your core contribution roles are.

2. Clarify the specific **goals, desired results** or **ideal performance outcomes** that are expected in each role.

3. Identify the **core competencies required** to achieve success in each role. A competency has four building blocks: natural ability (talent), the will to do (motivation), knowing what to do (knowledge) and knowing how to do it (skill). The best method to identify core competencies is to observe the most successful performers in the role and determine what specific knowledge and skills they possess that makes them so effective. In other words, what do the best performers do really well that makes them the best performers? Remember to apply the 80/20 rule, which means there are only a few skills (20%) that contribute to 80% of results. These are the "core competencies" of success.

4. Once you have recognized the few key abilities that contribute most to success, you now must conduct an objective self-assessment to identify

which competencies are your strengths and which create knowledge and skill gaps.

This process should help you identify what you need to learn and develop a learning plan that will target the highest ROLI (return on learning investment) knowledge and skills you need to develop.

Learning How to Learn

Now that we have strategically identified WHAT we should be learning, let's turn our focus to HOW to make our learning efforts more effective and efficient. Recent research has shed new light on the operation of the brain, allowing us to better understand some of the principles and practices on how to accelerate our learning.

Motivation

People learn to the degree that they are motivated to learn. If you are not naturally motivated to learn something, then first focus how you will benefit from learning the new knowledge or skill and the negative consequences of failing to learn. There is a direct link between emotion and memory; the greater the motivation to learn, the faster and deeper learning occurs.

Belief

People only learn if they believe or have the confidence that they are capable of learning. That's why the best teachers act as if their students are fully capable of comprehending what they are teaching.

Learning Styles

We all learn through all the styles, but each of us has a dominant learning style or two through which we learn most efficiently. The primary learning styles are listening and reading. Regardless of your primary style, I always recommend that when attempting to learn something, you write notes. I once heard a scientist suggest that writing is a psycho-neural muscular activity that integrates mind and body. I'm not sure what it means; I just know when I write something, it sticks with me.

Association

The process of *linking* is the physiological process of creating memory. This is primarily why stories and metaphors are such powerful teaching tools. I recommend that you always begin with a holistic overview of the subject you're attempting to learn, which then allows you to integrate or link each individual component into the whole, just as you would do with a jigsaw puzzle

Outstandingness or Uniqueness

Anything that is unusual, unexpected, surprising, weird, shocking or out of the ordinary stimulates the memory. So, when making your links, it is best to connect them to weird or unusual associations.

Whole Brain (Right and Left)

By integrating both sides of the thinking brain (cerebral cortex), retention can be dramatically increased. The left side is automatically involved though speech; the key is to activate the right side through the use of music, rhythm, colour, visuals, metaphors and conceptual thinking.

Repetition

Learning is the process of *transferring* information from the short-term memory to long-term memory. Memory development is a physiological process. When the brain learns something new, it forms connections between neurons, and with each review of the new knowledge, the connection gets reinforced to the point that it becomes long-term memory, allowing for instant recall. The only way to effectively create these learning connections is through the process of "spaced repetition" or "interval reinforcement." The ideal repetition pattern is within ten minutes, one hour, the next day, ten days, thirty days, three months and then six months.

Organization

There are three parts to the memory process – input, storage and recall. Research is clear that the more organized the input, the more effective the storage, and the better and easier the recall.

Primacy and Recency

The most potent times for learning are at the beginning and the end of the learning session; the typical retention pattern is u-shaped. Thus, we need a strategy for overcoming the learning sag typically found in the middle of the session.

Relaxation

When people experience stress, the mental energies are automatically channelled to the lower instinctive (protective) brain away from the upper thinking brain. **Stress and anxiety reduce learning capacity in a dramatic fashion. Optimum learning takes place when one is relaxed.** Positive emotions support the release of two specific chemicals (noradrenalin and acetylcholine) that grease the electrical connections, making them smoother and more effective.

Changing Habits

Now it is application time. It is not what you know that counts; rather, it is what you *do* with what you know that counts. To learn means to change behaviour, and the old adage is true: to learn something and not change behaviour means you never really learned it in the first place. Given the vast majority of behaviour is governed by the force of habit, this means that to make any meaningful and lasting behavioural change means changing habits.

The importance of habit has been long recognized throughout philosophical, psychological and wisdom literature. The great American philosopher Ralph

Waldo Emerson said, "Sow a thought, reap an action; sow an action, reap a habit; sow a habit, reap a character; sow a character, reap a destiny." In the late 1800s, William James, Harvard professor and considered to be the father of American psychology, wrote the original literature on habits and how to change them. He put forth that the vast majority of our decisions and behaviours were not a conscious choice, saying, "All our life, so far as it has definite form, is but a mass of habits." His writings have stood the test of time better than the work of his European contemporaries. Most recent behavioural research largely validates and occasionally challenges James's theories. When you look at the sum and substance of all the research and philosophy, the one inescapable truth is that it is your habit patterns that will ultimately determine the degree of success you achieve in the short time that you are on this planet.

The good news is that the process of changing habits is really quite simple; however, please be clear that I'm not saying that changing habits is easy. The process outlined below is simple, but let's not kid ourselves, it is important to recognize and accept that there are no mystical, magical or secret shortcuts to changing habits. There are no substitutions for hard work in the form of resolve, self-discipline and self-accountability to succeed in your habit-changing efforts.

Recent discoveries in the field of neuroscience provide some very valuable insights into how the brain naturally needs to develop habits so it can free up RAM for other mental activities. As mentioned previously, we all have three distinct and separate memory systems – long-term, short-term and what scientists call your "non-declarative" or "procedural" memory system, which you know as your habit memory. The procedural memory's basic operational principle is that anything you do for twenty-one to thirty days (this duration is now in dispute) the brain automatically transfers from the conscious brain to the unconscious brain and you now have a new habit.

Beware, because this process happens naturally, you risk developing destructive habits before you know it. The great educator Horace Mann said, "Habit is a cable; we weave a thread of it each day and at last, we cannot break it." I disagree that habits cannot be broken; however, I do admit the forces of human inertia is an incredibly powerful gravitational pull that requires true commitment and willpower to overcome.

In the 1950s, the renowned psychologist Abraham Maslow hypothesized that there are four sequential stages of the learning process. I believe this four-stage process applies directly to behaviour change or habit development.

1st Stage: Unconscious Incompetence – This is obviously not a good state to be in, as it means you don't even know that you don't know. You are not consciously aware of your destructive behaviour or knowledge and skill deficiencies.

2nd Stage: Conscious Incompetence – You now become aware of your knowledge or skill gap and ideally what it is costing you.

3rd Stage: Conscious Competence – You consciously work at learning the new skill habit. The new behaviour will feel uncomfortable at first because it is unnatural; however, with persistence, the new behaviour becomes more and more natural.

4th Stage: Unconscious Competence – The new behaviour or skill has now become habit or second-nature, no longer requiring conscious thought. You have now achieved what scientists called "behavioural automaticity."

My role in this book is to move you through stages 1 and 2 so you are fully aware of your productive habits and the non-productive habits you could most benefit from changing. My role in Stage 3 is to offer you solutions, strategies and techniques to apply so in time your "keystone habits" reach Stage 4 status and are truly automatic.

Changing Habits - Best Practices

Habit patterns are controlled by the subconscious part of the brain and thus we can run on autopilot for a long time in the wrong direction if we are not careful. Once the habits that need to be changed are identified, the change process must begin. The following are what I consider the best practices when it comes to changing habits:

1. First off, to make the desired habit changes, you must be highly motivated to change. Given the degree of willpower, self-discipline and determination required to make the change, you simply will not be able to sustain the behaviour-change process without the desperate desire to change. To understand human motivation is to understand that it comes down to the brain's pain/pleasure principle. You must confront yourself with objective, logical reality by performing a cost/benefit analysis to get clear of the true costs (pain) of failing to change and focus on the benefits (pleasure) that will occur if you do succeed. The more tangible and meaningful you can make the costs and benefits, the higher the likelihood of success. Warning – enter this change process at your own risk. Unless you are fully committed to make the change, I strongly recommend you do not try. Failure to make the change will only do more damage to your psyche and you will be worse off than before. Stephen Covey said it best: "Integrity is the value we place upon ourselves."

2. Start immediately. Remember that humans are also subject to Newton's "law of inertia," which states that an object in motion will remain in motion until impacted by an outside force. The first step of the journey is the most important and most difficult. Engineers have explained to me that when a rocket leaves the ground, the vast majority of energy (fuel) is consumed in the first few feet. The good news is that once begun, the change process becomes increasingly easier, requiring less conscious commitment.

3. Once started, don't stop. The analogy William James used is that starting a new habit is like rolling up a ball of yarn – if you drop it once, you have to start the entire process all over again. Recent research proves to be a little more forgiving, as the researchers also found that missing one opportunity to perform the behaviour did not materially affect the habit formation process. In other words, it doesn't matter if you slip up every now and then. Building better habits is not an all-or-nothing process, and the key is to re-commit to the change process immediately once stopped.

4. James insisted that you begin the change process in a flamboyant manner. I suspect he meant you should begin with a strong emotional commitment,

an impact statement or a memorable activity to signal the beginning of the process. To really commit to something, I recommend making a public declaration – social commitment can be a powerful motivator to hold yourself accountable to make the change.

5. The old axiom is that to form a new habit, you have to stick with the new behaviour or habit for twenty-one days. This also originated with William James over a hundred years ago, based on the idea that it takes a chicken twenty-one days to hatch an egg. A more recent study on how long it takes to build a new habit, conducted at University College London and published in the *European Journal of Social Psychology*, examined the habits of ninety-six people over a twelve-week period. Each person chose one new habit for the twelve weeks and reported each day on whether or not they did the behaviour and how automatic the behaviour felt. At the end of study, the researchers analyzed the data to determine how long it took each person to go from starting a new behaviour to automatically doing it. On average, it takes more than two months before a new behaviour becomes automatic, or sixty-six days, to be exact. How long it takes a new habit to form can vary widely depending on the behaviour, the person and the circumstances. The hard truth is that it probably takes anywhere from two months to eight months to build a new behaviour into your life. More important than the actual duration of the change process are the intensity of the commitment and consistency of the effort to change.

6. Visualize yourself successfully making the change and feel the resulting benefits. The subconscious mind is the seat of all habit and it operates on a visual basis. The more vivid you can make your visualization of yourself succeeding and enjoying the benefits, the greater the potency of the process.

7. I suspect you have heard the old saying, "What gets measured gets done." Over the years I have come to appreciate just how true this statement really is. If you are committed to making a change, then you must document and measure your progress. Documentation provides feedback that is vital

to holding yourself accountable. It also allows you to enjoy the progress of your tangible success.

8. Don't give up!

Remember that the time is now! Your time on this planet is short, the clock is ticking and the sands of the hourglass are falling; each moment of time wasted is a non-refundable fragment of eternity.

You don't become a leader by reading books or attending seminars on leadership any more then you become a car by standing in the garage. Leadership is about becoming the person you need to become. Obviously, I place great value on leadership books and seminars, as they can be catalytic; however, real leadership development is a lifelong journey that involves hard work, taking wise risks, suffering failures and persisting through and learning from setbacks and difficulties.

There are no quick fixes or shortcuts to leadership development; the hard truth is that becoming a highly effective leader is a deeply personal journey that requires the pain of failure and the real work of reflection and self-discovery.

CHAPTER 12: LIFE LEADERSHIP –
THE POOR SAILOR BLAMES THE WIND

As Shakespeare said, "The world is a stage," and it's just been announced that you have been given the lead role.

A few decades ago, Peter Drucker said, "The biggest challenge we will have into the twenty-first century is not dealing with massive technological changes but rather it will be the realization that we are responsible for ourselves again." As I suggested in Chapter 4, when we entered the new millennium, everyone was given a new title: CLO (chief life officer), and tragically many people have failed to accept the responsibilities of their new title and are unmoored and cut adrift in a whitewater world to be tempest-tossed and forever buffeted by the cold winds of fate, circumstance and other people's opinions.

An old English proverb says, "The poor sailor blames the wind." Perhaps I can best make my point by referring to an eloquent poem written in 1916 by Ella Wheeler Wilcox titled "The Winds of Fate." The poem begins with the line, "One ship sails East, and another West, by the self-same winds that blows; 'tis the set of the sail and not the gale that tells the way we go."

I believe Ella's profound poetry has far greater relevance today than it did when it was written. To extend the analogy, I suggest that in the hundred-plus years that have passed since the poem was written, the ocean of life on which we all must now navigate is far more turbulent and unpredictable than it was a century ago. The process of leading your life and setting your life sail is more important and more challenging. Just a few decades ago the world was much more stationary and stable, and life was much more predictable. That stagnant world is now long gone and we find ourselves in a world that is turbulent and ever more volatile.

The key lesson to garner from this poem is that if a person ends up someplace they don't want to be later in life, they don't get to blame the wind, because the same wind blew all of us; the real problem will have been that the person never took the time or made the effort to set their life sail. My fear is that many people are just drifting and have failed to take charge of their lives, which might have been okay just a few decades ago but not in today's whitewater world. There are two basic approaches to living life – by action or accident, choice or chance, decision or default, direction or drift. A hallmark of highly effective leaders is that they are proactive creators of circumstance and not reactive creatures of circumstance. Highly effective leaders act on life as opposed to having life act on them. To successfully take charge and lead your life, all you have to do is effectively answer the following four interrelated life-leadership questions.

Life Leadership Question #1 – Who Am I? (Know Thyself)

Aristotle said, where your natural talents intersect with the needs of the world, this nexus is your vocation.

To truly "know thyself," as the great philosophers enthusiastically encouraged, is simple in concept, but it is not an easy endeavour because it is a lifelong process of self-discovery achieved through ongoing reflection and feedback; a truly daunting and arduous challenge that may never be fully complete.

The brilliant Peter Drucker said the key success principle is to "play to your strengths and organize around your weaknesses." When attempting to recognize a person's strengths and weaknesses, an important insight is to first understand that they are both frequently on the same continuum, because a natural talent once overextended becomes a natural weakness. For example, I once asked an engineer, who was gifted at analysis, if she was indecisive and she responded, "Well, yes and no. I used to be, but I just don't know anymore." The great strength of analysis can quickly become analysis paralysis. This principle holds true in my own life, in that one of my strengths is my emotion, which serves me well as a public speaker; however, my emotions can quickly become my worst enemy in crucial conversations.

You're on the planet for a very short period of time. The key to success is to leverage your natural strengths and to push your natural weaknesses and go very small corner of your life, and the self-evident starting point is to understand who you really are. Here are a few questions to guide you in your efforts to achieve deeper self-understanding.

- What are your natural talents?
- What are your weaknesses?
- Which of the four temperaments is your primary and secondary type? (Study your MBTI type)
- Study "birth order" research and test the validity of the impact it had on who you are as an adult
- Under which conditions are you most productive? In a relaxed state or under deadline pressure?
- What time of day are you most productive?
- Are you a generalist or a specialist?
- Should you be in a leadership (decision-maker) or support (advisor) role?
- How do you make your best decisions?
- Are you better with things or people?
- Should you be in a large, more structured, stable organization or in a smaller, dynamic, more entrepreneurial one?
- Do you work better in a solitary manner or in a team?
- How do you best relax (recreation)?

Gallup recently conducted extensive research to identify the competencies that make the best managers. The findings were clear – the single most important ability that contributed to managerial success was the ability to identify what a person's natural talents were and put that person in the right job. Jim Collins's research suggested the starting point of organizational success is to get the right people on the bus in the right seats. Everyone's goal must be to put themselves in the right place where they can make the biggest contribution, create the greatest results and enjoy the greatest life success. People who earn a living doing what comes naturally report that work is more fun than fun, which means they never have to work another day in their lives.

A proven method of identifying your natural strengths is a century-old technique called "feedback analysis." The process is simple – whenever you make a key decision or take a key action, write down what you expect will happen as a result. After six to twelve months, compare the results with your expectations. Those predictions with the highest degrees of accuracy provide a clear indication of what your natural talents are.

Life Leadership Question #2 - Why Am I Here? (Life Purpose)

One of my all-time favorite speakers who had a huge influence on my thinking was Jim Rohn; he had a beautiful way of being eloquently simple without being simplistic. He proposed that the purpose of life was "to see what you could do with it."

To quote James Allen once again, "The majority of people are adrift on the ocean of life. Aimlessness is a vice, and such drifting must not continue for them who would steer clear of catastrophe and distraction. They who have no central purpose of their life fall and easy prey to petty worries, fears, troubles and self-pitying." I think the great playwright George Bernard Shaw was expressing the same idea when he said, "This is the true joy in life, being used for a purpose recognized by yourself as a mighty one; being a force of nature instead of a feverish, selfish little clod of ailments and grievances complaining that the world will not devote itself to making you happy."

Perhaps one of the most influential personal development books is called *Man's Search for Meaning*, written was by Viktor Frankl, a Jewish psychiatrist who survived the horror of the World War II Nazi prison camps. He was perplexed as to why some of the biggest and physically strongest people quickly deteriorated and soon perished while other prisoners who were weaker and frailer somehow survived. He concluded that the reason some people survived was they saw a purpose in their suffering, and those who did not didn't have a purpose. He said, "Those who have a why to live, can bear with almost any how." The father of humanistic psychology, Abraham Maslow, suggested that the most psychologically healthy people had a noble purpose in life outside of themselves that was bigger than them.

When you read wisdom literature on the purpose of life written by philosophers, poets, artists and scientists, you will see a central theme has emerged consistently throughout the ages – "to serve others." Early in my career as a public speaker, when giving a speech to a group of high school seniors, one student asked me what was the best definition of life success was. I responded "good question," which is my standard response when I don't have an answer. Another student who saw I was struggling offered a definition of life success, and it's the best I've ever heard to this day. She said the best way to measure your life's success is to ask how many people are better off because you were here.

I believe when all is said and done and you are looking back over the landscape your life, the question you will have to ask yourself is "Did you do more lifting than leaning, more contributing than consuming, more building than breaking, and more giving than taking?" One of the most mysterious and paradoxical truths is that the more you give, the more you get, and the more you take, the less you have.

Life Leadership Question #3 – Where Am I Going? (Vision)

Deathbed research reports that over 85% of North Americans confess on their deathbed, as they look back over the landscape of their life, that they did not get what they wanted out of life and that it was a disappointment. A quick examination reveals that the number one reason people fail to get what they want is that they never took the time or made the effort to define what they wanted. It doesn't matter how accurate a shot you have; the simple truth is that you cannot hit a target you do not have.

Trying to live your life without a vision is like trying to come back from someplace you've never been. I think everyone would agree that life would be a lot easier if we could live it backwards. To a degree, the unique human endowment of creative imagination gives our species this capacity. Stephen Covey's second habit is "begin with the end in mind." He suggested that you picture your own funeral and imagine what you want people to say about you, and then all you have to do is reverse-engineer your life accordingly.

The human endowment of **creative imagination** allows us to ask and answer two key questions:

1. Who do I need to become? My **ideal self?**
2. What do I want my life to look like? What does my **ideal life** look like in five, ten or twenty-five years?

Socrates suggested that "the unexamined life is not worth living." From time to time, we all must step back and take an aerial view of our life, and I recommend this lifeline tool. The purpose of the lifeline is to provide a holistic perspective of your life so you may better understand where you've been, where you are now and, most importantly, what you want your future to look like. The best way to predict the future is to create the future.

1. Write your date of birth at the far-left end of the line
2. Draw shallow loops on the bottom of the line to represent where you were living and your occupation
3. Using arrows of different lengths to indicate significant events in your life on top of the line
4. Mark today's date on the line
5. Ask yourself the value of everything to the left of today (the past)
6. Ask yourself the value of everything to the right of today (the future)

Review your lifeline every six to twelve months.

Significant Life Events

Where you're Living / Education or Employment

Creating a vision for your life is no guarantee of success because there are too many unpredictable variables; however, the greater clarity you can achieve, the more power the subconscious brain has to bring it to fruition.

Life Leadership Question #4 – What Really Matters Most to Me? (Values)

What is truly important to you? Values ultimately govern our behaviours, and what complicates any attempt to clarify values is that they are not at a conscious level. As mentioned previously, when you ask people to articulate their values, most people struggle because values are held deeply within the subconscious brain.

We must live in harmony with values. The calendar never lies; does your calendar reflect your values? If we observe how people spend their time, this is a good indication of what they truly value. Without clear values, you are bound to be a walking weathervane, always buffeted by other people's opinions.

Many people don't figure out what's truly important to them until they have a significant emotional event in their life or a "wake-up call," and suddenly, in the blink of an eye, what's truly important to them becomes painfully evident. It usually happens at a funeral parlor, graveyard, hospital emergency ward or doctor's office. Tragically, most people realize in this moment that they are off-track in that they have been majoring in the minors, drowning in detail, trapped in trivia and caught up in the thick of thin things.

Values determine what truly matters most to a person and also how they will treat others on their journey down the pathway of life in pursuit of their vision. Equally important to achieving your life vision is *how* you achieve it and whether you can pass the mirror test. Aristotle said, "The softest pillow of all is peace of mind."

A central topic in Chapter 13 is setting priorities, and without clarity of values it becomes increasingly difficult to do so. The guiding principle of priority setting is best expressed through the following trite but true statement: "The main thing is to keep the main things the main thing." The biggest problem most people have is that from day to day, week to week and year to year, they're not even aware at a conscious level of what the main things are. This is hugely problematic when it comes to setting priorities because everything is important and nothing is important without clarity of values, and the inevitable consequence is life imbalance. Further deathbed research explains that people report having two pools of regrets: they regret some things they've done, but the deeper regrets are always found in the important things they failed to do.

CHAPTER 13: GETTING THINGS DONE – OPTIMIZING PERSONAL PRODUCTIVITY

In Chapter 7, we established that the essence of leadership is the capacity to gain influence with people and explained Aristotle's essential and sequential process of gaining influence with people: **ethos–pathos–logos.** The establishment of ethos is the foundational starting point of gaining influence with people. To review, ethos is comprised of two distinct components – character and competence. Character is the source of trustworthiness, whereas competence is the source of credibility. Competence is defined as the capacity to achieve desired results or, simply put, to get things done. This capacity is widely referred to as time-management skills, a term coined mid- twentieth century. Still, today I find that much of the literature on the subject of time management is deeply rooted in an industrial-age paradigm. We have explained how the information-age workplace is fundamentally different than the industrial age; the challenges we face are not only different in degree, they are different in kind than those our parents and grandparents faced. The game of work has changed, and if our mindset, skillset and toolset have not changed, these prevalent and painful problems become highly predictable when trying to solve new problems with old, dangerously obsolete solutions.

Allow me to redefine what you currently know as "time management." To manage means to control, and it is obvious that we cannot control time, as the hands of time are marching on in lockstep conformity and the sands of the hourglass are dropping at precisely the same rate of speed. Will Rogers once said, "You can no more manage time than you could lasso the wind and tie it to the fence." Time management is a misnomer; what we are really talking about is **personal productivity** skills or how to become more effective and efficient in your work, or in plain talk, how to get more done in less time.

Are you feeling caught between a clock and a hard place? I strongly suspect the answer is yes, because we are now in a stripped-down, more-with-less, every-job-counts workplace world. The demand for my time-management workshops has grown dramatically because many people who feel overwhelmed, beat-up, burnt-out and trapped on a tedious treadmill are searching for new strategies – new challenges require new solutions.

Information-Age Workplace Time-Management Challenges

Over three decades of facilitating these workshops, participants have described their most significant time- management challenges and frustrations with growing intensity. I have condensed and organized their pain points into the following common themes:

Increasing workloads – Perhaps the most widespread and significant organizational changes over the last few decades was labelled "downsizing" or, in more justifiable terms, "right-sizing." In an attempt to trim the organizational "fat," many executives use their scalpel to excess, cutting far more than the going rate down through the muscle to the bone. This trend has caused ever-increasing workloads. Departments that used to have eight people are now down to five, and the five people are expected to produce more than the eight did. Many people lament that they are doing a job that in the near past was done by two or three people. Far too often, I observe the mindless pursuit of the golden eggs, with short-term quarterly profits, as the organizational goose gets sicker and sicker. The central strategy behind downsizing is to strip out layers of management and "flatten" the organization. This trend has resulted in broader and more ambiguous job descriptions, meaning people have to wear a lot of different hats and many are suffering from role confusion. Peter Drucker said, "The greatest challenge knowledge workers are going to face in the twenty-first century is trying to figure out what their job really is."

Greater urgency – Customers' demands for instant responses facilitated by technology has dramatically ramped up the pace of business. This operational acceleration has empowered the forces of urgency in the workplace. The great risk is when people confuse what is urgent with what is truly important. This confusion results in allowing urgent tasks to consistently trump the important tasks, which inevitably leads to a death spiral of ever-increasing reactivity. Far too many people are not acting on things but rather are being acted upon.

Greater unpredictability – Our MTBS (mean time between surprises) is dropping, which is creating an environment of constantly shifting priorities. Many people report having to consistently push important tasks and projects to the back burner because of an urgent operational problem, crisis or issue. To-do lists can become instantly irrelevant with one crisis email or phone call. Many people complain that they feel like firefighters in their jobs because there seems to be one fire to put out after the next. The truth is, many are the arsonists themselves.

Constant contact – The advent of "never out of touch" technology and 24/7 availability is blurring the line between people's personal and professional lives, undermining work–life balance.

Information and communication overload – A common lament I hear people say is that they get to the office, respond to voicemails and texts, handle their emails and it's time to go home. One senior executive recently said that trying to manage information in her organization is like trying to sip water from a full-blown fire hose. Dealing with an avalanche of information coming at increasing rates of speed from multiple directions is a major challenge, with no simple solution in sight.

Greater interdependence – The information explosion has driven increasing complexity into the nature of work. Just a couple of decades ago, the vast majority of knowledge required to complete our tasks was in our own heads. Today the amount of self-contained knowledge required to complete our work has consistently decreased, which has accelerated the need for greater interdependence, requiring constant and instant interaction with coworkers. Many people complain that their entire workday seems like one big interruption.

I suspect many of you can relate to these information-age workplace challenges, so it's good to know you're not alone. Most of the traditional time-management strategies and techniques are obsolete and no longer work like they used to. These new problems require new solutions, such as the ones I suggest in the rest of this chapter.

Time Wasters – The "7 Deadly P's"

Ben Franklin said that "if ye value life, then squander not time for it is the stuff of which life is made." I think Ben is trying to tell us that if you waste your time, truth be known you're wasting your life. Time and life are the same substance with a different label. A frightening statistic is that twenty minutes a day wasted equates to eleven days a year down the drain! Perhaps a good way to define "wasting time" is when you are in a state where you are not achieving "productivity value" or "recreational value." Research shows that most productive people are those who have overcome life-threatening illnesses because they truly value time and therefore don't waste it! Here are seven of the most common and devastating counterproductive time wasters to avoid:

1) *Preoccupation*

> Our conscious brain (the part of the brain required for concentration) can only hold one thought at time, so it is true to say that every moment you are preoccupied you are not on task. The key to achieving efficiency in your efforts is focus or concentration, which explains why people are so much more productive the last day before a two-week vacation. Being preoccupied is the opposite of being focused. Low-EQ people are constantly self-interrupting, which is the bombardment of the conscious brain with negative self-talk, magically turning what should be a ten-minute task into an hour-and-ten-minute task.

2) *Pleasing*

In the highly interdependent and dynamic information-age workplace, the truth is that many times we have to say yes to sudden requests from customers, coworkers and bosses; however, from time to time we must learn to say NO. Every time we say yes to something, we have automatically said NO to something else. The key question becomes – what's giving? The truth is, something is, and the more consciously aware of what you're giving up, the more empowered you are to kindly, gently and tactfully say no to requests from others. Beware: low-EQ people who are subconsciously seeking approval and validation from others are very susceptible to saying yes when they should have said NO.

3) *Perfectionism*

People lose perspective on the true importance of a task and thus are highly susceptible to committing a cardinal sin of personal productivity, which is spending **major time on minor things**! The guiding principle is simple – just spend major time on major things and minor time on minor things. Written communication and perfectionist tendencies are a particularly deadly time-wasting combination.

4) *Personality Conflicts*

In Chapter 2, we learned that knowledge workers spend 70% to 80% of their waking hours in one of the four forms of communicating: reading, writing, speaking or listening. The real key to effective and efficient communication is the quality of the relationship. When the relationship is right, the communication is flowing, spontaneous, effective and efficient. But when the relationship is broken, communication becomes trying, guarded, protective and time-consuming. The time costs associated with broken relationships are impossible to measure but are incredibly expensive.

5) *Politicking*

Low-trust organizational cultures are a major restrictive factor on employee's productivity, as far too much time is predictably spent on completely non-value-adding activities such as protecting, defending, justifying, gossiping, rumor-milling, game-playing and confessing each other's sins by the photocopy machine. In toxic organizational cultures, people tend to spend excessive amounts of time on activities that serve no other purpose then to protect themselves from any possible blame for anything that goes wrong. This results in time-consuming, formal, "pursuant to our discussion" types of written communications. Peter Drucker suggests that 80% of written communication serves no other purpose that to CYA (cover your anatomy).

6) *Posturing*

This time waster is different from politicking in that it is not defensive in nature; the purpose is self-aggrandizement and image enhancement. This means unwarranted amounts of time are spent on activities that do not value add to any stakeholders. This behaviour is particularly destructive because it wastes other people's time as well. Posturing shows up in a few different ways; first, by writing to impress and not express, resulting in emails that should be written in two minutes taking twenty-two. Secondly, it shows up as grandstanding and showboating in meetings and taking ten minutes to say something that could be said in two minutes. The third time waster created by posturing is too much time spent "managing up" (some might call it kissing up), which means excessive amounts of fawning, flattery and feigning interest in the boss's hobbies.

7) *Perplexing*

To maintain my alliteration, I took the grammatical liberty of using the noun as a verb. What I mean by perplexing is being in an unproductive state of deer-in-headlight overwhelm, indecision, bewilderment, wheel-spinning, picking stuff up and putting it down, stopping and starting, looking for stuff and chronically asking yourself the question, "Now where was I again?" It's when you have confused activity with accomplishment. Being in this state provides the appearance of being busy, but at the end of the day, there's not much to show for it.

I enthusiastically encourage you to attempt to answer these four questions as thoroughly as possible:

1. To what degree are you guilty as charged of each of the above personal productivity traps?
2. If so, what are these habits and behaviours truly costing you? (Maybe twenty minutes a day or more?)
3. What would it mean to you if you did overcome these counterproductive behaviours?
4. What do you intend to do about it? What are you going to do differently?

The Principles & Practices of Optimizing Personal Productivity

Optimizing personal productivity is really about producing the most desired results in the least possible amount of time. In more technical terms, it means becoming more effective and efficient. Evidently, many people are confused on the meaning of these two words because they tend to toss them around as if they were synonyms, and they are definitively not. Being effective and being efficient are both fundamentally important and fundamentally different.

Effectiveness is about results, outcomes and direction. Efficiency is about speed or getting results quickly, with the least amount of time and energy. The essential self-evident sequence of the two productivity principles is that direction must precede speed. The best definition of a fanatic is someone who gets lost and decides to double their speed only to become lost twice as fast. The great playwright Noël Coward reaffirmed this sequence when he said, "Many young people get lost in the rapid and efficient ascension up the career ladder only get to the top ladder and discover it's the wrong wall."

Peter Drucker, in his classic 1967 book on personal productivity *The Effective Executive* (probably the most influential book ever written on this subject), simplified the two fundamental personal productivity principles with these trite-but-true statements:

1. Effectiveness is about doing the right things
2. Efficiency is about doing things right

Almost all business books written in the 1960s are now terribly outdated, and yet Drucker's book, which was designed for executives in the industrial age, ironically should be read by everyone in organizations today. The book is about how to make decisions and set priorities, which in the industrial age was the domain of managers and executives. Ducker's book's increasing relevancy is best explained through the central theme, which is that in the twenty-first-century-empowered workplace, everyone must be a leader and act like an executive making decisions and setting priorities for themselves.

The four fundamental personal productivity practices are illustrated by the **Personal Productivity Pyramid.** In the relatively stagnant industrial age, where job descriptions were more fixed and clearly defined and work was more quantifiable, the key to success was an efficiency mindset – more and faster. The base part of the productivity pyramid was largely irrelevant to most employees because it was handled by top managers and a few executives. However, the information-age workplace demands much more of an effectiveness mindset by all employees because being empowered means we have to become our own bosses and decide what needs to be done when and how.

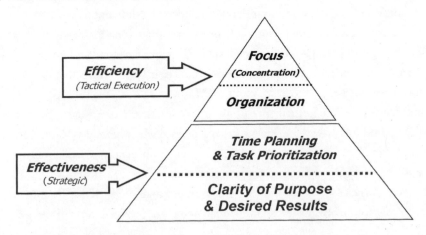

Enhancing Effectiveness - Best Practices

1] Create Contribution-Based Job Description

The primary guiding principle of optimizing personal productivity can be summarized and simplified by this statement once again: "The main thing is to keep the main things the main thing." If this is true, then the obvious starting point is to gain and maintain clarity of what the main things truly are – the purpose and desired outcomes at both job and task level. Unless we are talking about very basic jobs, traditional job descriptions that focus people on tasks and activities are dangerously obsolete for jobs of medium-to-high complexity.

Everyone in all roles has a new job description – make yourself valuable! Or make the biggest possible contribution to the organization you can. We must reconceive our jobs in terms of the results, value or contributions we are compensated to create and deliver. The all-important questions of the day are "How am I uniquely positioned to deliver value to the organization? What contributions can I make that the people above and below me can't?"

We must develop a contribution mindset by creating our own "contribution-based" job description.

If you already know the purpose and desired outcomes you are compensated to produce, then there is no need to do the following exercise. However, if you do have an ambiguous job, wearing multiple hats and suffering from role confusion, I highly recommend the following process to get clarity as to the value you are compensated to make.

The starting point is to break your job into "contribution roles." Roles provide structure in an ambiguous world and yet are still fluid and adaptable. They provide a framework for objective/priority setting and self-accountability. You may have two roles or ten depending on the nature of your job. For example, I have four roles. I have a "revenue-producer" role in which I speak at conferences and do training. I have a "research and development" role in which I read, write and develop material. I have an "administrative" role, which is running the operational side of the business and I have a "marketing" role. The last two roles I have largely delegated to my associate.

1. Break job down into each KCR (key contribution role)

2. Clarify all stakeholders in each KCR

3. Clarify/negotiate expectations with all stakeholders

4. Write statement of purpose for each KCR (one sentence)

5. Clarify KPIs (key performance indicators) or ideal outcomes in each KCR (what success looks like)

6. Set annual/quarterly/monthly goals in each KCR

7. Clarify/negotiate performance expectations with boss

The old adage "if you don't stand for something, you'll fall for anything" is so true. Without clarity of purpose and desired results, you will say yes to things when you should have said NO, which means you will be working on priorities, all right; the problem is, they are someone else's priorities.

2) Set Priorities – Best Practices

The process of setting priorities is the process of keeping the main things the main thing. It sounds simple enough, but our MTBS (mean time between surprises) has been steadily dropping, which means in today's dynamic and even turbulent workplace setting achieving priorities is not easy. When setting priorities, I recommend the use of two principles to guide your practices. First, remember the Pareto's principle, which you know as the 80/20 rule. When applied to priority setting, it means 80% of your results will flow from 20% of your tasks and activities. The obvious best practice is to identify and focus on the 20% high-return tasks and activities.

An even more practical principle is called the "urgent/important principle," which says "things that are important are seldom urgent and things that are urgent are seldom important." These are the two primary forces that drive choices as to how we spend our time, day in and day out. Many organizations and individuals make the mistake of confusing urgency with importance. I always ask this in my time-management workshop: "How many people have very important projects, which if you did manage to complete, would make a big contribution to the organization, but they're constantly pushed to the back burner by problems, crises and operational issues?" Consistently the vast majority of people raise their hand with frustrated enthusiasm.

The importance of a given task is defined by the **consequences** of completing or failing to complete the task. The urgency of a task is defined by **time pressure** and deadlines. What's important is largely an internal issue of your own values. Urgencies are driven externally – the ringing phone, the beeping emails, the people knocking at your doors. If you are constantly being bothered by external forces, then you will have a sneaking suspicion that you are not in control; you are being controlled by the urgent demands of others.

Whether you are aware of it or not, there are four types of tasks we engage in. "A-type" tasks are important and urgent. "B-type" tasks are important but not urgent. "C-type" tasks are urgent but not important. "D-type" tasks are neither important nor urgent. The forces of urgency driven by customer demands for instant responses facilitated by ever more user-friendly technology have grown dramatically through the years, which has resulted in many people and organizations being sucked into the powerful vortex of A- and C-type work.

The cornerstone of true, sustainable personal productivity success is to focus time and energy on B-type work. We must say no to D-type work, shrink C-type and find some time each day to do B-type work that will have long-term significant payoffs – but no one's pressuring you. Many people today report being trapped by urgency. Metaphorically, people in our whitewater world are in an old, leaky wooden boat and they are so busy bailing (A- and C-type work) they never take time out to patch a hole (B-type work) and thus they are doomed to a life of never-ending reactive bailing.

3) Use at Least Two Task Lists

Task or to-do lists are the foundational tools of the **Personal Productivity Planning Process**, and yet many people suffer from to-do list frustration, which means their lists are longer at the end of the day than at the beginning. This is self-defeating and never ending and leaves people feeling behind, overwhelmed and more likely to make the misguided decision to give up using to-do lists.

To properly build and manage to-do lists, we must start by understanding that lists serve two distinct purposes. The first is to gather, and the second is to guide. If you're only using one list, you are officially at cross purposes. The key list management practice is to keep at least two lists.

To-do lists clear the psychic decks by gathering everything that you could, should or might do some day to get it out of your mind, onto paper or into a trusted repository so you're not self-interrupting and spending time and energy trying not to forget what you need to remember.

Their second purpose is to **guide** our **actions**. The primary best practice of list management is that the only tasks and activities that make it onto action to-do lists are those you realistically think you can complete within a given timeframe. By making good action lists, you are setting yourself up for success; at the end of the day or week you should have most of your tasks completed, providing a sense of accomplishment and being on top of things.

4) Plan Weekly

To help gain clarity of what is truly important, we must apply the "perspective principle" – which means the longer the period of time you take into account, the more you automatically clarify and empower what is truly important. We must all adopt the habit of a meaningful weekly planning session with ourselves. I am not saying to abandon daily planning; I am saying it is vitally important to make a week the primary context of your time planning! The first critical step towards a life of proactivity (where you are acting on your job as opposed to having your job act on you) is to shift your primary planning efforts from daily to weekly. If you are only planning daily, you are unknowingly empowering urgencies (largely driven by the demand of others) in your life. The key strategy to becoming more proactive and less reactive is to commit to spending a half hour late on a Friday afternoon to regroup and take charge of the next seven days. Doing this will provide the highest ROI of the week – taking thirty minutes to take a degree of control over the other 167.5 hours of the week must become the cornerstone of your time-planning efforts.

There are multiple benefits from a meaningful weekly planning session:

- It helps you focus your time and energy on what is truly important and not urgent
- The more holistic perspective is the key to achieving work–life balance
- Weekly planning gives you much greater flexibility; it can change without discarding the entire plan
- It allows you to better compartmentalize your life (leave work at work) by emotionally completing your week
- It supports your capacity to schedule the essential chunks of time needed to focus on what is truly important
- Greater awareness of near-future events and due dates results in better preparation and fewer surprise crises

Here are some basic guidelines; however, I highly recommend you develop and customize a more extensive and systematic approach to your weekly planning session.

✓ Use the "week at a view" scheduling tool to block out fixed time commitments such as appointments and meetings. This allows you to see how much discretionary time you have available to work with..
✓ Build a weekly task list:

  ☑ Review and clean all your lists
  ☑ Review your "Current Projects" files
  ☑ Review your monthly goals in each KCR and set weekly priorities to accomplish in each role

☑ Look ahead at the next couple of weeks to identify deadlines and commitments. Is preparation required?

✓ The key step to proactivity is to schedule or block out time for the most important tasks and activities.

✓ Build your daily task list for Monday, which should cascade down from your weekly plan.

5] Plan Tomorrow Today

Always create your daily to-do list for tomorrow as one of the last things you do today! This simple habit creates many benefits. It allows you to better enjoy the evening as you have "emotionally completed" the day, which means leaving work at work and being more present with people in your personal life. This strategy also supports your ability to hit the ground running the next morning.

6] Implement the "4 D's" Workload-Reduction Strategies

Unlike just a few decades ago, the rate of change in the whitewater workplace of the information age requires constant reassessment of task relevancy. The "obsolescence trap" is nipping at our heels; this is where time is spent on tasks that have been rendered obsolete by technological changes. Lots of people are still spending valuable time on tasks that have become redundant, and if they stopped doing so, no one would notice. The larger and more bureaucratic an organization, the greater the severity of this problem.

At least once a quarter, we all need to step back and employ the workload-reduction strategy of reengineering our work by deleting, diminishing, delaying or delegating tasks that do not add value to self or stakeholders. Identifying and implementing workload-reduction strategies will mostly require conversations with stakeholders.

Delete: Create and update your "not to-do list." What can you stop doing? Tasks that are obsolete or redundant or do not add value to self or to stakeholders.

Delay: Which tasks will not be costly if put off? Examine the frequency of your standard operating reports and procedures. Do they really need it that often? Ask your stakeholders. Instead of weekly reporting, how about monthly? Instead of monthly reporting, how about quarterly?

Delegate: Which tasks can someone else do better, faster and cheaper? Develop complementary teams where tasks flow to people who are best suited for them, and get the right people doing the right work.

Diminish: Lean thinking! What reports and tasks could be minimized, downsized, streamlined or simplified in size, structure and scope?

7) Reverse-Engineer Projects & Tasks

In the industrial age, work was usually self-evident; there was a clear starting point and stopping point. As knowledge workers, more and more we must determine for ourselves what needs to be done. Stephen Covey's habit 3 is "begin with the end in mind." From the world of architecture, there is an expression that "form follows function," which means an architect first needs to identify the purpose and desired outcomes of the building, and once clarified, can reverse engineer the form to serve its function or the purpose of the building.

The starting point of planning your complex tasks and projects is always to develop clarity of **purpose and outcomes**. Developing crystal clarity as to why you are doing the task or project and what specifically you are trying to achieve provides these vital benefits:

✓ It is the task or project's "north star," providing direction for all other decisions downstream in the project
✓ It is vital to the process of motivating your lower brain by developing commitment
✓ It is the key to unleashing the creative powers of the lower brain
✓ It helps determine what "done" looks like

Enhancing Efficiency - Best Practices

The real key to efficiency or speed is to develop a systematic approach to all your activities and efforts so they become second nature, allowing you to flow through your tasks. When you're emptying the dishwasher, you don't have to stand back and ask yourself, "Now where do those plates go?" You do it automatically or subconsciously, without requiring upper-brain engagement and breaking your concentration.

1) Get Organized

As the world becomes more complex, confusing and fast, we all have to deal with ever-increasing amounts of information coming from more directions and multiple sources, so organization of your tools and information becomes increasingly important.

Remember that getting organized is a means to an end. Organization allows extended periods of deep concentration without having to stop and start to look for things. The primary principle of organization is found in the tried but true phrase, "A place for everything and everything in its place." Within three to four weeks, you can create a second-nature flow environment where you no longer have to stop and consciously look for things.

Organization is not an event; rather, it must be seen as an ongoing process

Most people have confused neatness with organization. Let's clarify – you are organized to the degree that you can locate things without having to consciously look for them. Neatness refers to appearances, i.e., having a clean, clear, clutter-free environment. I've seen many people who have a pristine environment but can't find anything. I've also seen some dishevelled workspaces where people can find whatever they need without having to look for them. Having a neat and organized workplace is truly an issue of different strokes for different folks. For extroverts, clutter is a concentration killer, so having a neat environment is much more important for extroverted people who struggle with concentration. Having a neat, clutter-free workspace is less important for introverts, who can concentrate regardless of how noisy their environment is.

Another key practice of organization is to stay **lean**! Always remember that your wastepaper basket delete buttons are your best ally in the battle of organization. Everyone's new mantra must be "When in doubt, throw it out!"

Risk alert! *Don't over-organize.* Beware the "law of diminishing," which means a little time spent organizing pays big dividends. I know some people who spend so much time getting organized they never seem to get much accomplished because they are always cross-referencing, colour coding and labelling things.

2) Create a Master Organizing System

In today's frenzied, frantic, frenetic, forgetful workplace, we all need a COS (central organizing system). There are multiple tools you can use for your COS – laptop, desktop, tablet, smart phone and paper-based systems. Each tool has advantages and disadvantages depending on the nature of your job. Most people use a combination of tools, and it still surprises me that many experiment with technology and end up going back to a primarily paper-based COS.

Whatever tool you choose for your COS, it needs to be holistic (for both your personal and professional lives), integrated (to avoid redundancies if using multiple tools), portable and comprehensive, in that it must manage the four core functions:

- Calendar/schedule events
- Task lists
- Contacts
- Notes/documents

3) Go to Work on Your Stakeholder Relationships

Your stakeholders essentially define the value you bring to the organization. To make things happen today in organizations, you must develop your "power grid" of stakeholder relationships with your key stakeholders (most likely your internal customers). The starting point of providing the required holistic perspective of your job is to apply a tool called "stakeholder mapping." This is a simple process of placing yourself or your team in a small circle in the middle of a page. Then draw lines out from the circle to connect with all stakeholders. The effort you put into improving stakeholder relationships brings forth many significant personal-productivity benefits:

✓ As you develop a deeper understanding of what is truly important to stakeholders, you can clarify the difference between stakeholder wants and needs, which supports your ability to set priorities and streamline your efforts.

✓ Improved stakeholder relationships will save a lot of time in much more open, spontaneous and efficient verbal communication, requiring minimal written communication.

✓ Improved stakeholder relationships result in fewer time-consuming misunderstandings, disagreements and conflicts.

✓ A strong stakeholder relationship helps your capacity to focus on and complete priorities, because stakeholders will offer more support and flexibility. It is easier to say no and deal efficiently with interruptions when the relationship is strong. Remember, when the relationship is right, the details are insignificant; when the relationship is wrong, the details are insurmountable.

4) Consolidate Your Discretionary Time into Chunks of Time!

Peter Drucker said, in his quirky way, that "four fifteen-minute periods of time does not an hour make." In other words, it is impossible to get anything of complexity done in little bits of time. It is of fundamental importance that we learn to consolidate our discretionary time into chunks of time for our most important and complex tasks that demand the deepest form of focus and concentration in uninterrupted periods (ninety minutes is ideal). I fully realize that today's workplace is marked by rings, pings, dings, buzzers, beeps and bells, and it's increasingly difficult for most of us to sequester ourselves and get chunks of time.

Beware the common myth of multitasking. The time costs associated with multitasking increase directly proportional to the complexity of the task. It is okay and perhaps even beneficial to multitask when you're working on things that do not require a great deal of mental horsepower or focused concentration. However, it is vitally important that you become a monomaniac on a mission when working on complex tasks. According to *Harvard Business Review*, people risk losing up to 40% of their productivity when attempting to multitask on complex work.

To support your ability to maintain focus, it is important to clear the psychic decks and perform a RAM dump to vacate the short-term memory banks. The most counterproductive, devastating interruptions are not external like the ringing phone, beeping email or people knocking at the door; they are internal. It is of particular importance to prevent self-interruption so you "eat your vegetables first" – in other words, it is vital that you get distasteful or unpleasant tasks and activities behind you as quickly as possible to prevent self-interruptions. If you have a root canal at 4:00 p.m., I suspect you will not have a productive day, as you will be preoccupied with thoughts of needles, drills and drooling. Mark Twain put it this way: "If you have to swallow a live frog, it's best not to stare at it too long."

Principles & Practices of Successful Decision Making

The ability to make decisions is a fundamentally important personal productivity competency. Priority setting is about making decisions, while procrastination is frequently a function of indecision. Every definition of wisdom involves the word "judgment" because the quality of your life is governed by the quality of your decisions. Simply put, the capacity to make decisions = personal power, while indecision = powerlessness and procrastination.

In the very recent past, the boss made most of the decisions; however, in today's empowered workplace, all employees must now make decisions. The capacity to make fast and prudent decisions is becoming increasingly important and simultaneously more challenging given the following factors:

- Greater uncertainty, ambiguity and unpredictability
- Growing complexity with ever more information to process
- Increasing urgency decreasing the time frame to make decisions
- Increasing employee involvement, meaning more consensus for team-based decisions, which are frequently complicated by interpersonal issues
- Greater number of alternative choices

When assessing your capacity to make decisions, there are two factors to consider. Judgment refers to the effectiveness or quality of a decision. Decisiveness means how efficiently or how fast you make decisions.

Guiding principles of successful decision making:

- The clearer your personal life **vision** and **values** are, the easier making becomes.
- Let the common sense "time allocation/importance principle" guide you. The more important the decision, the more time you should invest, and the less important, the less time you should spend.
- We must strive to achieve the delicate balance between head and heart or intellect and intuition. My suggestion when you are making "thing" decisions is to rely more on logic and reason; when making "people" decisions, rely more on intuition and gut feelings.
- Emotions cloud logic! The more emotional the decision, the greater the need for an objective third-party perspective.
- I highly recommend that when making important and complex decisions, you should write your thoughts on paper. The physical act of writing something activates the subconscious emotional brain, which is the true source of creativity and problem solving. A few centuries back, the famous French scientist Blaise Pascal said, "The heart has reason that reason will never know." After writing, I recommend you sleep on it. Many people have reported going to bed with a difficult problem and

waking up with clarity. This is because the subconscious brain never sleeps and has all the solutions to your problems.

- Our choices are frequently only as good as we make them. A truly effective decision is defined by a full, unconditional commitment to a choice. Many decisions fail not because of bad choices but rather due to a lack of commitment to implementation.
- The essential best practice or method of successful decision making is to apply a systematic **problem-solving process.**

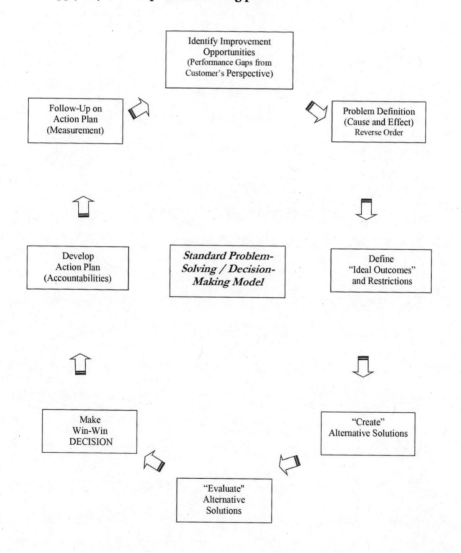

To conclude, in the industrial age, "time-management" skills, which we now know as "personal-productivity" skills, were a nice luxury to have; however, in the stripped-down, every-job-counts workplace, personal-productivity skills are now absolutely essential for anyone who hopes to achieve work–life balance. Allow me to reemphasize that the ability to get things done and produce results is the cornerstone competency of developing credibility, which is foundational to becoming a highly effective leader.

LEADING FROM EVERYWHERE

THE PRINCIPLES & PRACTICES OF CHARACTER-BASED LEADERSHIP

PART 5: INTERPERSONAL LEADERSHIP – PEOPLE SKILLS 101

14. Negotiating – The Tactical Side of Leadership
15. The Natural Laws of Interpersonal Dynamics
16. Three Leadership Core Conversational Competencies

CHAPTER 14: NEGOTIATING – THE TACTICAL SIDE OF LEADERSHIP

Negotiating is leadership in action, as it is through the day-to-day, ground-level, face-to-face and ear-to-ear interactions that leaders do to make things happen through people. The ability to negotiate is a fundamental core leadership competency. Leadership effectiveness or the success you achieve is directly related to your **ability to negotiate**.

A common and costly misunderstanding is that people don't realize they negotiate every day of their life, which is the biggest mistake you can make when negotiating. Like it or not, we are all negotiators! *Newsweek* magazine once referred to negotiating as the "game of life." Most people believe negotiating is what happens at the car dealership, with the real-estate agent, at the merger-and-acquisition table or when management sits across the table from the union. Negotiating is a fact of life. We all negotiate every day, and the only difference is the degree of formality. Returning a defective product to a retailer without a receipt; choosing what restaurant to meet a friend at, what TV show you're going to watch, what movie to go to or where you're going on vacation; or agreeing on bedtimes – are all are forms of informal negotiating.

The confusion around what it means to negotiate becomes instantly evident when I ask my workshop participants to create a complete definition of negotiating. To define negotiation by its simplest terms, any conversation where you

EXAMPLES OF DEPOSITS

- ❏ Giving credit away
- ❏ Requesting, asking and empowering
- ❏ Believing in the other person
- ❏ Making people smile or laugh

EXAMPLES OF WITHDRAWALS

- ❏ Moralizing, lecturing
- ❏ One-upmanship
- ❏ Chronic complaining, negativity
- ❏ Boasting, bragging, conceit

Of all the deposits you can make, there is one that stands out far above in terms of its potency: the simple act of listening. Every time you really listen to someone, you are giving them psychological air and you can watch their self-esteem slowly grow. I used to think you had to agree with people to make a deposit. I've since learned that it's not the agreement but rather how much you demonstrate that you value their opinion. Allow me to repeat the paradoxical truth that you persuade by speaking and gain influence by listening.

This principle is a little bit of magic; however, the magic only works if the deposits are made unconditionally. The intention is not to have you turn the relationship into a trading game. Be patient, because like all natural systems it takes time to realize the benefits of your efforts (but this is guaranteed to work unless you're dealing with a sociopath).

There are no "quick fixes" to repair broken relationships. Rebuilding and relationships take time and effort. There is one possible exception: a sincere, heartfelt, eye-contact apology can be a massive deposit and repair years of damage if the promise to change proves to be real and permanent.

A note of caution: be particularly careful what you say when emotions are running high because the potency of withdrawals are magnified in moments of conflict anger. As mentioned in Chapter 11, emotions activate access to long-term memory banks so what you say in anger cuts deep, as the long-term memory banks are laid bare. That's why, when emotions run high, it is always best to break off and reschedule.

are trying to get something from someone or have someone do something (or vice-versa) is negotiating.

There is little argument that the most significant book on the subject of negotiating is *Getting to Yes*, written by two Harvard professors, Roger Fisher and William Ury. What makes this book so unique is that it introduced a new style of negotiating based on principles as opposed to positions. The original industrial-age literature on negotiating was largely based on a win/lose competitive philosophy. It was about manipulation, truth-twisting trickery, pressure, deception and gambits. It was a zero-sum-game mentality where both sides would stake out an inflated "position" in preparation to "split the difference." These beliefs are still widely held today, which explains why many people associate negotiating with conflict and being adversarial and combative. The traditional industrial-age model of negotiations was about winning over people, whereas the new model is about winning people over.

The book *Getting to Yes* introduced a new philosophy and strategy of negotiating based on collaboration, not competition. The essence of this new approach is to turn the conversation into a problem-solving effort where you work together to achieve the optimum outcome for both parties. This more diplomatic approach to negotiating is perhaps best explained as the art of letting other people have your way. The only criticism levelled at this breakthrough book is that it was somewhat idealistic and not entirely applicable. Clearly, the best approach with those who are willing to collaborate is a win–win, but the world is full of people who have no interest in getting your needs met. The question that remains unanswered is: what then? We will cover how to identify and defend against hardball negotiators in this chapter.

At the risk of sounding mercenary, I've learned through the years that the most tangible, holistic and practical way to frame all interpersonal affairs is through the lens of negotiating. Negotiation skills are synonymous with interpersonal or people skills. In the most basic of terms, whenever you're dealing with people, you are negotiating.

The Ever-Increasing Importance of Negotiating Skills

I am consistently disappointed when I ask recent graduates from high-end business schools if they've ever had a class in negotiation skills. A very small percentage will raise their hand. Sadly, the first thing they do upon graduation is negotiating. These graduates are sent unprepared into a world where the harsh reality is that you do not get what you want, need or even deserve; you get what you negotiate.

When you consider the fact that almost all major life decisions involve other people, then negotiating is the preeminent form of decision making that shapes our lives, and the importance of negotiating skills should have always been self-evident. But hold on – the accelerating rate of change has created a "negotiation revolution," which is and will make negotiating skills even more important into the future because we will all find ourselves in more frequent and more challenging negotiations driven by the following factors:

- *Increasing rate of change* – The faster the rate of change, the greater the need to negotiate! The implementation of change initiatives requires negotiating of new agreements, strategies, priorities, policies, procedures, systems, contracts, mergers, work roles and workloads.

- *Job churn* – Say goodbye to lifelong employment. In 2015, approximately half the Canadian workers with full-time jobs had been in their current jobs less than two years. Younger employees see themselves as "free agents"; they are more aware of their options and are more willing to take advantage of them.

- *Less workplace structure* – The workplace is becoming less rigid and more boundary-less, with fewer rules than in the industrial age. As larger organizations downsize and strip out organizational layers, the vast majority of new jobs are being created by small entrepreneurial businesses, not major corporations. This means fewer people are restricted by rigid human resources policies and traditional fixed-salary ranges. More and more people are operating within flexible and performance-driven compensation structures, and they are increasingly free (and responsible) to negotiate for their true worth.

- *Interdependence* – In the recent past, the boss made the decisions, but today teams are most commonly making decisions. The process of building consensus decisions necessitates more negotiating.

- *More demanding customers* – Customers today are more sophisticated, informed and demanding. They have higher expectations and are more willing to complain, which means frontline customer-contact employees are going to be involved in more difficult negotiations on a more regular basis.

- *More demanding employers* and *employees* – Competitive pressures are forcing employers to demand more from their employees, while simultaneously employees are more willing to push back and ask for what they want, which in the main is better work–life balance. These two opposing forces pushing against each other create a greater need for more everyday negotiating.

- *Hyper-competition* – Across all industries there is increasingly fierce competition resulting in significant downside pressure on profit margins. This means a critical profit driver will be ensuring that all employees who deal with suppliers and customers must have well-developed negotiating skills.

- *Moral deterioration* – The vast majority of books and training programs on negotiating now all focus on taking a win–win collaborative approach. Paradoxically, whenever I ask my workshop participants if negotiating practices are becoming more collaborative or competitive in their industry, the vast majority lament that the reality is that their industry is becoming more competitive, dog-eat-dog, cutthroat and hardball, with lower ethical standards. It is a sad comment on our society, but we all have to learn to keep our negotiating guards up, as there are ever more scammers with fewer scruples who are ready and willing to take advantage of people's good nature.

Some Random Thoughts to Contemplate on Negotiating

- The response I get from my workshop participants over the years is that the vast majority (upside of 90%) of their negotiations take place within the context of ongoing relationships, as opposed to one-off deals. I then ask what percentage of their organization's revenues are coming from existing customers. The answer is consistently 90% plus. This means that most of our negotiations must be seen as a "parallel process." There are always two considerations to balance: the deal at hand and the quality of the relationship. If it is a one-off deal, it is okay to compete; however, the only viable long-term negotiating philosophy is "win–win or no deal." Guiding principle – to the degree the relationship matters, we must take a win–win collaborative approach.

- You can get anything you want if you first help other people get what they want. When I first heard this line spoken by Zig Ziglar, one of the original motivational speakers, I used to think it was corny and simplistic. However, over time I have come to realize the validity and deep wisdom in this seemingly simple statement. An effective negotiator is someone who can acquire what they want and need; a highly effective negotiator is someone who also enhances the relationship in the process by ensuring other people get their needs met as well.

- Many people hold the false impression that the negotiations take place near the end of a conversation. Given the common misconceptions around negotiations, this may sound a little cold-hearted; we will learn that the relationship is a source of negotiating power, which means negotiations begin as soon as two people first meet.

- Compromise is far too common and is seldom win–win. We have been conditioned to quickly jump to compromise when frequently there is a better solution for both parties that could be achieved through the process of creative collaboration. A common negotiation phrase is "let's split the difference." Any time you hear this phrase, beware and approach with caution because it has the appearance of fairness, but upon further consideration it may not be fair at all. If we are going to split the difference, is important that we do it on our terms, which we will discuss later in this chapter.

- The "people paradox" is that when dealing with "things," fast is fast, but when dealing with people, slow is fast. If you rush into a negotiation without building trust, then predictably the communication downstream will be guarded, arduous and time-consuming. However, if you take the time upfront to build a relationship, then the communication downstream flows more naturally, openly, easily and efficiently.

- Negotiating is more of an art than a science, and seldom is there a clear-cut, black-and-white situation! All negotiations are unique, and thus appropriate negotiation practices are highly situational, so you must be able to play different games. The answer to the often-asked question "What should I do in this situation?" is almost always "It all depends." We must accept that there is no magic, secret negotiating success formula – nothing works all the time. Some people are simply unreasonable, unchangeable and thus impossible to reason with.

- There are two basic styles of negotiations: competitive (win–lose) and collaborative (win–win). I am a firm believer in the win–win philosophy, but we must accept the fact that many people are not. A lot of people operate on the basis that "what is mine is mine and what is yours is negotiable." They may not have malice towards you but are willing to take advantage of you if you let them. It is a fundamental importance with negotiating to know what game you're playing so you can adjust your strategies and tactics accordingly. If you have dealt with a person over a period of time, it should be easy to identify their negotiating style and how they approach negotiations. But what if you don't know the negotiating counterpart well? How do you know what game the counterpart is playing? What are the indicators that tell you whether you're dealing with a collaborative or competitive person? Learning how to identify what type of negotiations you are in is essential to success. We must learn to identify people who don't think win–win and how to best defend against the use of manipulative, deceptive, aggressive strategies and tactics. The sooner you can accurately identify what game you are playing, the better off you will be. Here are some indicators to look for to determine whether your counterpart is in a competitive or collaborative negotiation mode:

- ✓ Watch the person's demeanour or presence. Some people walk into the room and say, "Here I am!" whereas others walk into the room and say, "Oh, there you are."
- ✓ Are they doing more asking or telling?
- ✓ Are they applying time pressure and appear to be in a rush? If so, that's a major red flag.
- ✓ How much information are they are willing share? This is a good indicator.
- ✓ Notice how much they listen and really attempt to understand you and your needs.

The **Negotiations Style Continuum** below is designed to provide context or a frame of reference for the chapter. It serves two practical purposes:

1. It's a self-assessment tool
2. It supports your ability to identify the negotiating styles of the people most commonly dealt with

Given that negotiating skills are a core leadership competency, they can and must be learned. The starting point of learning is accurate self-assessment of your constructive and destructive negotiating behaviours. I promise there is great value in attempting to answer the following questions. Where do you tend to fall on the continuum below? If you are not down the middle, what is it costing you? Why do you possess these inclinations? Most importantly, what do you intend to do about it? Where do the people you negotiate with most frequently tend to behave on this continuum?

| Competitive | Collaborative | Compliant |

WIN/LOSE	WIN/WIN	LOSE/WIN
Too hard (bully)	Leadership	Too soft (wimp)
Goal – victory	Best possible agreement for all	Peace and harmony
Adversaries	Problem-solving partner	Friends
Insensitive	Focus on facts, not feelings	Overly sensitive
Domination	Reasoned collaboration	Capitulation
No/low trust	Negotiate on the merits	Too much trust
Dig in on position	Focus on needs and interests	Change position easily
Demand concessions	Create options for mutual gain	Make concessions
Insist on position	Insist on use of objective criteria	Insist on agreement
Get bigger piece of pie	Grow the pie	Keep piece of pie
Position focus	Fairness by facts focus	Relationship focus
Aggressive	Assertive	Passive

Most Common Negotiating Mistakes People Make

Research conducted by the **Harvard Negotiations Project** (which was the genesis of the book *Getting to Yes*) produced a list of the most common mistakes people make when they are negotiating. Here they are:

- ❑ Not realizing when negotiations begin
- ❑ Underestimating your power and thus settling for less
- ❑ Giving concessions too often, early and easily!
- ❑ Assuming you understand the needs or what is truly important to the other party
- ❑ Not preparing effectively
- ❑ Allowing the negotiations to become adversarial
- ❑ Letting your ego get in the way
- ❑ Having a mindset that it is rigid, failing to listen and understand the other party
- ❑ Saying yes to things you have not previously thought through
- ❑ Failing to call time-out when emotions get out of control
- ❑ Not knowing when to walk away
- ❑ Failing to recognize when you are not dealing with a win–win negotiator

I also value this list as a powerful self-assessment tool. I challenge you to answer the following questions honestly: Are you guilty as charged on any of the above? If so, what is it costing you? Why do you possess these propensities? Most importantly, what do you intend to do about it?

Points to Ponder on Negotiating Power

What determines who has more power when negotiating? The power dynamics that govern the strength of your bargaining position are impacted by the different types of negotiating power (as listed below) that can vary dramatically given the scenario. The answer to who has more power is the answer to the all-important question "**Who needs whom more than who needs whom?**" and is governed by the **first two basic primary sources of negotiating power:**

1. The quality of your BATNA (best alternative to a negotiated agreement). This acronym is from the book Getting to Yes. When you think about it, it's just common sense; the more options you have, the more power you have. When it's salary negotiation time with your current boss, if you have three outstanding job offers, how much power do you have? If you have no outstanding job offers, how much power do you have?

2. The perception of the distinctive value you offer (how much they want what you have or bring that they can't get elsewhere). In the world of marketing, they call this concept "differentiation." The basic purpose of marketing is to explain to the customer how your product or service is different than the competition, which justifies a higher selling price. If you fail to convince the customer of the difference, the only way to get business is with price. The problem with this approach is twofold: first, you don't make much money, and second, you have zero customer loyalty. We will learn in Part 7 that the only purpose of a business is to drive value to the customer as perceived by the customer so you can increase your prices and profits.

   - Relationship power – The degree of influence you've gained with the other person.
   - Information power – Power goes to the person with the most relevant information. Risk grows to the degree that you know less about the issue at hand than your counterpart does.
   - Personal power – The attitude, mindset or degree of self-confidence you demonstrate.
   - Position power – Official status, formal authority.
   - Persuasion power – The power of a convincing explanation.
   - Planning and preparation power – Achieving clarity of ideal outcomes and your walk-away point.
   - Resource power – The capacity to allocate resources to the negotiations by hiring better lawyers, accountants and various experts.
   - Time power – Power almost always goes to the person with the most time.

Power is in the eye of beholder; it can be real or perceived. Perception of power is power! Power should be politely tested. Until someone pushes back, you don't know how much power you have, and you will likely end up with less than you could have had. People tend to naturally underestimate their power because they are much more aware of their own limitations and restrictions than their counterpart's. You probably have more negotiating power than you know. The question is – are you using it?

Planning & Preparing for Your Negotiating

The amount of time, effort and energy you should invest in planning and preparing for a negotiation should increase directly based on two variables. The first and most obvious is the degree of importance: what is at stake? The second is the degree of competitiveness: the more competitive, the more the preparation. Accepting the fact that no plan survives its collision with reality, you must be prepared to adjust your plans on the go as you learn new information. The guiding principle is that any time you are surprised by new information, you should automatically call for a timeout.

Four Strategic Preparation Questions

1. Who is involved in the negotiation? Conduct "stakeholder analysis" to ensure you are aware of everyone who will be involved. Attempt to assess how much authority and influence each person has. It's important to identify the "pen" (the final decision maker).

2. Who's got the power? Assess the balance of power by answering the key question: Who needs whom more than who needs whom? The answer is largely determined by each party's BATNA.

3. What game is being played? Assess and anticipate the nature of negotiations that you expect using a rating on the collaborative/competitive continuum.

4. What time pressures are both parties under? Evaluate whose side time is on, remembering that power goes to the person with time.

Eleven Tactical Preparation Questions

1. What do you want to have? What are your ideal outcomes?

2. What do you absolutely *need to* have to make it a viable business deal? What are your basic outcomes?

3. What information is relevant or important? What information do you currently have? Where are your information gaps? What information do you need to access? Determine what information you need to understand about the other party/person and then plan (on paper) your questioning approach.

4. Determine what information is important for the other party to know about you and plan your explanation.

5. What is truly important to the other party and what pressure are they under?

6. At what point is it in your best interest to walk away? When you have conceded all your wants or when your BATNA becomes better than the deal at hand?

7. What is your opening position going to be (if this is a highly competitive scenario)? The proven principle is the higher the aspiration level, the better the outcome. Or, simply put, the more you ask for, the more you get. The risk is asking too much, which could result in the loss of credibility or antagonizing the counterpart. The key is to identify your MPP (maximum plausible position), which is the highest you can possibly request and justify with the power of a good explanation.

8. What concessions are you prepared to make? Anticipate what concessions will be requested (ideally that the other party's values don't cost too much).

9. What will you request in exchange for requested concessions?

10. What is the best way to open the meeting or conversation?

11. When is the best time and where is the best place to meet?

Collaborative Negotiating – Basic Best Practices

- To avoid a "**fixed pie**" of single-issue negotiations, which end up in a "take it or leave it" situation, it is vital to build in as many variables as possible to allow for trade-offs leading to win–win outcomes. This avoids the risk of a one-issue, take-it-or-leave-it, win–lose situation. Here are some common negotiating variables to build in:

  - ✓ Deliverables
  - ✓ Pricing
  - ✓ Terms and conditions
  - ✓ Quantities
  - ✓ Customization
  - ✓ Service support
  - ✓ Delivery
  - ✓ Timing
  - ✓ Warranties
  - ✓ Training

- To ensure FAIRNESS, insist on the agreement upfront of **objective third-party criteria** or **processes** whenever possible. An objective criterion when selling a house is the multiple-listing services. When selling or buying a used car, objective criteria would be the Kelly Blue Book. In other cases, depending on the situation, you may wish to propose an agreement based on:

- ✓ Market value
- ✓ Precedent or tradition
- ✓ What a court would decide
- ✓ Objective third party (appraiser)
- ✓ Professional standards (engineer or accountant)

- Never say yes to anything of significance that you have not thought through.

- Cardinal rule of all conversations: whenever a disagreement arises, **ask questions, listen and then prove that you fully understand the other person.**

- When emotions begin to get out of control, call for a time-out or cooling-off period before the emotional damage is done. The time-out allows the blood to go back to your cerebral cortex so you're much better able to have a mature, reasonable and productive conversation.

- When in complex and protracted negotiations, it is vital to keep track (on paper) of what has been accomplished and agreed to and what issues still need to be discussed. It's important to periodically step out of working "in" the conversation to work "on" the conversation by reviewing notes. The benefits are many:

  - ✓ Gives structure, organization, timing and focus to the conversation
  - ✓ Prevents confusion, which tends to break down negotiations
  - ✓ Provides opportunity to prove you have been listening to them, which builds trust
  - ✓ Creates a sense of progress and a "swing towards agreement"

- When dealing with a shark, the ideal objective is to move your counter-part from a competitive to a collaborative mindset. Metaphorically, move to the same side of table, turning the conversation from a face-to-face discussion into a side-by-side dialogue. The first step is to convince the adversarial counterpart there is more in it for them if they collaborate instead of competing.

The central strategy to shifting the conversation into a collaborative, problem-solving mode is to understand the needs and interests driving their position. You must discover what is truly important to other party or what is motivating them. Best practice – define the negotiation in terms of needs and interests, not positions!

The essential tactic is to begin by asking questions about their needs and interests. Then listen, listen and listen some more to build trust so they slowly open up. Restate what you have heard until you prove that you understand them to their satisfaction. It is very difficult to argue or fight with somebody who is sincerely trying to understand you.

Allow me to illustrate the strategy by telling a short story about two old men who live together. It's a mid-Sunday afternoon and they both end up in the kitchen at the same time looking for a snack. One of the old men grabs an orange, and the other one says, "That's a good idea, I'll have an orange too." Realizing there are no oranges left, the discussion ensues. "I want the orange, no, I want the orange, but you had the second-last orange yesterday so that makes this mine, but I carried them home from the grocery store so I think it should be mine..." Predictably, after a brief squabble, they agree to compromise and split the orange in half. One guy grabs his half, goes back to watch TV and eats it. The other guy stays in the kitchen and starts to rummage through the cupboards looking for a peeler; he wants to make orange muffins and only wants the orange peel. One simple question opens the problem-solving door: "Why do you want the orange?"

Competitive Negotiating – Best Practices

If you have to negotiate with a shark and cannot walk away, then the guiding principle of competitive negotiations is to **win the best possible deal for yourself or your team without making the counterparts feel like they lost.**

- Beware of rushed or fast negotiations. Hardball negotiators throw fastballs that are behind you before you know it. A common tactic is called *fait accompli,* i.e., acting as if the deal is already done. Slow down and learn to say yes slowly. Try to be the reluctant seller and the unenthusiastic buyer, always demonstrating "walk-away" power. Patience is a cardinal negotiation virtue.

- Deadlines are often designed to make things happen. Realize that often "deadlines" can be moved or changed. When you suspect a false deadline, politely ask why they are asking for it. If they hesitate at all, this is a good indicator of a fake deadline.

- When dealing with a hardball negotiator who is attempting to use a manipulative technique, the best counter-tactic is to "name the game." Say with a smile, "You wouldn't use that old trick on me, would you?" and they will have to stop using the tactic.

- Don't bite on baited hooks. If dealing with an aggressive or abusive person, the strategy depends on the severity of the situation. Don't overreact to threats and intimidation; try to demonstrate **"assertive pacifism"** using the following countertactics:

    o *Selective inattention* – Ignore specific words or phrases
    o *Strategic withdrawal* – Leave with a plan to come back at a better time
    o *These boots are made for walking* – Leave with no intention of returning

- Always ask for more than you expect, because you just might get what you ask for, and if you don't get what you ask for then it leaves room to haggle.

- If you are planning to "split the difference," then play the game on your terms by tactics referred to as "bracketing." This means you start with the asking price then drop it to what you want to or can pay, then drop it the equal distance again to determine your opening position, landing on your original goal. This will illustrate the strategy:

Their asking price = $17,000
You want to pay = $15,000
Bracketed offer should be = $13,000

- If you are the buyer, it is important to request cost breakdown. If you are selling, it is important to try not to give cost breakdowns.

- Mark Twain said, "There are three kinds of lies: lies, damn lies and statistics." Tactfully test their estimates, statistics, averages and facts. Gently encourage them to reveal the source of the facts and statistics.

- Opinions on who should make the first offer is the subject of some debate in negotiating literature. I believe that in most circumstances it is best to get the other party to make the first offer because it could be more than you expected. Exceptions would be in circumstances that are ambiguous or if the counterpart is uninformed – you may want to make the first offer in an effort to anchor the price range. It is equally important not to say yes to the first offer in order to avoid the "winner's curse," which is the remorse that develops in the counterpart if you take their first offer. The first thought that enters their minds is "I should've offered less" and the second is "What hunk of junk did I just buy?"

- Never give without a get! This is also called "contingency" or "trade-off," and it elevates the value of the concession and stops requests for further concessions. Don't trust the old "I'll make it up to you later" line.

- Discover other people's "degree of authority" as soon as possible to prevent the use of the higher-authority technique commonly used at car dealerships where you will hear, "I will have to check with my boss."

- Making concessions – best practices:

    ✓ Conserve your concessions, and try not to make one first (unless absolutely necessary).

    ✓ Make small concessions slowly, loaded with regret or pain to ensure the counterpart fully appreciates the value.

    ✓ Watch your pattern; the second concession should be smaller than the first.

    ✓ Make the last concession so the person walks away feeling good and fully committed to live up to their end of the deal.

- Don't be fooled by "funny money." A commonly used manipulative technique is to break the cost into the smallest possible increments such as, "It's only the cost of a cup of coffee a day." The key question to answer is, "What is the true cost in hard cash?"

- When confronted with the request for a concession, apply the **YIKES** techniques! When the other party makes any request for a concession or favour use the **wince**, or in extreme cases on major requests use the full-body **flinch** or what I call the "Kramer." This technique demonstrates the pain and will ideally prevent any further request for concessions.

- Take good notes! The basic principle is "The lower the degree of trust, the higher the number of notes." Power goes to the person with the best documentation. Furthermore, it is important to make it obvious to the other party that you are taking notes, because people are more cautious and clearer in what they say when someone is writing it down.

- As a last resort, when confronted with an unacceptable offer, try saying, "I'm having a hard time seeing how this deal works for me. So, if you were in my position, how would you justify this deal?"

To conclude, negotiation skills are to being a leader what skating is to being a hockey player. Negotiation and strategy skills can and must be learned if you hope to be a highly effective leader.

CHAPTER 15: THE NATURAL LAWS OF INTERPERSONAL DYNAMICS

Human nature is the only constant in all of human history. Effective leaders that truly understand people must first understand human nature. The concept of natural laws was introduced in Chapter 9, where we learned the cause-and-effect dynamics of all natural systems, such as interpersonal relationships, are governed by natural laws or principles that are timeless and changeless. In this chapter, I will explain the natural laws that apply to interpersonal communication and relationship dynamics. What makes it challenging to identify, grasp and teach these forces at work is a function of the emotional, subconscious lower brain. In Chapter 8, we learned that the lower brain is physical, primitive and powerful in that it governs pretty much everything we do while operating below conscious awareness. It is the nature within us that explains why human behaviour is largely determined by natural laws. These laws, which highly effective leaders seem to intuitively grasp, once understood and applied will dramatically enhance your capacity to effectively communicate and build better relationships. In Chapter 16, we will focus on the core competencies or the practices to implement these principles.

Allow me to borrow a phrase from one of my favourite philosophers, Jim Rohn, who said, "Things don't just happen; things happen just." In other words, if you have excellent relationships in your life as evidenced by deep, rich, spontaneous communication, it is not random, accidental or a quirk of the cosmos. There are fixed laws or principles of cause-and-effect that predict and explain why relationships either build and sustain or sputter and break down. Of the seven laws I will cover, the first three laws are the primary laws that govern relationship success or failure.

1] The Law of Harvest

The law of harvest is considered the master law of the universe and has been given many labels throughout the ages. Scientists call it the law of cause-and-effect. Covey called it the law of the farm. Philosophical literature calls it the law of sowing and reaping. Sociologists call it the law of social reciprocity.

In its simplest terms, the law of the harvest explains that you will get out in direct proportion to what you put in, and that there are no shortcuts or quick fixes in natural systems. Shortcuts may appear to work in short-term "social systems" like schools. My social group really thought we had it figured out in university; we learned how to play the game and beat the system, and we would charm the professors, cram for exams, using Coles or Cliff notes to study. This explains the sad truth of my post-secondary education; I often confess that I did get a degree but I'm not sure I got much of an education. I pretty much got out in direct proportion to what I put in. Do you think the same principle holds true in your career? Is it true in your relationships? Is it true in your life? Sadly, many people fail to understand this basic law and think they can somehow get more than they put in. I'm sure Confucius was trying to deliver the same message when he said, "One must sit in chair for very long time with mouth open if waiting for cooked duck to fly into it."

In natural systems, there are growth sequences or steps that simply cannot be skipped or sidestepped. There is no possible way a baby can learn to run until they can walk, and they cannot walk until they learn to crawl. An engineer once explained to me that you cannot possibly learn calculus until you learn algebra, and you cannot learn algebra until you have learned basic math. Similarly, you cannot achieve success at organizational leadership until you achieve success at team leadership, you cannot succeed at team leadership until you have succeeded at interpersonal leadership and you cannot succeed at interpersonal leadership until you succeed at personal leadership or self-mastery.

There are a few fundamental success sequences in life that cannot be circumvented. First, in order to have something you first must do something and to do something you first must become something, by demonstrating personal leadership through fulfillment of potential.

Specific to the interpersonal dimension there are a couple self-evident principles that many intelligent people don't seem to fully appreciate. An example we have already covered is that you cannot persuade people using logic and reason until you have first gained influence with them per Stephen Covey's premise that there is no way one can develop sustainable, productive relationships with others (habits 4, 5, 6) until they first have a good relationship with themselves (habits 1, 2, 3). The American philosopher Will Rogers put it this way about a hundred years ago: "If you don't like yourself very much, there is a very good chance you're not alone."

We have already defined the relationship we have with ourselves as self-esteem. High-self-esteem people naturally tend to make deposits with no conscious effort, whereas low-self-esteem people naturally tend to take withdrawals, for two basic reasons: First, you cannot give something you don't not have. Second, nature abhors a vacuum, which means these people who do not have internally driven self-esteem are unconscious "psychic vampires" who not only fail to build self-esteem in others but tend to take it.

A hard truth of our quirky species is that people do not love or like you for who you are nearly to the degree that they love or like you for how you make them feel. So, the key question now becomes, how do you make other people feel? Covey expressed this natural law through the metaphor that all relationships are like a bank account into which you make deposits or take withdrawals, and that at any point you can assess the quality of the relationship by simply looking at the bank balance. The relationship currency is self-esteem or, simply put, how you make people feel. Covey called it the "emotional bank account." I also like to call this the influence bank account because making people feel valued and important is the core central strategy of how to gain influence with people.

I am particularly enamoured with the use of this practical metaphor because it is simple without being simplistic, as it is on the far side of neuroscience complexity. To quote Will Ferrell in his movie *Anchorman,* "It's science!" There are twelve watts of electrical energy in our brain that activate neurons with either a positive or negative charge. Our brain has associated a bundle of neurons to every person you know. This bundle of neurons (the relationship) has either a positive or negative charge, massive or marginal, but there is no neutral.

Deposits are any behaviour or attitude that builds a person's self-esteem. Withdrawals are behaviours or attitudes that make other people feel less valued and important. Some examples are listed below.

EXAMPLES OF DEPOSITS

- ❑ Listening to understand
- ❑ Caring, spending time
- ❑ Acceptance
- ❑ Keeping commitments
- ❑ Holding people accountable
- ❑ Apologizing for withdrawals
- ❑ Compliments and praise
- ❑ Acts of courtesy or politeness
- ❑ Acts of kindness, consideration and generosity
- ❑ Valuing someone's opinion
- ❑ Open-mindedness
- ❑ Remembering key dates
- ❑ Letting people "save face" when wrong

EXAMPLES OF WITHDRAWALS

- ❑ Ignoring and indifference
- ❑ Interrupting
- ❑ Judgment
- ❑ Breaking commitments
- ❑ Criticism, put-downs, sarcasm
- ❑ Acts of discourtesy or rudeness
- ❑ Acts of selfishness, self-centeredness
- ❑ Acting superior, condescending
- ❑ Forgetting important dates
- ❑ Making people feel stupid
- ❑ Ordering around, any attempt to control
- ❑ Manipulation
- ❑ Having low expectations

2] The Law of Character

The law of character is really an extension of the law of harvest, as it explains the simple truth that **trust can only come from those people who are trustworthy.** From character flows trustworthiness, from trustworthiness flows trust and from trust flows deep, rich, spontaneous communication. It is obvious that the essential ingredient in all interpersonal communication and relationships is trust, which is far more important than any skill or technique. In my workshops, I challenge participants to debate me on the validity of this principle, and they always promptly conclude that there is really nothing to debate – the statement is true because it is a principle.

People can fool others for a period time with their projected persona in the cosmetic charm, synthetic smiles and artificial niceties; however, eventually people will figure out who they really are, who they're out for and what their real motives are. This realization of the truth won't happen when things are going well and the sun is shining; true character will be exposed when the going gets tough and storm clouds are on the horizon and fast approaching. I fear it took me too long to learn the vital life lesson that, in the long run, you cannot keep talking your way out of problems you behave your way into.

3] The Law of Equilibrium

The law of equilibrium makes clear that any relationship that is not win–win in time will eventually become lose–lose. In any relationship, professional or personal, when needs go unmet, resentment builds just as surely as water flows downhill. Throughout the years, engineers have explained to me that, once energy is created, it cannot be destroyed and that it must and will manifest. Wise people understand that unexpressed emotions never die; they get buried alive to fester, ferment and come back later in ugly ways.

True interdependence is based in the capacity to build and sustain win–win relationships. The only way to sustain a relationship is to ensure that both sides are getting their respective needs met. To achieve this essential balance involves the two fundamental interpersonal competencies: empathy to ensure other people get their needs met and assertiveness to ensure you get your own needs met.

Most of our communication challenges are predictable because they are a function of our temperaments. Type-A individuals tend to be naturally assertive and need to make conscious efforts to work on their empathy. The great tragedy is that type-A people with low self-esteem who desperately need to empathize really struggle because of deep subconscious fears of being wrong, losing face or, even worse, losing control. As a result, the people they live and work with fail to get their needs met, and resentment builds and eventually manifests in destructive ways, breaking the relationship down. Type-B individuals tend to be naturally empathic and need to make conscious efforts to work on assertiveness. The great tragedy is that type-B people who desperately need to assert themselves really struggle because of deep, subconscious fears of conflict or not being liked and accepted. As a result, they don't get their own needs met, and predictably resentment builds and eventually manifests in explosive love–hate or passive-aggressive destructive conversations and dysfunctional relationships.

Empathy and assertiveness are the core communication competencies essential to making all relationships sustainable. They are the fundamentals because failure in either will inevitably result in a series of broken relationships. The critical question is what do you need to work on – becoming more empathic or more assertive? Why do you think you have this challenge? Are there relationships with specific people or situations in which you would benefit from becoming more effective in this area?

4] The Law of Perception

The law of perception has two dimensions: inside-out and outside-in. First, it explains how we perceive the world, and then how other people perceive us.

The menu is not the meal (does the burger they serve at the fast-food restaurant look like the picture on the wall?), the map is not the territory, the portrait is not the person and your perception of reality is not reality, but rather representations of reality. The first key learning point about perception is that we do not see the world as it is but rather as we are. Effective leaders realize their perception of reality is incomplete, distorted, biased and limited. No one has a complete or fully accurate perception of reality. Maslow said that one of the characteristics of the most psychologically healthy (self-actualized) people on the planet is that they have an efficient perception of reality. What he's trying to say is that the higher your EQ, the more accurate your perception of reality becomes, which shows up as common sense and decision making.

The significance of understanding and applying this law is huge, in that highly effective leaders consistently welcome disagreement. A hallmark of good leaders is they value disagreement because they recognize that their own perception is incomplete, distorted and most likely biased. They realize that if they are mature enough (or have high enough EQ) to really listen to the other person's perspective (perception) upon disagreement, it provides an excellent opportunity to learn and get a more accurate perception of what's really happening. I suggest to my workshop participants that if they agree with everything I say, it becomes painfully evident that one of us is not necessary.

As mentioned, people do not perceive you as you are but rather as they are subconsciously motivated to perceive you through a positive or negative lens. They are either motivated to perceive the good in you and your ideas or the bad in you and your ideas, and they're going to find exactly what they're looking for every single time. In marketing they call this phenomenon "selective perception," and in psychology they call it a "scotoma," commonly known as a "blind spot." In practical terms, it means that once a leader has gained influence by making deposits, people become blind to the leader's weaknesses and those once-annoying habits become perceived as charming idiosyncrasies. People that you have gained influence with will support and defend you when people badmouth you, and for some unknown reason (to themselves) will have a propensity to want to buy what you're selling. In reverse, if you have been taking withdrawals and making people feel unimportant, then you could present a program with ten good points and one small bad point and all the people you are trying to persuade will only perceive and latch onto the bad point like a dog with a bone.

5) The Law of Indirect Effort

This law has been expressed in the old axiom, "You can lead a horse to water, but you can't make it drink." Reduced to its simplest terms, the law of indirect effort explains that pressure begets resistance! The more you push and try to force someone to do something, the more our natural reaction is to push back. Ben Franklin put it this way: "A person convinced against their will is of the same opinion still." Type-A people push back aggressively with the use of verbal violence. Type-B people passively push back with the secretive silent treatment.

Highly effective leaders realize people do things for their own reasons. Given that the use of formal authority or force to get somebody to do something is becoming less effective by the day, we are now down to two basic methods: motivation and manipulation. Manipulation is when I get you to do something for my reasons, and it may work in the short-term. However, effective leaders understand that motivation is getting someone to do something based on their reasons. You can't force a horse to drink, fair enough, but good leaders realize you can put a little salt in their oats (ha-ha) and present them with cold, clear water. The fundamental principle of motivation is to provide people with a motive to take action. Effective leaders understand that everyone listens to the same radio station WIIFM (what's in it for me) and always focus on helping people understand how they will benefit from taking the action.

6) The Law of Expectations

We have already established that the best measure of leadership effectiveness is to what degree leaders develop, grow and bring out the best in people. The law of expectations states that people will live up to or down to expectations.

A hallmark of effective leaders is in their natural (with no strategic thought or effort) capacity to see the oak tree in the acorn. High-self-esteem people naturally perceive others' potential and strengths, whereas low-self-esteem people have a psychological need to perceive weaknesses and shortcomings in others. As a result, high-self-esteem people naturally grow people because they perceive the best and thus expect the best in them, and people live up their high expectations. When you hang out with people who tend to see the best in you, the best part of you grows.

7] The Law of Distortion

The law of distortion says that, when you're dealing with people, little things mean big things. An example is when you're on an airplane and you pull down your tray. You have not had any coffee and yet there's a big coffee stain on your tray, so you simultaneously see careless maintenance of the aircraft engine. Or if you see crumbs and dirt under the table in a restaurant, you simultaneously see rats in the kitchen. We must remember that the subconscious brain is symbolic and representational. I've learned that, when relationships break down, it usually starts with the little things. The first thing to go are the smiles, laughter and the little things, and then people find themselves in a downward spiral to the point that they can't stand to be in the same room with the other person. Effective leaders realize it's the little things that count because, to the lower brain, little things mean big things.

The Anatomy of Relationships

To conclude, here is a holistic perspective on interpersonal relationships: every relationship has three distinct components that are driven by separate and distinct causal factors.

Many people are confused about the difference between trust and respect. Would you rather have a competent doctor who's honest or a dishonest doctor who's incompetent? I know some people who would lend $20 to but I'm not sure I value their opinion, and vice versa. Some say if you lend someone $20 and never see them again, it's probably worth it. I know some accountants who are brilliant with numbers but I do not trust their billing practices, and I know some accountants who are honest and trustworthy, but I'm concerned they really don't know much about accounting. The point is that you can trust a person and not respect them and vice versa.

The Anatomy of Relationships

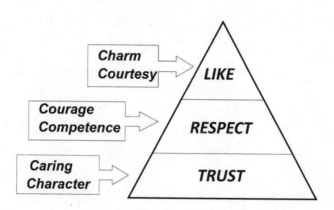

Points of clarification on the above diagram: I am trying to be cute with the use of alliteration, so allow me to clarify that by using the word "caring" I mean **empathy**, and that by using the word "courage" I mean **assertiveness**.

Highly effective leaders need to build complete relationships by working on all three components of the relationship. A difficult realization for me was that it is much more important to be trusted and respected as a leader than to be liked. The word "charm" comes from the Latin word that means charisma. At first, as many people do, I believed charisma was essential to effective leadership. I now realize that the bottom two components of the relationship are fundamental to leadership success, and charisma and being liked is a bonus; the icing on the leadership cake, if you will.

CHAPTER 16: THREE LEADERSHIP CORE CONVERSATIONAL COMPETENCIES

We have established that all of life occurs in relationships, but to be more precise, all of life occurs in conversations. Relationships are built or broken one conversation at time. If you want your life to work, your relationships have to work, and if you want your relationships to work, your conversations have to work. Creating a constructive conversation seems like a simple and straightforward process, and yet all of us have felt the painful sting from the splinters of fractured conversations. This chapter is about the tactical, core-communication competencies that allow us to build constructive conversations while enhancing the relationship.

Remembering the motivation equation – influence plus persuasion equals motivation – let's turn our focus to the competencies that result in a leader's capacity to communicate persuasively. A competency is defined as the capacity to achieve desired results, which we will examine in greater detail in Chapter 19 when we cover coaching. For now, let's just say that a competency has two basic components: the will to do something and skill. Will refers to the person's attitude or degree of motivation. Skill refers to knowing what and how to do to it to achieve desired results.

Carl Rogers, who did seminal work in the study of interpersonal communications, best defined the essential attitudes that highly effective communicators demonstrate. He distilled it down to three basic attitudes that foster truly effective communication: acceptance, empathy and genuineness. Highly effective leaders demonstrate these attitudes naturally because all three attitudes are the natural and sweet harvest of healthy self-esteem. Low-self-esteem people demonstrate precisely the opposite because instead of accepting people for who they are, they have a psychological need to judge people. Their egocentricity cripples their capacity to empathize with others, and because of their need to constantly project a persona or façade, they lack genuineness or authenticity.

It is worthwhile to draw a distinction: our goal is empathy, not sympathy. The Latin root words of empathy mean, "to see through the eyes of another." Empathy is about understanding, not feeling. A wise person once said "empathy is about *your* emotions, and sympathy is about *my* emotions."

The focus of this chapter is the skill component of competencies required for creating constructive conversations. We will cover the best practices of the following three core conversational skills sets:

1. Questioning skills
2. Listening skills
3. How to speak so people will listen, believe, understand and remember what you say

Before proceeding to skill development, I would like to create context by providing an explanation of the basic anatomy of interpersonal communications. Albert Mehrabian, a UCLA Communications Studies professor, wrote a landmark book called *Silent Messages* in which he introduced the concept that there are three levels or channels of face-to-face communications. He described them as the "3 V's." The **verbal** channel, which is the words we use, the **vocal** channel, which is the tonality and tenor of our voice, and the **visual** channel, which is body language. His research centred on trying to determine what percentage of the meaning of the whole message (the meta message) was driven by each of the channels. His findings were stunning.

The "3 V's" - Key Learning Points

- You cannot not communicate! Even when people are not speaking, they are still sending messages. Ralph Waldo Emerson put it this way: "Who you are screams so loudly in my ears that I cannot hear what you are saying."

- We must learn to listen to the whole person. The ironic truth of interpersonal communication is that you listen more with your eyes than your ears. We all speak distinct and separate languages – the language of logic and the language of emotion or sentiment. People communicate what they are thinking (upper brain) through the words they use. People communicate how they are feeling through their tonality and body language.

- When speaking on the phone, you are down to only two channels. Be aware that 86% of the meaning of the message is through tonality and only 14% is though the words. This model also helps us understand just how limited and ineffective the written word is relative to face-to-face or ear-to-hear conversations. However, in today's workplace it is increasingly difficult to get face time with people, and the face time we are able to get is fraught with distractions, disturbances, interruptions and cross conversations. One person recently lamented in a workshop that in her workplace, trying to have a meaningful conversation is like trying to send smoke signals in a windstorm.

- Our ultimate goal as a communicator is to be believable, and the key to believability is to channel congruency. The key to congruence is to be your natural self, and the key to being your natural self is to focus on genuinely trying to help the person or audience you are speaking to. You are always at your best when you are trying to help people; I know for certain that it is true. The Chinese philosopher Lao Tzu said in the sixth century, "When pure sincerity forms within, it is outwardly realized in other people's hearts."

The highest and most effective form of a conversation is dialogue. The words "discussion" and "dialogue" are not synonyms; they are two different types of conversations. "Discussion" has the same Latin root word as the words "concussion" and "percussion." A discussion is more of a competitive debate. The root word of "dialogue" is the Greek word *dialogos,* which means two (*dia*) people having a logical (*logos*) and objective exchange of ideas. Dialogue is a much more effective form of conversation, as it is collaborative and reserved for high-self-esteem people. What best characterizes a true dialogue is when one person is introduced to new information and is willing to change their mind and position. Low-self-esteem people can't or won't change their minds for fear of being wrong and losing face. As the great economist John Maynard Keynes said, "When the facts change, I change, pray tell, what do you do?"

Core Communication Competency #1 - Questioning Skills

After nearly three decades of teaching interpersonal skills, I am fully convinced that questions are the master communication tool in all circumstances. Socrates realized the best teachers don't give students answers, but rather they ask questions. One of the best books ever written on tactical selling skills is called *SPIN Selling* by Neil Rackham. The research he conducted before writing the book concluded that by far the single most important competency correlated to sales-cycle success is most frequently the ability to ask questions. So, whether you're selling, teaching, resolving conflict, coaching or simply conversing, the most powerful communication tool leaders have is questions.

Benefits of Asking Questions:

- Questions are the best method to activate a conversation. Sometimes you have to ask a firecracker question to spark a conversation.
- Questions are the best way to guide the conversation; they give you control of the conversation without appearing to be domineering.
- Perhaps most importantly, questions create an opportunity to listen, demonstrate your intentions, and build trust and the relationship.

- Asking questions in a strategic and systematic fashion is a great way to establish credibility without being boastful.
- Questions involve the other person, holding interest and avoiding a monologue.
- When the other person is talking, it allows you time to work on the conversation and strategize the next appropriate comment or question.
- Asking questions is the most potent form of persuasion without being pushy or forceful.

Guidelines to Asking Questions:

- Ask door-opener question, which are a non-coercive invitation to talk. "Looks like you had a tough day; would you like to talk about it?"

- Ask mostly open-ended questions, which invite an expansive response. "How do you feel about?" or "What are your thoughts on …?" Limit use of closed-ended questions, because too many, too fast can turn the conversation into what seems like an interrogation, eroding trust and restricting open communication.

- Don't ask leading questions such as "Are profits important to you?" because it indicates an attempt to manipulate the person.

- To gather (or give) complete information, use a systematic approach like the "5 W's" model from the world of journalism – who, what, when, where and why. The **why** question is usually the most important, but be careful because it's also the most dangerous question for evoking defensiveness.

- The most effective method of persuasion is the art of asking questions that bring people to their own reasons for taking action. This set of questions is designed to provide people with their own motives for action (motivation):

1. **"Ideal-outcome" questions** – To clarify and pinpoint the specific result the person needs/wants.

2. **"Gap" questions** – To identify the gaps that exist between current results and desired results.

3. **"Leverage" questions** – To identify, clarify and make tangible how the person will benefit from closing the gap, and the costs associated with failing to do so (this is the key step in the persuasion process).

4. **"Next-step solution" questions** – To identify ideas and solutions on how to close the gap (ideally created by the person).

Core Communication Competency #2 - Listening Skills

"Good listeners are perceived as powerful, compassionate, trustworthy, accurate, keen and intelligent, whereas poor listeners are perceived as weak, ineffectual, selfish, shallow, ignorant and dense."

– William James, 1897

Effective leaders are effective listeners, period. Warren Bennis suggested in his excellent book *On Becoming a Leader* that "highly effective leaders will need to take a sabbatical every six months because they are so exhausted from all the listening they've been doing."

One of the most common delusions I encounter is that people think the speaker is the active role and the listener is the passive role in a conversation. However, the subterranean truth is that it is the listener and not the speaker who largely determines the quality and quantity of the conversation. When you really listen, it is like a word magnet or as if you are putting oil on their jaw. The best conversationalists are not the most talkative people; they are the best listeners.

As stated in Chapter 3, knowledge workers spend 70% to 80% of their time in one of the four forms of communication: speaking (30%), reading (16%), writing (9%), listening (45%).

Our educational system has provided all of us with years of training in speaking, reading and writing. However, very few people have ever been trained in the most common and important form of communication. The research is clear: most people are poor listeners, as it is estimated that people only remember about 25% of what they hear. The research done in the area of emotional intelligence has validated what most of us know intuitively – women are naturally more empathic and better listeners than men. Men in particular must appreciate that there is a big difference between listening and hearing. To hear something means there are little bones vibrating in your head, whereas to listen means physical, emotional and mental exercise to truly understand the other person.

Becoming a great leader is about becoming a great listener, which is about developing two basic skill clusters: **attending** skills and **reflecting** skills.

Attending Skills - The Demonstration of Interest & Caring

❑ To attend means **being present** and **providing feedback** to the speaker to prove that you are paying full attention. The best example of how lack of feedback kills conversations is when you are speaking on the phone and the other person asks, "Are you there?" and we respond, "Yes, I'm here, I'm here." The basic principle is when feedback dies so does the conversation. So, when speaking on the phone, use "verbal attends" such as "uh-huh, really, hmmm, okay, yup" to provide feedback.

❑ Create a posture of relaxed involvement by leaning in slightly and slowly. Maintain open body language to demonstrate acceptance and sit squarely toward the person to avoid giving the "cold shoulder."

❑ Establish appropriate distance to the person, ideally three to six feet. Research shows that inside of three feet anxiety gets created and beyond six feet there is a loss of connection.

❑ Avoid any distracting behaviours. I recommend "steepling" your fingers to demonstrate calmness and that you are really focused on the speaker.

❑ Ask clarifying and confirming questions. A powerful technique to prevent interrupting the speaker that proves you are listening is the technique of "connecting questions." Once the speaker completes a thought and pauses, say, "A few minutes ago you mentioned such-'n-such; could we go back there for a moment?"

❑ If appropriate, take notes, but in a limited fashion. This demonstrates that what the person is saying is important to you. The risk in taking too many notes is that it can dramatically inhibit open communication if the person thinks every word is being recorded.

❑ Use the power of the **pause**. It's essential to wait for a second or two when someone finishes speaking before you begin speaking, because it gives the impression that what was just said was important. If you jump in and speak instantly, you risk the person thinking you were not listening but rather waiting for your turn to talk.

Reflecting Skills – The Confirmation of Understanding & Acceptance

A paraphrase is a concise response to the speaker, which states the essence of their content in your own words. An effective paraphrase cuts through the details and gets to the meta-message or the central meaning and reflects it back to the speaker for confirmation. I like to use the phrase "So, let me see if I understand, and correct me if I'm wrong." A complete reflective statement has two parts: first, a statement of the facts or content, and then reflection of how the person feels. A word of caution: if it's obvious to both parties that you have a clear understanding, I recommend not paraphrasing or it's going to sound forced, fake and like you have just come from a communication-skills workshop.

Communication Competency #3 – How to Speak So People Will Listen, Believe, Understand & Remember What You Say

"When the conduct of a person is designed to be influenced, persuasion, kind, unassuming persuasion, should ever be adopted. It is an old and a true maxim that a drop of honey catches more flies then a gallon of gall. So with people. If you would win a person to your cause, first convince them that you are their sincere friend. Therein is a drop of honey that catches their heart, which, say what they will, is the great high road to their reason, and which, once gained, you will find but little trouble in convincing their judgment of the justice of your cause, if indeed that cause really be a just one. On the contrary, assume to dictate to their judgment, or to command their action, and they will retreat within themselves, close all the avenues to their head and their heart. Such is a person, and so must they be understood by those who would leave them."

– Abraham Lincoln, 1842

Remember the motivational equation: **influence + persuasion = motivation**. Now that we understand how to gain influence, let's turn our focus to persuasive communication skills so we can prevent the common problem of what you say "going in one ear and out the other." This section is a crash course in presentation skills, and the strategies and techniques apply whether you're speaking to a group are having a one-on-one conversation.

- The first principle of successful conversations is that the more important the conversation, the more strategic you must be – 95% of your conversations are somewhat inconsequential, but there are about 5% that are crucial. These 5% crucial conversations are when talking turns tough and there's a lot at stake, a lot of money or emotion involved. They call them "crucial conversations" for a good reason – because it's the outcome of the 5% of crucial conversations that governs the rest of your life. Before entering into a crucial conversation, you must have clarity of purpose and desired outcomes before you speak.

- The key is to be "participant centred," not "content centred." This means the speaker identifies desired outcomes from the perspective of the audience/person. As a result of my presentation, what do I need my people to understand, accept, think, learn, believe and do?

- Remember the "primacy and recency" principle. The opening and ending of the conversation are the most important, so use the "3 Tells" formula: Tell them what you are going to tell them, tell them, and then tell them what you just told them: OPEN – BODY – CLOSE.

- When delivering your message, the real key to successful communication is not to be dynamic but to be your natural self.

- Remember, a person's head is on the far side of their heart! To connect with the audience/person, they must believe that you genuinely care about them, and the best way is to prove you understand them.

- Tell stories because they have a magical ability to help people learn. All great teachers have taught in parables or short stories. Stories hold people's attention, create comprehension and drive retention. Maybe it's because until about 5,300 years ago, when somebody first picked up a hammer and chisel to record human history, all previous history was passed down around campfires through the telling of stories. Tell stories to make your points but keep them relevant and concise, and try not to make yourself the hero.

- Use analogies and metaphors, especially those that conjure visual images. Metaphors take something you understand and apply it to something you have yet to understand. It is a powerful way of driving comprehension and retention. When someone asks how big the piece of property is and you respond that it is about 8,500 feet, the best way to remove the confused look from the person's face is to say it's about the same size as a football field. Analogies can increase the impact of your message. For example, to make a powerful point on how much a billion dollars is, explain that the time difference to count out one million dollars at the rate of one per second relative to counting out one billion dollars at the same rate is eleven days to thirty-one years.

- **Eye contact** is the most important method of connecting to people. The nerve tissue that connects the eyes to the brain is twenty-two times greater in magnitude than the nerve tissue that connects the ears to the brain. When you make eye contact with a person, it is almost like physically touching the person, so be careful of not enough or too much. Be aware of the "4 I's" of eye contact. What we want is "**involvement**," which means holding eye contact for two to four seconds. We don't want "**ignoring**" (no eye contact) or too much eye contact, which can result in "**intimidation**" or "**intimacy**."

- The old expressions "seeing is believing" and "a picture is worth a thousand words" have been validated by the most recent neuroscience. When communicating, use visual aids as much as possible, such as PowerPoint, flipcharts, whiteboards, diagrams, graphs or models. The major benefits to using visuals are that they focus and hold attention, activating the right brain and driving up retention. They also help overcome language barriers. The research for the use of visuals conducted by Harvard is very convincing, indeed:

  - Comprehension was 7% when verbal was used and jumped to 87% when visuals were added
  - Retention increased 71% when visuals were used
  - 28% less time was consumed when visuals were used
  - Speakers' goals were met 34% more often when visuals were used
  - Achieving consensus increased 28% when visuals were used

✓ Watch the use of your vocabulary; the key is to use plain, simple, straightforward words. Big words are a good indicator of a big ego and are highly counterproductive as a communicator because they usually serve only to distance and distract you from the audience. When the speaker uses big words that the person or audience doesn't know, how do you think that makes the people in the audience feel about themselves?

✓ Remembering that pressure begets resistance is important so you are suggestive as opposed to forceful when presenting your ideas. I recommend when proposing ideas that you soften your approach to make ideas more palatable to the audience by using such phrases as "in my opinion, I think we should ..." When you couch your ideas with this phrase, the unspoken words to the other person are "what's your opinion?"

Being an effective and persuasive communicator is central to effective leadership. The good news is that anyone can enhance their communication skills because it's more of an art than a science. The bad news is, like all other endeavours, it takes hard work and the willingness to accept feedback. I enthusiastically recommend that everyone take a course on presentation skills that involves video feedback. It will most likely be a shocking and even painful experience, but it is a critically important exercise to see yourself in action so you can accurately assess what you're doing well and what you need to work on to become a more effective and persuasive communicator and leader.

LEADING FROM EVERYWHERE

THE PRINCIPLES & PRACTICES OF CHARACTER-BASED LEADERSHIP

PART 6: TEAM LEADERSHIP – LEADING A HIGH- PERFORMANCE TEAM

17. Teamworx – High Performance Team & Team Players
18. Seven Roles of a Highly Effective Team Leader
19. Coaching and Feedback

CHAPTER 17: TEAMWORX - HIGH PERFORMANCE TEAM & TEAM PLAYERS

In the fundamental power shift in organizations in the last few decades, the traditional model of management, problem solving and decision making was the domain of managers. As discussed, the power has shifted from management into teams who are now expected to solve problems and make decisions. The sheer volume of information and increasing complexity of the world today means no one individual can know it all anymore. The broadening of the marketplace, the information explosion, rapid technological investment and the imperative of innovation means that teams, especially cross-functional teams that operate from a holistic organizational perspective, are now the only way to solve problems and make effective decisions. The trend towards team-based organizations began in the 1980s, and many companies rushed to the concept. However, it became evident, despite the overabundance of teambuilding books and seminars, that many people were not prepared or equipped to operate within the new model, resulting in teams struggling and breaking down. As a result, many organizations retreated to the safety and predictability of the hierarchical, formal authority, command-and-control philosophy.

When it comes to giving teams the power, it's a high-leverage, good-news/bad-news story. The good news is that, if the team is performing well, it can be incredibly creative, innovative, fun, energizing and ultimately highly productive.

However, if the team breaks down, it can be incredibly costly in a number of painful ways and difficult if not impossible to repair without blood on the floor. Broken teams are counterproductive because time and effort is diverted from driving value to customers and consumed in bickering, backbiting, game-playing, gossiping, allocating blame and trying to fix interpersonal issues. It seems to me that when teams are good, they are getting better and when teams are bad, they are getting worse.

High-performance teams and teamwork are becoming ever more important, and unfortunately, simultaneously, they are becoming ever more uncommon. This trend was explained in Daniel Goleman's *Working with Emotional Intelligence*. The research shows that the average IQ in the western world is increasing. US Army recruits have IQ scores twenty-four points higher than those recruited during the First World War. Data indicates the same type of IQ growth in most developed countries. Psychologists believe the rising IQ scores are related to factors such as better nutrition, smaller family sizes, more children completing more schooling and more time spent playing challenging computer games.

When it comes to EQ, there is evidence to show that since late last century, average EQ scores are dropping. The research specifies that EQ is dropping across all Western countries and all socioeconomic groups, from the wealthiest suburbs to the inner-city poor. Research conducted by Thomas Achenbach, a psychologist at University of Vermont, had findings that were particularly disturbing, as it indicated that there was a steady worsening of children's emotional intelligence. The research beginning in the 1970s indicated that with each successive generation, children were becoming lonelier, angrier, nervous, unruly and more prone to worry, and experiencing higher rates of depression. These are the children that are now entering and populating the workforce today.

I don't suspect many readers will be surprised that the research finds dropping levels of EQ, because there are telling signs sadly evident throughout society today, from rising divorce rates to increasing drug abuse, higher rates of depression and suicide, more bullying in schoolyards, eating disorders becoming more common, kids dropping out of school more frequently and teams in the workplace breaking down.

Some teams and team players are highly effective while others are highly ineffective. My strategy is to provide you with a clear depiction of what high-performance teams and team players look like. The examples I provide can be used as self-assessment tools. I enthusiastically encourage you to use these tools to identify the strengths and opportunities for improvement in your teams.

The most significant book on the topic in the last couple decades is *The Five Dysfunctions of a Team* by Patrick Lencioni, in which he listed the five most common and destructive dysfunctions that plague teams.

1. Absence of trust
2. Fear of conflict (lack of open, honest dialogue)
3. Lack of commitment/engagement
4. Avoidance of accountability
5. Inattention to results

Four Simple Truths About Team Performance

1. A team is successful to the degree that it can **solve problems** that are obstacles to accomplishing its performance objectives.

2. A team can only solve problems successfully to the degree that it **communicates** effectively.

3. A team can only communicate successfully to the degree that its **relationships** are right (trust-based).

4. The quality of relationships is determined by the degree of **leadership** (self-esteem, EQ, character) demonstrated by each individual team member.

This cause-and-effect sequence of team success further validates the title of this book, which is that everyone must demonstrate leadership from everywhere. It also explains the subtitle, character-based leadership, in that the essential ingredient is always **trust**, which can only come from people who are trustworthy or people of good character. People who are not trustworthy are metaphorically killing the immune system of the team, which is the team's ability to communicate. If the team can't communicate, it cannot solve problems, which renders it dysfunctional and unproductive. Duplicitous individuals with hidden agendas erode trust, which cripples communication, and the team becomes so dysfunctional it can't even decide what pizza toppings to order and dies the death of a thousand cuts.

Nathaniel Branden, who has written a number of books on self-esteem, said in his book *Six Pillars of Self-Esteem* that "self-esteem has always been of paramount psychological importance and now in the highly interdependent workplace self-esteem has become of paramount economic importance." What Branden is trying to tell us is that if you cannot be an effective team player, you are of little value in the workplace of the twenty-first century. It only takes one low-EQ person to create havoc on the team, as these people are not non-productive; they are actually counterproductive to the team's effectiveness.

Synergy - The Essence of Teamwork

Synergy is more than just a biz babble buzzword; rather, it is a force of nature that is not yet fully understood. Some examples from the world of physics are that one Clydesdale horse can pull 8,000 pounds, two Clydesdale horses can pull 18,000 pounds, and if you train them to work together in harmony, they are capable of pulling up to 25,000 pounds. If two people each hold the end of an eight-foot-long 2" x 4" piece of wood, and we ask a third person to begin placing bricks on the two-by-four, under the weight of the tenth brick, the wood snaps. If two people hold two two-by-fours together, the wood can withstand the weight of more than twenty bricks before snapping. This mystical, magical force in nature called "synergy" also applies in the interpersonal dimension.

Synergy is synchronized energy. When energy is harmonized, it somehow creates an expansive, combined effect. When synergy is present, the whole is in some way greater than the sum of the parts. Synergy is when 1 + 1 = 3 or 5 or 10.

It's true in our physical world and it's true in our interpersonal world: the ultimate goal for every team is to achieve synergy. The only possible way it's achieved is by having everyone on the team subjugate their personal needs and interest to those of the team. What this means is that low-self-esteem or EQ people with big egos ("I" in Greek) can never really be an effective team player because when push comes to shove and the going gets tough, they're really out for themselves. John Wooden, who led his UCLA basketball team to a record number of national championships, is widely considered to be the greatest basketball coach in history. I think he said it best in his response to a newspaper reporter who asked for the secret of his success: "It is amazing what a group of people can do when no one is concerned about who gets the credit."

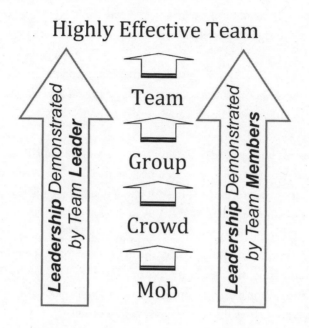

Highly Effective Team

Team Performance – Meetings Tell the Story

In the 1960s, Douglas McGregor wrote a book called *The Human Side of Enterprise*, which is considered an all-time classic in management literature. In his last chapter, he outlined the characteristics of both high-performance and low-performance team meetings, which I believe is an excellent, real-world, ground-level description of team dynamics. I do not have to eat the whole cake to know what it tastes like, and I don't have to hang around a team meeting very long to know how functional the team is, because meetings tell the story. I challenge you to contrast McGregor's eleven descriptors of high-and-low performance teams and determine which more accurately reflects your team's overall effectiveness.

Descriptors of High-Performance Team Meetings:

1. The atmosphere, which can be sensed in a few minutes of observation, tends to be informal, comfortable and relaxed. There are no obvious tensions. It is an atmosphere in which people are involved and interested. There are no signs of boredom.

2. There is a lot of discussion in which virtually everyone participates, but it remains pertinent to the task of the group. If the discussion gets off the subject, someone will bring it back in short order.

3. The task or the objective of the group is well understood and accepted by the members. There will have been free discussion of the objective at some point until it was formulated in such a way that the members of the group could commit themselves to it.

4. The members listen to each other! The discussion does not have the quality of jumping from one idea to another unrelated one. Every idea is given a fair hearing. People do not appear to be afraid of being foolish by putting forth a creative thought even if it seems very extreme.

5. There is disagreement. The group is helpful with this and shows no sign of having to avoid conflict or to keep everything on a plane of sweetness and light. Disagreements are not suppressed or overridden by premature group action. The reasons are carefully examined and the group seeks to resolve them rather than to dominate the dissenter. On the other hand, there is no "tyranny of the minority." Individuals who disagree do not appear to be trying to dominate the group or express hostility. Their disagreement is an expression of a genuine difference of opinion, and they expect a hearing in order that a solution may be found. Sometimes there are basic disagreements that cannot be resolved. The group finds it possible to live with them, accepting them but not permitting them to block its efforts.

6. Most decisions are made by a kind of consensus in which everyone is in general agreement and is willing to go along. However, there is little

tendency for individuals who oppose the action to keep their opposition private and thus let an apparent consensus mask real disagreement. Formal voting is at a minimum; the group does not accept a simple majority as a proper basis for action.

7. Criticism is frank, frequent and relatively comfortable. There is little evidence of personal attack, either openly or hidden. The criticism has a constructive flavour in that it is oriented toward removing an obstacle that faces the group and prevents it from getting the job done.

8. People are free and expressing their feelings as well as their ideas both on the problem and on the group's operation. There is little pussyfooting; there are few "hidden agendas." Everybody appears to know quite well how everybody else feels about any matter under discussion.

9. When action is decided upon, clear assignments are made and accepted.

10. The group leader does not dominate, nor does the group unduly defer to the leader. Leadership shifts from time to time depending on circumstance. Different members, because of their knowledge and experience, assume leadership roles. There is little evidence of power struggles. It's not about power; it's about getting the job done.

11. The group is self-conscious about its own operations. Frequently, it will start to examine how well it's doing or what may be interfering with its operation. The problem may be a matter of procedure, or it may be an individual whose behaviour is interfering with the accomplishment of the group's objectives. Whatever it is, it gets open discussion until a solution is found.

Descriptors of Low-Performance Team Meetings:

1. The atmosphere is likely to reflect either indifference or boredom. People are whispering to each other or carrying on side conversations and there are individuals who are obviously not involved. Tension is just below the

surface and there are palpable undercurrents of hostility and antagonism, stiffness and undue formality. The group is clearly not challenged by its task or genuinely involved in it.

2. A few people tend to dominate the discussion. Often their contributions are way off point and little is done by anyone to keep the group clearly on track.

3. From the things that are said, it is difficult to understand what the group task is or what its objectives are. The chairman may have initially stated these but there is no evidence that the group either understands or accepts a common objective. On the contrary, it is usually evident that people have different, private and personal objectives they are attempting to achieve that are often in conflict with each other and with the group's task.

4. People don't listen to each other. Ideas are ignored or overridden. The discussion jumps around with little coherence or sense of movement along a track. There is much talking for effect, and people make speeches that are obviously intended to impress someone else rather than being relevant to the task at hand. Conversations with members after the meeting reveal that they failed to express ideas or feelings they may have had for fear they would be criticized or regarded as silly. Some members feel the leader or the other members are constantly making judgments of them with evaluations of the contributions they make so they are extremely careful about what they say.

5. Disagreements are not dealt with effectively by the group. They may be completely suppressed by those who fear conflict or it turns into open warfare. Disagreements are resolved by vote where a small majority wins, leaving the minority resentful. "Tyranny of minority" is evident; this is when majority gives in to an aggressive person or sub-group to preserve peace. In general, only the more aggressive members get their ideas considered because the less aggressive people tend to either keep quiet altogether or give up after short, ineffectual attempts to be heard.

6. Actions are often taken prematurely, before the real issues are either examined or resolved. There is a lot of discussion and complaining after the meeting by people who did not like the decision agreed to but they did not speak up. A simple majority is considered sufficient for action, and the minority is expected to go along. Most of the time, however, the minority remains resentful and uncommitted to the decision.

7. Action decisions tend to be unclear, with no one really knowing who is going to do what. Clear assignments of responsibility are not made; there is often considerable doubt as to whether they will be carried out.

8. The leadership remains clearly with the committee chairman, who may be weak or strong, but always insists on sitting at the head of the table.

9. Criticism may be present, and it is embarrassing and tension-producing. It often involves personal hostility, and the members are uncomfortable and unable to cope with it. Criticism of ideas tends to be destructive. Sometimes every idea proposed will be "clobbered" by someone else. Then no one is willing to stick their neck out.

10. Personal feelings are hidden rather than out in the open. The general attitude of the group is that they are inappropriate for discussion and would be too explosive if brought up.

11. The group tends to avoid any discussion of its own maintenance. There is often much discussion after the meeting of what was wrong and why, but these matters are seldom brought up and considered within the meeting itself where they might be resolved.

The High-Performance Team Player

In Part 1, we referred to research that confirms the single most important ability valued today – outside of specific, required technical skills – is the capacity to be an effective team player. The best way to precisely pinpoint the characteristics and competencies of highly effective team players is to ask you to perform a self-assessment using the Team Player Inventory below. As you answer each question, I challenge you to consider whether each descriptor has more to do with IQ or EQ. I suspect it will become evident very quickly that being an effective team player is synonymous with being an effective leader.

Team Player Inventory

Always	Frequently	Sometimes	Seldom	Never
5	4	3	2	1

1. I take responsibility for maintaining a clear focus on my team's purpose and objectives   ____

2. I clearly understand my role and what contributions are expected from me   ____

3. I take responsibility for building and maintaining productive working relationships with teammates   ____

4. I understand what is most important to each of my teammates   ____

5. I voice my opinions and my needs clearly and concisely   ____

6. I listen carefully when my teammates are speaking   ____

7. I participate actively in team meetings   ____

8. I invite and value feedback from my teammates   ____

9. I eagerly help my teammates when they need it, sometimes   ____
    even if they don't ask for it

10. I can disagree with teammates without being disagreeable   ____

11. I fully commit to implementing team decisions, even those I   ____
    do not fully agree with

12. I attempt to resolve conflict with my teammates in a   ____
    constructive win–win manner

13. I can compromise my positions for the good of the team   ____

14. I do not participate in gossiping about my teammates behind   ____
    their backs

15. I carry my full weight in terms of making my expected   ____
    contributions to the team

16. I will change my mind or position when presented with valid   ____
    evidence that suggests I should

17. I share recognition when things go right   ____

18. I accept my fair share of responsibility when things go wrong   ____

19. I contribute new and innovative ideas when the team is   ____
    solving problems

20. I am patient and tactful when communicating with and   ____
    providing feedback to teammates

Total Points   ____

<u>**Scoring Guide**</u>

80+ points – Star team player

60+ points – Solid team player

40+ points – Serious self-assessment required

20+ points – Brush up your resume

Note: I believe the answer to Question 11 is the truest test of team-player effectiveness.

Four Reflective Questions to Noodle On

1. How effectively is your team currently performing?
    * Where is your team on the synergy continuum?
    * Which of Lencioni's five team dysfunctions is your team guilty of?
    * Of the eleven descriptors of high- and low-performance teams, which is a more accurate reflection of the current reality of your team?

2. How would the members of your team score on the twenty-question **Team Player** Inventory?

3. Where are the biggest gaps between where your team is and where it should or could be?

4. What would it mean if you were to close these gaps or if you fail to close these gaps?

5. What do teams and team players need to do differently to close the gaps?

CHAPTER 18: SEVEN ROLES OF A HIGHLY EFFECTIVE TEAM LEADER

In Chapter 2, we covered how the philosophy or paradigm of managing the human asset has evolved and changed over 150 years in the western world, and like everything else the rate of change has dramatically increased in the last few decades. The four roles of the traditional industrial-age manager were planning, organizing, commanding and controlling, which came straight out of Henri Fayol's book *Principles of Administration*. The problem is that circumstances have changed dramatically, but the old management paradigm has not. Some remnants of this out-of-date management paradigm sadly still exist today. This obsolete model grew very deep roots and is hard to shake off, as it was the bible of business schools for almost the entire last century. There are five powerful primary driving forces that command a new model of managing the human asset:

- Employees today are no longer subservient, dutifully following orders from above like people did in the industrial age, but rather are insisting on and even demanding involvement and empowerment.

- Customers want instant responses and are no longer willing to wait for someone to "check with the boss"; they want to deal with someone who has been empowered to make on-the-spot decisions.

- TQM (total quality management) has had broader adoption and deeper integration into Western management philosophy; originally it was rejected by North American industry right after the Second World War but was quickly embraced by the Japanese, providing them with a significant competitive advantage for decades. A central guiding principle of TQM is that **the people in the organization solving the problems should be the people closest to the problems.**

- In the industrial age, the boss typically had more experience, knowledge and know-how than the employees; however, knowledge power is shifting to the employee as more and more commonly the frontline worker has deeper knowledge and intellectual capital than the team leader.

- Organizations have been flattened in the last few decades as layers of management have been stripped out, which has expanded what they refer to in human resource management terms as "span of control," or the number of direct reports managers can have. In the industrial-age, command-and-control management philosophy, managers could have a maximum of five or six people reporting to them because they could only control, think and solve problems for five or six people. Today, most evidently in the high-tech sector, it is common for team leaders to have as many as fifteen or twenty people reporting to them, which requires an entirely new management approach.

It is no longer viable for managers to play the role of a **cop** using the carrot and stick to motivate people; rather, managers must become more of a **coach** who supports and facilitates people and the team's success. The job of the manager has literally been flipped on its head, and instead of people working for the manager, the manager works for the people. To succeed today, managers must become much more of a guide on the side and not the sage on the stage; instead of the manager doing the problem solving and decision making, the people will be solving problems and making decisions. Perhaps the most appropriate title that best describes the function of the twenty-first-century manager is "team facilitator." The root word of "facilitate" comes from the French word *facile*, which means "easy." The new role of managers is to make things easy for their people to achieve desired results.

In Chapter 13, we established that the starting point of personal productivity is to understand that everyone has a new job description, which is **make yourself valuable**. The refinement is how the person is uniquely positioned to bring value to organizations. Allow me to put this principle into practice by offering team leaders a new job description by reconceiving the mental model of their jobs into seven contribution roles that only they are uniquely positioned to make.

1] Pathfinding Scout Role

To paraphrase Napoleon, being a great general is not so much about making brilliant decisions upon the battlefield but rather it's about understanding the terrain. Peter Drucker said, some fifty years ago, that "the first job of the manager is to define reality." The challenge of the twenty-first century is that our reality and terrain is constantly shifting. Japanese organizations have always focused on long-term strategic planning; sometimes as far as 200 years. In the last few decades, they have also adopted the practice of quarterly or monthly strategic planning. As Churchill said, "Plans are useless, but planning is invaluable." I think he is trying to say that no plan ever survives its collision with reality, yet the process of planning is vital.

Because of our whirlwind environment, this first reconnaissance or navigational role has become much more important and much more challenging over the last few decades. This role is more important because as the pace of the world and the rate of changes accelerate, we are losing reaction time. A plan that is valid today can be rendered totally obsolete by one sudden totally unpredictable development. This role is much more challenging because, as mentioned in Part 1, our MTBS (mean time between surprises) is dropping rapidly as the world is ever more unpredictable.

While the team members are working away in the engine room, the more turbulent the seas, the more the team leader must be spending time on the bridge of the ship, constantly scanning the environment to understand marketplace dynamics, changes in customers, competition, economic and industry trends, technological changes, governmental changes and what's happening with all stakeholders, both internal and external. This role may be considered the front end of effective change management in that the more clearly the team understands what changes are coming, the more lead time they have to prepare.

A central focus of Part 7 is the simple truth that an organization's or team's success or failure is ultimately defined by the customer, which means the primary focus of this role is for the team leader to create and maintain an intimate understanding of the customer's needs and expectations and then saturate the team with the voice of the customer.

The appropriate title to give the team leader, which explains the second dimension of the scouting role, would be CDC (chief dot connector). Once the terrain is understood, the team leader must now show people the map by defining the big picture so the team has a current, clear and complete understanding of reality – what's really happening, what's about to happen, how it all fits together and what it means to them. British Prime Minister Margaret Thatcher perhaps best explained this role when she said, "I cannot manage the past. There are other people in my government to manage the present. It is my unique responsibility as the leader to shine a spotlight on the future and marshal the support of the people to create that future."

This role is unique from the others in that it does tend to hold more relevance for senior executives; however, even frontline supervisors must actively perform this role so their people feel in the know and can better anticipate and adapt to the coming changes within and external to the organization.

2) Performance Manager Role

This is the standard operational role of ensuring the team is achieving the desired results and outcomes. Before proceeding to the four practices, allow me to emphasize the primary underpinning principle of performance management: the performers must be responsible for their own performance. The team leader must transfer ownership of the work to the people doing the work.

This role has four integrated and sequential processes that the team leader must facilitate:

1) Alignment with organizational mission and objectives
2) Strategic planning
3) Performance measurement
4) Performance feedback

Alignment

If the mission, vision and values have been clarified and bought into at the organizational level, then the team-alignment process is simplified for the team leader. The mission is the basic purpose of the organization the team is designed to serve. The vision represents the ideal future state the team or organization is striving to become. The values are an agreement on how we will treat each other on the journey towards fulfillment of the team's mission and vision. If, however, there is no clear understanding or acceptance of the mission, vision and values, the team leader would be wise to facilitate the group to achieve clarity and buy in. This is fundamental to successful empowerment, as it metaphorically provides the team and team members with the empowerment compass or true-north guidance tool, which enables independence in their decision making downstream in the task or project.

At the risk of oversimplification, I believe all organizations have the same basic purpose or mission – to create and deliver value to the customer as defined by the customer. In the final analysis, the customer is the ultimate boss. Given the fact that the customer always defines performance, the first priority of the team leader is to be the voice of the customer by saturating the team with customer feedback so all team efforts and activities are correctly aligned with driving value to the customer.

Strategic Planning

A strategic plan is a concise description of the specific outcomes and results the team wants to achieve and how it will achieve them. The first focus is always on customer-based results that the teams need to achieve. Secondly, take the "balanced scorecard" approach by clearly defining the desired outcomes of the team's stakeholders.

Facilitating team meetings to achieve clarity of the team's strategic plan is vital to team members' capacity to effectively set their day-to-day priorities. Team members have to think about the big things while doing the small things so the small things go in the right direction.

Performance Measurement

Peter Drucker said, "If you want it, measure it. If you can't measure it, forget it." The processes of strategic planning and performance measurement are inextricably linked because it is through measurement that plans are brought into reality. I have learned through the years that "what gets measured gets done." I have taken the liberty to make a small addition to the old adage: "What gets measured gets done, and what gets measured and rewarded gets done well." So, it is simple; measure what is critical to team success. Whatever the team agrees to measure, when and how, it is always of supreme importance that you first measure customer satisfaction.

Performance Feedback

The team leader is the keeper of the scoreboard. Put down the carrot and stick, show people how they are doing and self-motivation will kick in. The scoreboard strategy is based on the principle that the team will make the required adjustments on its own when it knows where it stands. I recommend you keep the scoreboard simple and always present it in visual form such as charts and graphs because visuals are easy to grasp and have more immediate and greater impact on people.

3] Team Builder

The teambuilding role is about establishing a structure for the team by creating role clarity for each member and integrating everyone's roles into a cohesive unit. Teambuilding consists of two sequential parts or processes:

1) *Role Clarification* – This is the process of delegating (empowering) each team member by creating clarity of agreement of the desired results that each person will be held accountable to achieve (individual performance expectations).

I fear the second component of the teambuilding role is frequently overlooked, which results in role confusion among team members, and the predictable negative consequences are role overlap and underlap. Role overlap is when two or more people are doing the work and there are redundant efforts. Role underlap is when certain things don't get done because people think someone else is responsible for making them happen.

2) *Role Integration* – This is the process of synchronizing by helping all team members understand how their contributions fit into the big picture of team success. To prevent role confusion, the team leader must coordinate the team by helping all members understand the roles, goals, needs and expectations of other members so they can best help and not hinder their teammates.

When I ask people the difference between delegation and empowerment, I often get a quizzical look. It's a bit of a trick question, because the answer is that it's the same thing, which is the allocation of work to be done within the organization or team. The only difference is in the process of how you delegate. A lot of people have a negative association to the word "empowerment" because it means they have more work to do. Despite its bad name, empowering people is no longer an option; as you will learn in Part 7, it's an essential ingredient for employee engagement.

Some Thoughts on Delegation and Empowerment

- Most managers I observe are running out of time while their people are running out of work, for the simple reason that they don't know why, what and how to delegate properly.

- Empowerment is simply returning the power to its rightful owner. Highly effective leaders transfer ownership of the work to people who execute the work by giving people control over how it is to be best completed.

- To the degree that the job involves intellectual capital, the performer must be responsible for their own performance.

- When facilitating team and individual objective-setting, the guiding principle is called "essential tension," which means the goals that leaders help their team set should be out of reach, but not out of sight. Out of reach so people have to stretch and grow, but not out of sight because research is clear that when people do not think a goal is possible to achieve, it de-motivates them.

- Do not mistake, as many people initially do, this new style of management as a soft, touchy-feely "country club" approach. The goal of the team leaders is to create a state of "accountable freedom," which means providing as much freedom as possible; this is not a charity, and people will be held accountable for performance results.

- The process of empowering people is the same process as turning people into leaders (thus the title of this book).

- Truly empowered people must be given the freedom to try and to fail! However, it must be controlled risk, as we cannot afford mistakes that are metaphorically "below the water line of the ship" or on anything mission-critical.

- The starting point of effective delegation is making sure you're delegating the right job to the right person. The book *First, Break All the Rules* by Marcus Buckingham and Curt Coffman was based on research data from 70,000 managers conducted by Gallup in an attempt to identify what makes the best managers. They concluded that the single most important ability was the ability to identify what people's natural talents were and put them in the right job. Jim Collins further validated this strategy in *Good to Great*, saying the first job of a leader is to get the right people in the right seats on the bus. I realize that this could be considered somewhat idealistic, as it is not always possible to have the right people in the right roles as, more often than not, the team leader does not have a great deal of free choice as to who the team members are and they have to play the hand they are dealt.

- Accountability is not a zero-sum game. Empower people with caution, and always remember that, as a team leader, if the person you empower to do a task makes a mistake or creates a problem, at the end of the day, it is the team leader who is going to have to do the explaining.

- The following Freedom Scale is an effective way to frame the relationship leaders have with their people. The leader's responsibility is to grow and develop people so they can give them increasing amounts of freedom. It is the responsibility of the individual to earn increasing degrees of freedom from the leader by proving that they are worthy of more empowerment.

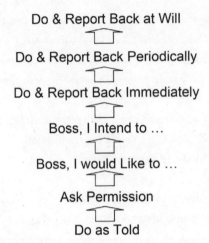

Do & Report Back at Will

Do & Report Back Periodically

Do & Report Back Immediately

Boss, I Intend to …

Boss, I would Like to …

Ask Permission

Do as Told

The basic principle of empowerment is to give your people the greatest degree of latitude to make decisions as to HOW to achieve the desired outcomes to the greatest degree possible. However, be aware that there are very real restraining factors on a manager's ability to empower people. The degree of freedom a leader can give a person is constrained by both of the following factors:

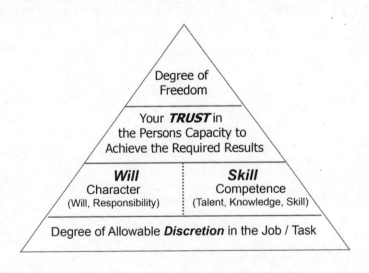

The degree of freedom a leader can give an employee is based on the nature of the work and the nature of the person.

Some jobs don't lend themselves to empowerment. For instance, they're not telling the tellers at your local bank to handle the cash in the most creative way possible.

Some people don't lend themselves to empowerment. As mentioned earlier, an increasing number of young people don't live to work as the previous generations have, but rather they work to live. In other words, they don't get their kicks out of work; they work to get a paycheque so they can buy a better snowboard or big-screen TV. These people could still be of value as they come on time, get their work done and don't cause problems with the coworkers. However, they are not really interested in being promoted or empowered. When attempting to empower certain people, it is predictable that they are going to say something like, "Wait a minute, you hired me ten years ago to do the 'doing' and now suddenly you want me to do the thinking *and* doing. No thanks, boss, that's not my job description; just tell me what you want done." I have learned through the years that, whereas type-A people really want the freedom of empowerment, type-B people tend not to jump on the empowerment bandwagon so quickly, as they don't want the risks associated with making their own decisions. What a type-A person would consider to be micromanagement would be a comfortable level of management for a type-B person.

Lastly, certain people are simply not capable of full empowerment, and it is very important that you do not set people up for failure by putting them in over their heads.

Delegation – A Seven-Step Process

The following is an effective and complete approach to delegation and establishing clear, **outcome-based performance expectations**. This process could be used to design a person's entire job (job description) or to delegate a task or project. Depending on the size, complexity or duration of the task or project, some of these steps could be minimized or skipped. Notice that each of the seven steps start with the word "agree"; this is to symbolize the essential collaborative aspect of this process.

1. *Agree on Purpose and Scope of Job/Project/Task*

   - Define the WHAT or the scope of the job
   - Ensure the person understands the purpose or WHY the task is happening (this is key to motivation and independent problem solving)
   - Define WHO is involved; all stakeholders must be identified
   - Clarify WHEN are the timeframes/deadlines

2. *Agree on Required Results/Outcomes*

   - Agree on the desired results, if it is a quantitative role (for example, a sales job where you can set hard sales targets or operating a machine where it is easy to set production goals of so many widgets per hour)
   - Agree on ideal outcomes, if qualitative; provide people a "picture of success" (for example, in a customer service job where results are difficult to quantify, the leader must make sure the employee is clear about what great service looks like)
   - Ensure the vital step of creating crystal clear PERFORMANCE EXPECTATIONS (the importance of this step cannot be overstated as this is the cornerstone of self-accountability)

3. *Agree on How Performance is Best Measured*

   - What will be measured (remember what gets measured gets done)
   - Who will collect the data
   - How data will be collected
   - How often

4. *Agree on Boundaries, Cautions and Degree of Freedom*

   - Define the level of freedom the person has and when they should seek advice

- Describe all relevant policies and restrictions
- Explain what not to do, the risks to avoid,. i.e., past problems and pitfalls
- To promote empowerment, define the boundaries on an "exception basis" – "You can do anything within ethical boundaries to achieve desired results, except for ..."

5. *Agree on Available Resources and Support*

- What support and resources (budgets) will be available?
- When and where does someone go for help?
- *Agree on the Natural Consequences of Success and Failure*
- Frequently, consequences are self-evident and this step is not necessary
- Clarify how the person, team or organization will be affected by achieving or failing to achieve desired results

6. *Agree on a "Refresh" Mechanism*

- This is reserved for when delegating more long-term projects
- Agree on when the "agreement" should be reviewed and updated
- What changes have to happen to trigger a change to the agreement?
- When delegating very long-term projects, hold "refresh meetings" at regularly scheduled intervals

4) Communicator

I positioned this role as the central #4 spot because it is integrated into all other roles. Communication is the lifeblood of the organization and team, and like everything else, communication within organizations has changed in significant ways. In the industrial age, it was largely confined to up and down within departmental silos, but today we must communicate with people from across the organization. In the industrial age, many managers would put forth information on a need-to-know basis and frequently felt that people didn't need to know, because they realized that information is power and they weren't about to give that away. Communication was limited to face-to-face, telephone calls and memos in the same time zones.

Team leaders must see their role as a two-way **information conduit**. The team leader is the voice of the organization to their people, and the voice of their people to the organization. The minute the team leader begins to supply information to their people/team, the process of empowerment has begun. The truth of empowerment is that without information, people cannot take responsibility, whereas people with information cannot help but take responsibility.

Whenever I ask workshop participants if there is a rumour mill alive and well within their organization, I consistently get the same sad answer. The British author C. Northcote Parkinson stated in his book *Parkinson's Law* that "nature abhors a vacuum. The void created in any organization by the absence of open, honest communication will quickly be filled with drivel, misrepresentation and poison." In other words, if people don't know what's going on, they are going to spend many of their waking hours making it up. A central component of the communicator role is that the team leader is the rumour-mill killer by keeping people informed and feeling in the know.

Many people complain that trying to manage information in their organization is like trying to sip water from a fully open fire hose. People today are drowning in data while thirsting for information. It is the team leader who is uniquely positioned to take the avalanche of raw data and organize and distill it into meaningful and actionable information to support the team's problem solving and decision making.

Information People Need to be Effectively Empowered

If the goal of empowering people is to have them **make decisions** as if they owned the organization, then it follows that we must provide the information (develop the understanding) so they are making **informed decisions**.

- **Industry** – Information about big-picture trends, current and anticipated changes in customers, competitors, technology, and comparative and competitive data

- **Organizational mission** – Information that provides everyone with a clear sense of organizational values (who we are, how we behave) and vision (where we are going)

- **Departmental context/stakeholder** – Information that helps everyone understand how their department/team fits into the big picture of overall organization (stakeholder mapping)

- **Job context/stakeholder** – Information that helps everyone understand how their work fits into the big picture of the overall department and organization

- **Performance objectives** – Information that ensures everyone has a clear understanding of what "great performance" looks like for the organization, department and team

- **Team member** – Information that helps team members understand other team members – their experience, roles, what is important to them, what they need help with and how they can best help others succeed

- **Customer-based performance feedback** – Information that helps people understand how the organization, the team and they as individuals are currently performing

- **Cost of doing business** – Information that helps people understand how their decisions financially impact the organization

5) Meeting Manager

When all is said and done, in the vast majority of meetings, there is a lot more said than done. I am sure we would all agree that there is a massive difference between a well-run meeting and a poorly run meeting. Poorly run meetings are probably costlier than the obvious expense of putting a group of highly paid people in a room for a couple of hours. Bad meetings are not only non-productive, they are counterproductive as they build frustration in people, create animosities, activate the rumour mill and waste time, and the team leader suffers a loss of credibility.

Team leaders must first ensure the team is having the right type of meetings – working IN meetings, the purpose of which is to solve operational problems and issues. High-performance team leaders ensure that their teams are periodically working ON meetings where the team reflects on how the team is working in an attempt to improve its capacity to solve problems. The team leader must determine the right meeting frequency and duration of team meetings. A word of caution regarding regularly scheduled meetings: while many people say they are fairly productive, beware because they also carry the highest risk of meeting for the sake of meeting. The following are some best practices for before and during the meeting that will assist the team leader to facilitate meetings that are both effective (produce decisions and desired action-based outcomes) and efficient (using the least amount of time).

Making Team Meetings Work

- Quality of a meeting is largely determined by the quality of preparation! Agenda is the vital tool. The primary purpose of an agenda is to induce participant preparation for meeting.

- Send the agenda to participants forty-eight to seventy-two hours in advance.

- Ideally, structure the agenda in question form whenever possible and say, "Please come to the meeting prepared to discuss the following questions."

- Scheduling meetings at 11:00 a.m. and 3:30 p.m. for greater sense of urgency drives decisiveness.

- Restrict interruptions; establish guidelines with the gatekeeper and participants.

- If you want to actively participate in the meeting, you should always delegate two key roles: scribe and timer.

- Always start the meeting on time. A hallmark of high-performance teams is that they start meetings as scheduled. When the leader does not start the meeting on schedule what inadvertently happens is the punctual people are being punished, the late people are being rewarded and conditioned to come late to the next meeting, and worst of all, it sends the wrong message and sets the wrong tone for the meeting.

- Open by restating and reinforcing the meeting's purpose and objectives. Gain agreement on a final agenda. The meeting leader must use this agreement to gently but firmly keep the meeting on track. If the meeting wanders into gossip, chitchat or irrelevancies, use phrases like, "Let's move forward as we agreed that we would stay focused and end on time."

- Set time frames for each topic. Almost never discuss any issue for more than forty-five minutes, as the conversation become circular and redundant.

- The leader must achieve closure by concluding each topic with a "commitment to action" by confirming the "3 W's" – *who* does *what* by *when*. Record all commitments to action, make copies and distribute to all participants before the meeting disbands.

- Always close meeting with a brief review of meeting objectives and outcomes, recap key decisions and a give a confirmation of all agreements and commitments to action.

Facilitating Team Problem Solving & Decision Making

I look back on my corporate managerial career of fifteen years with some regret, as it is only in retrospect that I realize I was guilty of giving away far too many fish. I suspect you're aware of the old Eastern adage that if you give a person a fish, you'll feed them for a day and if you teach them how to fish, you'll feed them for a lifetime. One of the most fundamental skills of effective team leaders is the ability to facilitate their people through the problem-solving/decision-making process.

The benefits of facilitating problem solving as opposed to just giving people answers are multiple:

- People and teams grow and develop as they learn to solve their own problems.
- This practice is consistent with the central TQM principle that the people solving the problem should be closest to the problem, which means the solution will have a high degree of practicality.
- The greater the degree of involvement solving the problem, the greater the degree of commitment to implementing the solution. Once again, people don't argue with their own solutions and ideas.

Clearly, it is ideal to have people and teams solve their own problems; however, a word of warning that this approach is time consuming. Recognizing the tempo and time pressure of today's workplace, realistically, team leaders sometimes just have to give the team the fish.

The management principle called "Completed Staff Work" was invented by Napoleon. This meant that if any general came to Napoleon with a problem he had not thought through to an alternative solution stage, he would be hanged. That would be considered somewhat extreme today, but the principle holds true in that your experienced, direct reports should be expected to come to you with a problem only after they have thought it through, ideally to the point of recommending alternative solutions. See the problem-solving process explained in the decision-making component of Chapter 13.

6) People Developer

To grow an organization means you first have to grow people. As team leader, you must begin this role by making a serious commitment to personal development and demonstrate to people that you are willing to learn, be coached and take feedback. I recommend a number of books for my participants to read, and I jokingly tell participants in my workshops that they don't necessarily have to read the books but just go buy a half-dozen and put them in their office in an obvious place so people get the impression they're a serious student. Demonstrating that you are coachable and committed to learning grants the psychological licence to coach others.

Allow me to clarify the difference between training and development. Training is learning knowledge and skills to enhance performance in a current role; development is the learning of knowledge and skills that prepares people for their next role. For ambitious people who want to move up the corporate ladder and get promoted, a key question becomes "Is your replacement ready?" The CFO of a very large coffee company told me that every time she picks up the CEO from his private jet at the airport, she has learned to anticipate being asked the following questions: "If a bus hit you today, who would be your possible replacements? What are their strengths, what are their weaknesses and what are your development plans for them?"

The foundational starting point of all development efforts is to facilitate objective self-assessment that leads to greater self-awareness of a person's strengths and weaknesses.

One of the most significant trends in the people-development dimension of human resource management is that we are no longer turning people into fix-it projects. Instead of focusing on people's "areas of development" and trying to fix weaknesses, the primary developmental focus should be on building a person's strengths. Effective team leaders deal with people's weaknesses by placing them in a team with people who have the natural talents to compensate for those weaknesses, which is the definition of a complementary team.

There are two basic methods of people development:

Active development – providing coaching feedback, mentoring and training, which we dedicate the entire next chapter to.

Passive development – developing people through delegation by empowering them to think for themselves and solve their own problems by providing them with ever more challenging goals and objectives.

7] Team Ambassador

This is the most overlooked and ignored of all the roles, and this neglect is becoming increasingly costly as the need for horizontal communication and interdepartmental collaboration grows. Many, if not most, organizations that I work with, and even my most sophisticated clients, still struggle with departmental silos and as a result there is broken interdepartmental communication and a lack of collaboration. The root cause of the broken inter-functional communication is because there's no one held accountable to make it happen since there's a lack of role clarity at the team-lead level.

It is the team leader who is uniquely positioned to ensure that the team or department is integrated and synchronized with the rest of the organization, with particular emphasis placed on managing the cross-functional value chain so the handoff from one to department to another is seamless.

This role also includes ensuring that the team is acquiring adequate resources from senior management and full support from departments such as IT and HR. Part of the ambassador role is that the leader must identify and remove organizational barriers and obstacles within the organization that prevent or hinder team success. Barriers can take the form of structures, systems, policies, procedures, processes, bottlenecks and even sometimes certain people. It might be said that the team carries the ball, and the role of the team leader is the lead blocker.

To conclude, I realize that for those who us who were raised in the command-and-control industrial age, this is a very difficult mind shift to make, and I see many people struggling. I think a lot of people intellectually grasp the concept of empowering people, but when push comes to shove it doesn't really happen. A very real restraining factor is that the managers always thought they did the thinking and the people did the doing. Now they've been told that the people have to do the thinking *and* doing, and the obvious question that enters the leader's mind is "What am I here for?" The answer is to be found in the seven roles. The role of the manager is still important, but we all must accept that it requires a new and very different approach.

CHAPTER 19: COACHING & FEEDBACK

Feedback is the breakfast of champions that is far too seldom served. The great coach John Wooden said, "An effective coach is someone who can give correction without causing resentment." The ability to give and the ability to receive feedback are vital twenty-first-century workplace competencies for people at all levels of the organization. If effective leadership is defined by the ability to grow, develop and bring the best out of people, then it follows that the ability to coach and provide feedback is a core leadership communication competency. The importance of coaching is never argued, and yet research clearly indicates that most managers spend little if any time coaching. My personal observations are consistent with the research, as in over three decades of working with both private and public sector clients as a leadership-development strategist, the most common lament I hear from human resources professionals and executives is that they just can't seem to get their managers and supervisors to have the difficult conversations with their people.

Allow me to share the confessions of my workshop participants as to the reasons they don't spend time coaching their people:

- Technical comfort zone (for technically talented people, there is an irresistible gravitational pull back to a **task focus** away from the intended **people focus**)
- No time for coaching

- Fear of offending
- Fear of conflict
- Fear of failure
- Don't see coaching as part of their job or responsibility
- Have never been effectively coached (no one to model) so they don't know how or where to start coaching.

Coaching and feedback are the flip side of the same process. The difference is that coaching is strategic, whereas feedback is tactical. An effective coaching strategy is about planning to have the right conversation with the right person for the right reason at the right time in the right place. Tactical feedback is about the skills and techniques used to deliver the face-to-face or ear-to-ear feedback.

Diagnosing Performance-Improvement Opportunities

The starting point of the strategic coaching process is to assess and identify performance improvement opportunities in your strongest, weakest and mediocre performers. The key is to understand *why* a person is exceeding performance expectations or *why* they are failing to achieve performance expectations. Understanding the anatomy of a competency or the four building blocks of performance will assist in the diagnosis process.

The Anatomy of a Competency

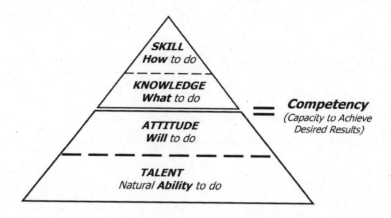

- There is a risk of over-simplification because all four components are interrelated, and it is usually a combination of components that contribute to superior or inadequate performance.

- External factors can also be a governing factor in determining performance, such as the environment, coworkers, tools, equipment and resources.

- Performance problems rooted in lack of knowledge or skill are easily fixable through coaching and training.

- The bottom two performance components are much more difficult to deal with. If the deficient performance is an issue of talent, it means you've got the wrong person in the wrong job, and training will not fix this issue. I believe the most challenging and time-consuming performance problems to deal with are attitudinal.

- One of the most successful airlines, Southwest, has a simple and obviously effective recruiting strategy – hire attitude and train skill. The bottom two performance building blocks must be addressed in the recruiting process.

I'm not sure that flowcharts and leading people go hand in glove, but below is a strategic approach to coaching. This model is designed to help the coach determine what is the right conversation to have with the right person at the right time in the right place and for the right reason.

Strategic Performance Coaching Process

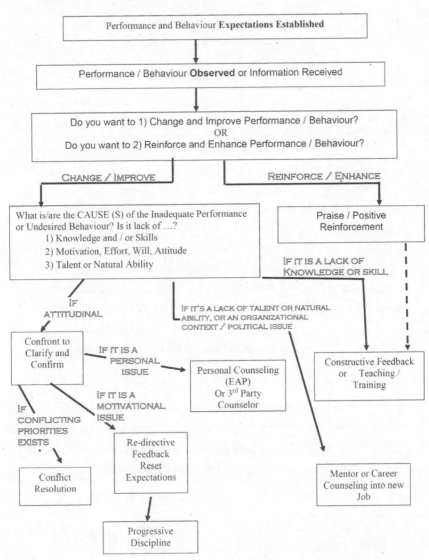

Delivering POSITIVE Feedback to Reinforce Behaviours

No doubt there will always be a need for corrective feedback; however, let me emphasize that I believe strongly that the most regular feedback a leader should look to deliver is positive "reinforcing feedback" or praise whenever possible. Praising constructive and productive behaviours will ideally crowd out unproductive or undesired behaviours. However, we all have weaknesses and blind spots, which means that inevitably we all can benefit from corrective feedback. A few years back I facilitated a workshop for all the coaches in the National Hockey League, and one particularly successful coach explained that he tried to implement a 4 to 1 ratio, in that for every corrective feedback he would give the player, he would try to give four positive feedbacks.

When to Praise

- Whenever possible! The role of the industrial-age manager was to catch people making mistakes and doing things wrong. The highly effective leader has a constant focus on catching people doing things right.

- When performance is partially successful. You do not have to wait until the entire job is done perfectly to offer praise.

- When performance exceeds standards.

- When standards are consistently met. Star performers receive plenty of accolades, and poor performers received negative feedback. I fear it's the solid performers in the middle who frequently get overlooked.

- Before delivering corrective feedback, try to find something positive to discuss that gives you the "psychological licence" to deliver corrective feedback.

Praising – Best Practices

When delivering positive reinforcement, allow the seven "S's" to be your guide.

Sincere

The con man says that once you can fake sincerity, you've got it made. I think it's evident that feedback delivered in a less-than-genuine manner simply won't take root and will not achieve desired behaviour change. False flattery may work on needy, low-EQ people, but most people will quickly recognize the praise as an attempt at manipulation.

Specific

Whenever delivering praise or giving credit, be as specific as possible. Specificity gives compliments credibility, power and potency. It also ensures that the coach is not reinforcing *all* aspects of the work and inadvertently reinforcing some counterproductive behaviours.

Soon

The sooner, the better. Positive reinforcement must be delivered in a timely fashion to create optimum impact and learning.

Selective

At the risk of contradicting myself, as much as you want to look for every opportunity to give praise, the risk of giving too many compliments is that, in time, they lose the desired effect – although I seldom if ever run into people who complain about getting too much positive feedback and appreciation. Mostly

I hear people say that the only praise they receive is when their boss tells them their paycheque is there.

Specialize

The old expression that it is best to "praise in public and reprimand in private" still holds true. However, the one qualifier I would like to add is that it is important for the leader to specialize the style and content of the praise based on the person who is receiving the praise. I've learned that extroverted people do truly value public accolades and recognition, but introverted people would much prefer a gentle tap on the shoulder and a quiet word of appreciation as opposed to being made the centre of attention. Introverts also place a higher value on written words of recognition and appreciation.

Significance

If needed, help the person fully appreciate the importance of what they have just accomplished. For example, the leader could say that by dealing effectively with a difficult customer issue, the person saved the organization about $10,000 to underline the importance of the accomplishment.

Standardize

The primary purpose of feedback is to have the person replicate the constructive behaviour into the future. So, unless it is straightforward and obvious, the leader must ensure people are aware of what they did and how they did it to standardize the positive behaviour. It is ideal to create a dialogue by using questions during the process of delivering praise, such as "How did you just do that?" "Do you know why you got the outstanding results?" "What do you feel were the main contributors to your success?"

Please note that it's likely not appropriate or necessary to use all the seven "S's" when you deliver a complement, but the first three (sincere, specific, soon) are always critical to the success of praise or compliments. I cannot think of a leadership activity that has a higher return on investment than giving people positive feedback. The time and energy costs are minimal, and the return is certain and sometimes immeasurable.

Planning & Preparing for Delivering Corrective Feedback

The English writer Samuel Johnson warned us 300 years ago when he said, "Advice is seldom welcome, and those who need it most like it least." On the subject of feedback, we must accept the tragic truth that the people who most need corrective feedback are the people least able to accept in a constructive manner, as they take all feedback personally and get defensive. The inability to accept feedback dramatically stunts people's growth and dooms them to be trapped in an endless cycle of failure or at best mediocrity.

These are some of the most challenging conversations a team leader will need to have in the course of their career. To be sure, there are very real risks associated with these conversations, as things could quickly become emotional, adversarial and destructive if not carefully managed. However, I do believe there is ever-greater risk in failing to have them.

Remember, the guiding principle is the more challenging the conversation, the more strategic you must be. I recommend asking yourself a series of questions in preparation for the feedback conversation:

✓ Can I live with the behaviour in question? Do the benefits of giving the person feedback and achieving the desired behaviour change outweigh the risks of delivering the feedback?

✓ Is it me? To what degree am I at fault for the poor performance? In particular, does the person clearly understand performance and/or behaviour expectations?

✓ Am I angry with the individual?

✓ How mature or emotionally intelligent is the individual? How open to feedback is this person?

✓ What is the quality of the relationship with the individual? Have I developed credibility and influence with this person?

✓ What is the specific purpose of the feedback, and what are the desired results of the feedback as defined by behaviour changes?

✓ Am I able to clearly describe the impact of the problem performance and/ or behaviour on all stakeholders, i.e., the customer, organization, team or team members, other teams, myself and the individual receiving feedback?

✓ What other factors (or people) could be impacting the performance outcome gap?

Before we look at the four-step, four-stage corrective-feedback process, I would like you to consider some general guidelines and best practices to follow when delivering redirective feedback.

Guidelines Delivering Corrective Feedback

- First and foremost, remember that you're dealing with the person's lower brain, which means it is essential that the intent be perceived by the receiver of the feedback to be supportive or helpful and not critical. The tone of the conversation must be inquisitive and not condemnatory.

- Feedback must always be purpose-driven, and the essential purpose of providing feedback is always to encourage effective future behaviour. Effective feedback is fundamentally future-focused.

- Remember, you are dealing with the lower brain, so it is absolutely essential that conversation be perceived as supportive or helpful. Tone must be inquisitive and not condemnatory.

- Effective feedback is always performance-based. It is about changing the behaviours that cause gaps between actual outcomes and desired outcomes or goals.

- Be as objective, fact-based and specific (with details) as possible. Avoid the use of "you always" or "you never."

- Stay calm, speak tactfully and rationally, and if emotions run high the antidote is always the same – ask questions and listen intently to defuse resistance or anger.

- Be concise; the clock is ticking. This can be done very quickly – stage one feedback can be delivered successfully in less than sixty seconds.

- It is important that the focus remain on the person's behaviour. It's not the person; it is their behaviour that is the issue. Using the word "behaviour" reduces the likelihood of the person perceiving it as a personal attack; behaviours can be changed.

- Use silence effectively. Silence can serve a number of purposes:

  o To emphasize a point

  o To allow time for a key thought to sink in

  o To evoke a response from the person receiving feedback

  o To change subjects

Delivering Corrective Feedback – The 4-Step & 4-Stage Process

STEP 1 – Request Permission to Give Feedback

☞ "Can I share an observation with you?" "Is it okay if I give you my perspective on something I've been noticing lately?" "Can I give you some helpful feedback?"

☞ If it's a sensitive issue or you observe defensiveness, call a time-out and then **explicitly clarify your purpose** and intentions by saying, "Here is what I am trying to do and what I'm not trying to do …"

STEP 2 – Describe Specific Behaviour

☞ Describe your observations in a non-blameful or attacking manner

☞ Provide examples and be very **specific** to avoid resistance, arguments and disagreements

☞ Use **action verbs**: "When you are late …" "When you rolled your eyes …" "When you said …" "When you raised your voice…" "When you failed to …"

STEP 3 – Describe IMPACT or Consequences Resulting from Behaviour

☞ Assume the impact was unintended. "You are probably not aware of the consequences of your behaviour …"

☞ List how the behaviour or performance gap impacts all stakeholders

☞ This is the key step in gaining **motivational leverage** for a person to change and is also a vital step in **reducing defensiveness**

☞ Confirm your motives by asking the person, "If you were in my situation, can you see why we're having this conversation?"

STEP 4 – Request or Suggest Behaviour Change

☞ Step 4 is not always required at stage one, as the ideal outcome of the conversation is to have the person take initiative and come up with their own solutions after Step 3

☞ Assist the person in identifying solutions to the problems and only suggest solutions when necessary

☞ Offer whatever help and support is available to assist the person in their efforts to change

Four Stages of Feedback

Stage ONE Feedback: Steps 1–3

Stage TWO Feedback: Steps 1–4

Stage THREE Feedback: Steps 1–4 plus firm commitment to change

Stage FOUR Feedback: Game-changer, now about integrity and broken commitment

Each stage of the feedback process is to be facilitated with greater specificity and rigour.

Guidelines & Considerations for Receiving Feedback

☞ Highly effective leaders request feedback that focuses on opportunities for improvement as opposed to one's strengths and successes.

☞ Always remember that even the very best get criticized.

☞ Don't telegraph the answers you want to hear.

☞ Listen attentively and try not to interrupt.

☞ Paraphrase to ensure and prove that you understand the spirit and central points of the feedback.

☞ Stifle the urge to rationalize or allocate blame and instead ask for examples and specific details.

☞ Don't overreact, and squelch the urge to counterattack. Ask for thinking time before responding.

☞ Immediately discount feedback given in anger or vindictiveness.

☞ Assess *validity* of feedback by asking yourself:

   o Is the person's motive for providing the feedback constructive or destructive?

   o What is the person's degree of competency or credibility?

   o How accurate is their perception of the situation and how complete is their information?

   o Are the suggested behaviour changes worthwhile? Will the change get me closer to my goals?

☞ If you believe the feedback is valid, request they suggest solutions or describe how they would have handled the situation. Then, if appropriate, explain how you will handle the situation the next time.

☞ Thank the person for taking time and making the effort to provide the feedback.

☞ If needed, take a quick moment to recall your list of strengths and remind yourself of some of your successes.

☞ If feedback is valid, develop an action plan to change behaviours and attempt to somehow measure the desired behaviour changes to hold yourself accountable.

LEADING
FROM
EVERYWHERE

THE PRINCIPLES & PRACTICES OF
CHARACTER-BASED LEADERSHIP

PART 7: ORGANIZATIONAL LEADERSHIP –
LEADING A HIGH-PERFORMANCE ORGANIZATION

20. The High-Performance Twenty-First-
    Century Organization
21. Creating a Customer-Focused Culture
    of Engagement

CHAPTER 20: THE HIGH-PERFORMANCE TWENTY-FIRST-CENTURY ORGANIZATION

In the industrial age, the key to success was about standardization, duplication and replication that drove operational efficiencies. It was the bigger organizations that had a natural competitive advantage because they could leverage economies of scale, allowing them to buy cheaper raw materials than their competition. The typical organization was rigidly structured, hierarchical, departmentalized, bureaucratic and slow-moving. In the information age, given the dynamic nature of the marketplace and the ever-increasing demands of our customers, organizational responsiveness and nimbleness are now critical success factors, which means size is no longer the significant competitive advantage it once was. It is now the smaller, more agile organizations that possess the natural competitive advantage, as they are better able to respond quickly to the unprecedented marketplace turbulence that all organizations must navigate. This explains why many large organizations are breaking themselves into "strategic business units" in a desperate attempt to become more responsive, innovative and entrepreneurial.

We have established that customers today are far more demanding for the obvious reason that they can be; as the number of competitive choices increases, so does their power. Welcome to the "value era" – a hyper-competitive reality when winning and keeping customers is increasingly challenging, and traditional, industrial-age solutions don't work anymore. In the information age, the key organizational strategic competitive advantages are now adaptability, responsiveness, rapid new product development and speed to market, all of which demand a fundamentally new organizational paradigm where leadership must be demonstrated at all levels of the organization.

The High-Performance ^Twenty-First-Century Organization Defined

It was Harvard business professor Rosabeth Moss Kanter, in her classic book *The Change Masters,* who first helped me understand that any organization that hopes to survive let alone thrive now and into the future will need to be increasingly defined by the "5 F's." I have taken the liberty of adjusting and adding a couple more F's. Every organization must become aligned with the following "7 F's," which also apply directly to all departments and teams.

1) *Focused on delivering VALUE to customers*

   The primary purpose for the existence of every organization is to create and communicate value to its customers. Customer value is so fundamental to organizational success that the balance of the chapter is dedicated to the concept of driving value to the customer.

2) *Fast*

   Customers want things now. It is simply not possible to operate at world-class speed if we have to wait for information to flow up one silo, across and down another and wait for decisions to come from above.

3) *Flexible*

   Obsolescence is nipping at all of our heels. All organizations must now be able to "turn on a dime" rapidly, if not instantly, adapting to new customer expectations and sudden new competitive challenges. Yesterday the customer wanted it this way, and today they want it that way. Yesterday we had a specific competitive advantage, and now, overnight, it's gone.

4) *Friendly*

The only sustainable competitive advantage in most markets is superior customer relations. Product and process competitive advantages can be quickly copied by the competition, but creating a culture that fosters excellence in customer service cannot be simply or quickly developed.

5) *Fun*

A positive work environment is essential for any organization that has any hope of recruiting and keeping the best people. The key to success today is innovation, and the key to innovation is creativity in problem solving and decision making. Creativity can only happen in a safe environment where positive energy predominates and people are free to take initiative and prudent risks in pursuit of their objectives. Negative energy kills creativity.

6) *Frugal*

Increasing competitive forces are putting tremendous downside pressure on profit margins across all industries; this has put pressure on organizations, which must then be very financially responsible by creating a "cost consciousness" throughout the organization. An ROI mindset must be prevalent, and resource allocation should be focused on those investments that add value to the customer or stakeholder.

7) *Fundamentals*

The instant appeal of quick-fix solutions is often irresistible to executives, and as a result the organization jumps from one flavour-of-the-month bandwagon only to serve growing cynicism throughout the organization. A strong word of caution: I far too frequently encounter organizations into the latest management fad that dominates organizational agendas, when the truth is that long-term success can only be founded upon the bedrock of success on the few simple basics. The evidence is clear that the organizations that have the best return on investment over the long-term are those that do the simple things exceedingly well; they are excellent on the basics. The real key to business success is not to be found in the implementation of the latest in-vogue management fad written by some consultant or academic but rather in the application of common sense and a perpetual focus on the fundamentals.

Points to Ponder on Customer Loyalty

The starting point of succeeding in the "value era" is for everyone in the organization to understand a few simple truths that help define current reality and that must underpin the operational paradigm or belief system of the organization. Everyone must crystallize, internalize and maintain top-of-mind awareness of the following basic customer truths:

The customer is the ultimate boss and always defines value. Organizations are successful to the degree that they develop repeat and referral customers, period. Over the years, I have witnessed an insane imbalance of resource allocation in many organizations between customer acquisition and customer retention. Research tells us that it costs somewhere between five to eight times as much to acquire a new customer than to keep an existing customer.

You develop loyal customers to the degree that you add distinctive value to them. If your organization fails to add distinctive value, you are relegated to marketing the lowest price. The problem with gaining customers by having the lowest price presents a couple of significant problems. First, you don't make much profit, and second, you have zero customer loyalty. The fundamental principle remains: to drive value to the customer, and to the degree the customer perceives distinctive value, you can (should) add the commensurate additional margin.

- Simply satisfying the customer is no longer good enough to maintain loyalty. One recent study indicated that over 70% of satisfied customers would defect if someone else offered them what they perceive to be a better value proposition. If we hope to develop and maintain loyal clients, we must develop an organization capable of consistently exceeding customer expectations.

- The research shows that most dissatisfied customers will not bother or take the time to register a complaint; instead, customers just vote with their feet and take their wallets with them and they are forever gone. The key is to invite customer complaints, as the research is clear that if you can get the customer to open up and complain, even a small remedial action will result in the customer coming back. Inviting customer complaints is the best and least-expensive form of market research.

- Each customer interaction must be seen from the correct perspective – only the "lifetime perspective" illustrates the true value of a customer! For example, if a grocery store can develop a loyal customer in their twenties who spends $100 a week, this equates to $5,200 a year. Over twenty-five years, the total revenue is $130,000. It is vital that the people serving these customers behave as if they are dealing with a $130,000-appreciating asset as opposed to a $100 transactional exchange.

Moments of Truth

Customer loyalty is built or broken one interaction at a time, which means each customer interaction, contact or communication is a "moment of truth" during which the quality of the customer relationship grows or deteriorates, thus determining the future fate of the organization. Whether customers are consciously aware of it or not (mostly not), there is a subconscious "value equation" that determines the level of customer satisfaction during and after every interaction and in the long run determines the degree of customer loyalty.

The Customer Satisfaction Equation

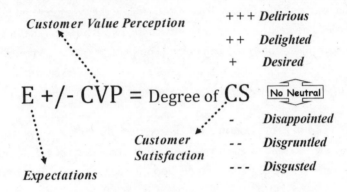

A key learning point from this equation is to understand that customer satisfaction is a function of the value the customer perceived they received relative to what they expected to receive. This is why there tends to be conflict in many organizations between the sales departments and the operational departments. Salespeople tend to over-promise to get the order and then hand it off to the poor operations and service people to deliver against the inflated expectations the eager salespeople created. In a high-end restaurant, if the maître d' knows it's a ten-minute wait for seating, he will tell arriving guests that the wait is twenty minutes. Bank A promises they will have the service completed by 2:00 p.m. and yet it is not ready until 2:15, whereas Bank B promises they will have the service completed by 3:00, and it is ready to go by 2:45. While Bank B is a full half-hour slower than Bank A, they will win the customer perception battle hands down every time. Always remember that the primary principle of creating customer satisfaction is to manage customer expectations by applying the old axiom "promise good, deliver better!"

The Only Thing That Really Matters - Customer Value Perception

Karl Albrecht wrote a book a few decades back titled *The Only Thing That Matters,* in which he makes a very convincing case that if you think about it long and hard enough, the only thing that really matters to any organization big or small is what your customers think about you. My accounting friends frequently argue that the only thing that really matters is bottom-line profits. My counterpoint is that truly successful organizations focus everyone on one simple, singular purpose, which is "driving value to the customer." The basic rule of business success is the more distinctive value the organization creates for the customer as perceived by the customer, the more the organization is able to increase the selling price and higher profit margins.

The starting point of becoming customer-focused is for everyone in the organization to achieve and maintain an "outside-in" perspective and see your organization through the eyes of the customer. The reasons people are loyal or not to a given business are largely a function of subconscious perception. To make the practices and processes of adding value more tangible, measurable and manageable, allow me to introduce the concept of the "customer value package" which is a composite of the four different types of customer value, which combined determine the only thing that really matters – customer value perception.

The Customer Value Package

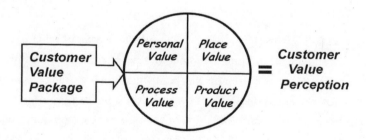

To provide a practical illustration of the four types of value, allow me to use the example of a grocery store, which everybody can relate to. **Place** and **product** are tangible forms of value, whereas **process** and **personal** are intangible, which are becoming more important to creating customers' loyalty. For many organizations outside of retail or any type of business where customers do not visit a location frequently place value can be a nonfactor.

PRODUCT VALUE

- ✓ Quality/reliability
- ✓ Selection
- ✓ In-stock position
- ✓ One-stop shopping

PLACE VALUE

- ✓ Location/proximity
- ✓ Cleanliness
- ✓ Aesthetics/lighting/signage
- ✓ Parking

PROCESS VALUE

- ✓ Hours of operation
- ✓ Speed and ease of buying process
- ✓ Fast-moving lineup at till
- ✓ Payment options
- ✓ Quick, easy, fair return policy

PERSONAL VALUE

- ✓ Emotional value (attitude)
- ✓ Intellectual value (knowledge)
- ✓ Responsiveness and quick decision making
- ✓ Follow-through/reliability
- ✓ Clear, concise, complete and caring communication

This question is frequently asked: which of the four types of value is the most powerful in building or breaking customer loyalty? A recent study conducted by the Forum Group out of Boston on why companies stopped doing business with certain vendors reported that 15% of the time it was product problems, 15% of the time it was pricing issues and 70% of the time people stop doing business with a given company because of a personal or attitudinal issue. Research conducted by TARP on customer loyalty in the retail business focused specifically on why customers stop doing business with a retailer, and the findings are as follows:

- *1% die*
- *3% move*
- *4% naturally float*
- *5% change on friend's recommendation*
- *9% can buy cheaper elsewhere*

- *10% are chronic complainers*
- *68% because someone treated them with indifference*

The research is crystal clear: time and again the conclusion is that the most potent value factor in determining customer perception is the **personal** component! The most common reason cited was that someone from the organization had treated them not with rudeness but with indifference. Remember that the opposite of love is not hate but indifference. The key question now becomes how do you get your frontline staff to care and go the second mile for the customer? I've learned that if the frontline people don't think the organization cares about them, the people quickly become careless with the organization's tools, equipment and resources and, most destructively, with customers.

Adding value to customers (internal or external) must be the primary purpose of everyone's job! Every job description in your organization must start with the following statement: **"Things I do day in and day out to get and keep customers are ..."** Everyone in the organization must see a direct line of sight between your daily efforts and how they create customer value. At IBM, there is a motto that perhaps best capsulizes the concept: "If you are not directly adding value to a customer, then you better be adding value to someone who is adding value directly to the customer. If not, then the question becomes why are you on the payroll?"

The Anatomy of High-Performance, Value-Driven Organizations

Given the incredibly competitive nature of the marketplaces today, if any organization hopes to achieve world-class levels of performance, it must do nothing less than fundamentally reconceive itself as a value-rendering vehicle. In other words, every organization must become "value driven." This simply means that the overarching, governing success principle is that every person, process, decision, activity, task and resource allocation must be driven by one central purpose: delivering value to the customer. The same success principle also applies to every department, team and individual.

Allow me to provide a holistic model or conceptual framework that supports a strategic approach for every organization, department or team to become increasingly value-driven. The model is based on the premise that the anatomy of every organization consists of four highly interconnected dimensions to every organization that must be considered when planning and implementing management initiatives. The four dimensions or components form an ecosystem, meaning no single dimension can be worked upon in isolation, as changes made in any component inevitably will impact the other three dimensions. This model is designed to provide a comprehensive and practical framework that leaders can use to guide all strategic-planning sessions. It is an all-inclusive organizational model that provides an excellent framework to assess current performance and identify performance improvement opportunities in each of the four dimensions.

To help you grasp the concept, allow me to apply the metaphor of human body to the organization. The strategy is the brain of the organization. The structure is the skeletal/muscular system of the organization. The systems are the internal organs of the organization. The culture is the heart of the organization. The strategy, structure and system dimensions of the organization can mostly be repaired at an executive retreat with the use of some flipcharts. However, if the organizational culture becomes sick, there are no quick or easy fixes.

The Anatomy of High-Performance Organizations / Teams

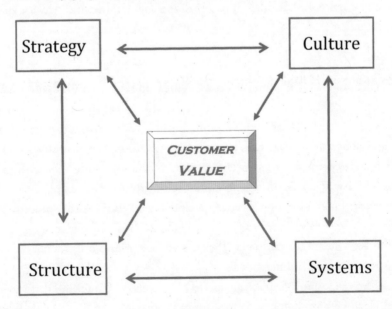

Systems and structures tend to be more a function of management, whereas strategy and culture are the domain of leadership, and in most organizations I've observed, are sadly over-managed and under-led. As we cover the principles and practices of success in each dimension, I challenge you to assess how successfully your organization is currently performing in each of the four dimensions and identify opportunities for improvement.

Strategy

An organization is strategically successful to the degree that it is acting on the marketplace (customers and competition) as opposed to having the marketplace acting on it. The strategic dimension of the organization has two components: the organizational mission (which includes vision and values) and the operational strategic plan.

The purposes of a mission statement are to inspire employees through serving a higher purpose, and more practically to provide everyone in the organization with the same compass that empowers people to make self-guided decisions without managerial consent, knowing that they will always be in alignment with the organization's mission. However, executives must be aware that there are very real risks when developing and communicating mission statements, and more often than not, mission statements do more harm than good. If the senior executives are walking the talk by consistently modelling the desired values and behaviours, it won't hurt to formalize and publish the organizational mission, but I don't suspect there will be any pressing need to develop an official mission statement.

However, the great risk is if the executives are not walking the talk. Then it is incredibly destructive for the executive team, guided by a consultant at a weekend retreat, to formulate a mission statement full of platitudes and proceed to put posters on the wall and purchase pens, hats, coffee mugs and mouse pads with the new slogan so everyone gets the message. This is a typical quick fix that many executives attempt to implement with the best of intentions, but like all quick fixes, the organization ends up worse off in the long run. When the executives have a wide "say–do gap" the unintended corrosive consequences of preaching platitudes are to drive cynicism deeper and deeper within the bowels of the organization. What do you call people who say one thing and yet do another?

The strategic plan is much more specific, as it defines and details what value, and when and how the organization will deliver the value to the customer and stakeholders through each of the four value channels of the "customer value package."

The research on the reasons strategic planning efforts frequently fail is consistent and clear. By far the most common causal factor is not the plan itself but rather the lack of buy-in or commitment from the critical mass of the people to implement the plan. To have a truly effective, value-driven strategy means everyone in the organization has a clear line of sight between what they do daily and the organizational value-delivery strategy. It is vital that everyone understands how their individual and team contributions impact customer value perception. Achieving clarity of the strategic plan and then effectively communicating to everyone in your organization is fundamental to empowering the frontline employees to independently set priorities and make spontaneous customer-keeping decisions.

The starting point of developing an effective value-driven strategy is to always and intensely listen to the customer so as to gain a deep and even intimate understanding of their needs, expectations and frustrations. The key to sustaining a relevant value-delivery strategy is to constantly monitor and measure customer opinion through a variety of feedback methods. Senior executives must be spending time with customers. All employees should have some form of customer contact. Encourage people from all levels and functions of the organization to do customer visits, and then saturate the entire organization with the voice of the customer to ensure every conversation that takes place includes the word "customer."

Structure

To become a truly customer-driven organization, the structure must be designed to support two essential outcomes. First, the informal organizational structure must redirect the vertical energy flow within the organization fully to the customer.

Secondly, the organizational structure must facilitate horizontal communication fluidity and operational functionality between teams and departments.

The Inverted Pyramid

To have a high-performance, value-driven structure means the traditional hierarchical pyramid structure has to be effectively turned upside down. I still see far too many companies with traditional "kiss up and kick down" cultures that are facilitated by vertical organizational structures that drive the energy flow up towards the "boss" and not to the customer. It is fundamental to organizational success to philosophically invert the traditional hierarchical power pyramid to effectively reverse the energy flow from the boss to the customer. The customer-contact people hold the future fortunes of the organization in their hands. Thus, it makes complete common sense to say that the only purpose all other people in the organization should serve is to support and enhance the capacity of the frontline customer-contact people to deliver value to the customer. I ask you to visualize an inverted pyramid with the CEO at the bottom peak holding up their hands to support the executive team that is holding up their hands to support the managers who are holding up their hands to support frontline supervisors who are holding up their hands to support frontline staff who are holding up their hands to support the customer. To make this simple and totally logical concept take root is a great example of something truly easier said than done. To activate the inverted pyramid concept and make it a reality within an organization requires a massive paradigm shift (particularly for more senior employees), and it demands that character-based or servant (ego-less) leadership be demonstrated at all levels of the organization.

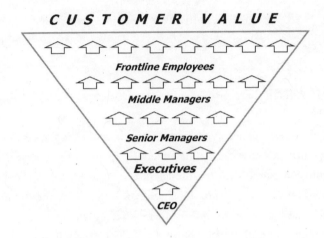

The Horizontal "Value Chain"

Every department team employee is a link in the "value chain," which ends with delivering value to the external customer. Everyone in the organization must see the direct link and understand how their efforts contribute to the organization's or department's ability to deliver value through to the final customer.

The structure of the organization should be designed (re-engineered) around horizontal "work-flow value processes" driven by a singular purpose – to deliver customer value through the value chain! For example, the R&D department hands off their product concept to the engineers to design the product, the engineers hand off their product design to production to manufacture the product, and manufacturing hands off the tangible product to logistics, which must work closely with sales and service marketing to distribute the product. The value chain is simply a sequence of horizontal or "customer/supplier" relationships that lead to the end customer. Horizontal fluidity that is driven by seamless handoffs between every department in the value chain is fundamental to an organization's speed and responsiveness. The old expression, with a slight variation, still holds true: the value chain is only as fast as the slowest link (department/team). It is essential to employ cross-functional teams to break down all interdepartmental walls, silos and barriers of the traditional departmentalized organization to solve customer problems. The real key to operational execution is to have accountability driven through the horizontal value chain by systematically ensuring crystal-clear performance expectations are established in all the internal customer–supplier relationships that make up the value chain.

I would like to make a quick observation on the frequently applied label of the "internal customer." At first it might appear I'm just messing with semantics, but I think not, because words carry connotations and meaning. I think there is a real risk in using the term "internal customers" in that it infers more of a competitive master/slave or win/lose relationship. I believe the true customers are those we send our invoices to. I prefer to refer to the people we deal with along the value chain as "internal partners," as it suggests more of an on-the-same-team, collaborative or win–win relationship.

Systems

The primary guiding principle of developing systems is straightforward: Form must follow function. Means must follow ends. Process must follow purpose. And all the systems of every organization must be designed and aligned with one singular purpose in mind – to support customer-value delivery! Systems in effect hardwire the organization in a manner that it maintains consistency of performance. Systems make things permanent and govern results.

Misaligned systems frequently become barriers to value delivery in the other three channels. Systems call the tune, and bad systems will always produce bad results. An example of a misaligned system is when an organization preaches teamwork and collaboration as a core value and then proceeds to create a compensation system that includes a "fixed-pie" bonus program for the executives that ends up producing destructive competition among the executive team as they each struggle for their piece of the pie. Or the sales executives create a short-term incentive program in the formula sales contest where the winner who sells the most gets a trip to Hawaii. The unintended negative consequence is that the salespeople are now competing against each other to win the trip at any cost, often to the detriment of long-term team and customer relations.

Keep in mind that there are two types of systems that must be developed and managed: the hard systems involve tangible equipment such as ERP software – financial, communication, inventory management, delivery and technology. Soft systems are the policies and procedures (standard operating procedures). The following are a few suggestions for guiding your system-development efforts. All systems must be constantly scrutinized to determine if they are still producing the desired outcomes.

✓ Any organization that has a policy and procedure manual that takes three grown adults to carry is a bright-red warning flag. It is vital is to minimize all rules and regulations, starting with the elimination of all "mickey mouse" bureaucratic policies and procedures to provide as much autonomy and latitude as possible to frontline service people so they can solve problems in creative ways and make fast decisions. A great example is Nordstrom's, headquartered in Seattle, Washington, which is one of the most successful, profitable and growing retailers in the world. Their policy and procedure manual for frontline employees is simply "use your best judgment at all times."

✓ The development of all systems must begin with the end in mind. The key is to first identify what results the system needs to produce and then reverse-engineer to achieve the desired outcomes. The design and development of all systems and processes must involve consultation and collaboration with the end user of the system to ensure functionality and commitment to the full use of the system.

✓ The KISS (keep it simple, stupid) philosophy must underpin all efforts when designing systems to ensure all people will understand and fully use as designed.

✓ Beware: the allure of the latest and greatest technology is very powerful, and it is often hard to resist the requests from the IT team who will always want to invest in cutting-edge technology. We must remember that systems are a means to an end – they must never be seen as an end unto themselves, particularly in the area of technology. Always follow the mantra "technology if necessary, but not necessarily technology!"

✓ Here are some of the systems that are critical to any organization hoping to become high-performance and value-driven:

- Customer-listening systems
- Customer-satisfaction measurement systems
- Employee-listening systems
- Employee-satisfaction measurement systems
- Customer-complaint recovery systems
- Human resource management systems (especially recruiting, performance management, compensation, and training and development systems)
- Competitive-information system
- Internal-communication systems
- Financial-reporting systems
- Strategic-planning systems

Culture

Culture is of the utmost importance, and yet it is very difficult to define it in any tangible manner. Academics would define the culture of the organization as it shared values and believes. Some more practical ways to define culture might be that it is the sum-total attitude of the organization or how people feel about working in the organization. It could be defined as the self-esteem of the organization. The mission statement is analogous to the personality of the organization (what it says it is). The culture of an organization is really the character (what it really is), and as we established earlier in the book, true, sustainable success can only be based on the bedrock of character. Character is as fundamental to team or organizational success as it is to an individual. The culture of the organization is impossible to measure in any specific manner, although you can assess the character of the organization in how they treat their employees and customers, particularly when problems or difficulties occur. Culture could be defined as the sum of the quality of the relationships within the organization. We established earlier that all relationships are governed by natural laws or principles, so the key to creating a healthy, high-performance culture is to align organizational **values**

275

(mores and norms) with timeless, correct principles. The most self-evident principle is that, if the organization wants to be trusted by its employees, then it first must become trustworthy. In *Built to Last,* Jim Collins reported on his studies of why certain companies stand the test of time, whereas their competitors failed. His central conclusion was the organizations that had achieved sustainable success were those that constantly updated their practices; however, what they called their "core philosophy" or principles remained a changeless constant.

Of the four organizational dimensions, culture is by a long stretch the most important dimension in terms of creating sustainable strategic competitive advantages. Culture determines the degree of energy and level of commitment to the organization's success. To have an effective value-driven culture means that you are optimizing the most important asset – the human asset. In the industrial age, the most important assets were capital assets (plant and equipment), and as a result, traditional management theory barely, if ever, even touched on the concept of organizational culture. A very common cause of cultural problems in management is still operating from obsolete, industrial-age, command-and-control management philosophies, which at very best can only obtain compliance from people. Today, in order to have even a hope of becoming a high-performance organization, we must obtain far more than compliance; rather, we must create a culture that supports and sustains commitment, collaboration and creativity in a spirit of continuous improvement. A healthy culture is so fundamental to becoming a high-performance organization that I dedicated the entire next chapter to the subject

Customer-service workshops, which tend to be feel-good smile training, may have a limited and short-term effect; however, when it comes to achieving excellence in customer relations, it's an inside job. It is simply impossible for unhappy, dissatisfied employees to create happy, satisfied customers. A healthy culture creates healthy employee attitudes that are projected to the customer. Employees who don't feel good about the company simply can't make customers feel good about the company. The fundamental truth is that the quality of the external customer relationships is always a reflection of the quality of the internal relationships, which means developing leaders at all levels of the organization is the real key to a high-performance culture!

CHAPTER 21: CREATING A CUSTOMER-FOCUSED CULTURE OF ENGAGEMENT

According to academic definition, an organizational culture is the shared attitudes, values and beliefs that create the psychological and social environment of the organization. My best and most basic definition is that culture is "the way we do things around here." Or, the "unwritten rules" of the organization. Once again, when you attempt to measure the all-important soft stuff like culture, you are doomed to imprecision. However, it doesn't take very long to get a feel for how healthy the culture is by simply listening to the conversations. Does the critical mass of the conversations in the boardroom and the lunchroom consist of an exchange of more positive or negative energy? Are the conversations focused more on the future or the past?

I believe that, of all the changes required to create a culture of engagement, it is the managerial roles that must experience the greatest transformation. It is absolutely essential that managers at all levels become leaders, which in practical terms is making the difficult but vital transition from being a command-and-control cop to becoming an empowering and supportive coach. Unless management makes this pivotal adjustment, most change initiatives will turn out to be nothing more than lip service that fail to produce any real or lasting change. The most significant cultural improvements I have ever observed over the years took place upon the implementation of "multiple-source" or "360-feedback" performance-appraisal systems. This means that the managers are truly held accountable for making the change as they receive feedback from their managers, their coworkers and most importantly their people. I have seen some very significant attitudinal and behavioural changes in managers and supervisors when the tables are turned and their people are allowed to provide regular feedback on their performance.

As stated in Chapter 20, there is no doubt in my mind that organizational culture is the key to achieving world-class organizational performance. However, as with most things in life that are truly important, culture is the most challenging to create, measure, manage or even define, whereas you can fix the organizational strategy, structure and systems in relatively short order because you're dealing mostly in the domain of logic or matters of the mind. However, if the culture becomes sick and toxic, there are no quick or easy fixes because you're now mostly in the domain of emotion or matters of the heart.

Recruiting is the single most important activity any organization ever performs. It is vital to recruit people whose values fit harmoniously into the culture. A word to the wise: too much uncontrolled growth too fast is a mortal enemy of a healthy organizational culture.

The High-Performance Twenty-First-Century Culture Defined

The following models illustrate in tangible, real-world terms what the characteristics of healthy and sick cultures look like:

The 4 C's that Define a Healthy Culture

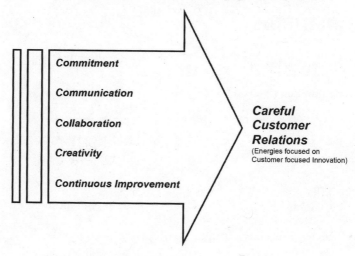

High Performance Culture of Engagement Defined

Commitment

Communication

Collaboration

Creativity

Continuous Improvement

Careful Customer Relations
(Energies focused on Customer focused Innovation)

The 4 C's That Define a Sick Culture

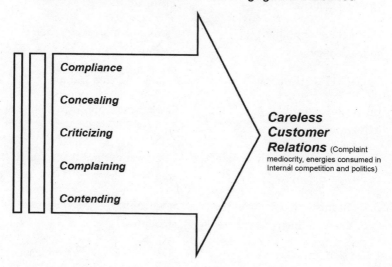

Low Performance Culture of Dis-Engagement Defined

Compliance

Concealing

Criticizing

Complaining

Contending

Careless Customer Relations (Complaint mediocrity, energies consumed in Internal competition and politics)

The Cultural Health Continuum

HEALTHY CULTURE

Holistic leadership

Empowered cross-functional teams

Ethics, integrity

Open, honest, free-flowing communications

External "customer-centred"

Optimistic, positive "can-do" mind-set

Long-term quality, service, excellence

Personal responsibility and accountability

People feel "in the know"

Innovation, creativity, breakthroughs

Conversations primarily exchange positive energy

Bias towards action and completion, follow-through

Learn from mistakes

SICK CULTURE

Hierarchical leadership

Silos, turf-building, pyramid structures

Hidden agendas, politics, game-playing

Lots of written CYA-type communications

Internal competitions "politics-centred"

Resignation, "why do it, it doesn't matter"

Short-term, strictly bottom-line focus

Victim, blame, excuses, pointing fingers

Highly activated "rumour mill"

Resistance to new ideas, cling to the past

Conversations mostly exchange negative energy

Stagnation, risk-aversion, fear of failure

Hide mistakes, bury problems

HEALTHY CULTURE	SICK CULTURE
Clarity of vision, values and priorities	Reactive, tasks and activities driven by urgencies
Highly engaged people	People in minimum daily requirement mode

Using the above as a reference, there is real value in taking a little time to contemplate the following questions:

- How healthy is the culture in your organization, department or team? (Healthy:10 – Sick:1)
- What are the causal forces creating the current cultural conditions?
- How "engaged" is the human asset in your organization, department or team? (From 1 to 10)
- What would it mean to you and your organization if you could improve employee engagement by just 10%?

Measuring "Engagement"

Early in my career I would talk a lot about morale and emphasize why it's so important for organizations to have good morale. One night when I was teaching a night course at a local college, a young student challenged me when she asked, "Are happy employees necessarily productive employees?" I answered, "Good question," which means I didn't have an answer. Driving home that night, I realized the student was really onto something, and it opened my eyes to the truth that happy people are not necessarily productive. I have observed some family-run businesses where everybody is happy with good pay, benefits and free Friday lunch, but there is little accountability, thus dooming the organization to be mired in "country-club" mediocrity. So, I shifted my focus to go beyond morale and teach what motivates and de-motivates people. I have shifted once again to focus on how to engage people. Although I am somewhat hesitant to adopt the latest human resources or management fad, I do believe the concept of "engagement" is legitimate, as it is a more holistic, meaningful and performance-orientated approach than simply talking about motivating people. The end goal is not to create happy people but rather to create high-performance people. I do not mean to diminish the importance of morale, because engagement cannot take place without good morale.

When I ask my workshop participants what engagement means, I mostly get blank stares. Academics would define engagement as the employees demonstrating discretionary effort. Once again, engagement means that an engaged employee thinks, decides and behaves as if they own the joint. Engaged employees act more like owners than renters. Whenever I invert the engagement question, it seems to resonate better with my audience. "How many people can look around at the people in the organization and see untapped talent, energy, creativity and commitment that is currently dormant within the human asset?" In every workshop, every participant immediately raises their hand. There are huge engagement gaps in most organizations, which means the organization is not even coming close to utilizing the full potential of its most important asset. It is important to emphasize that I'm not talking about exploiting people in any way; rather, that we can learn how to create a work environment or culture where people want to come early and stay late, and the boss has to shoo them out of the office to promote work–life balance.

Attempting to measure how engaged people are in any precise manner is a daunting duty indeed. Many large organizations employ formal engagement surveys, which are well-intended but fraught with potential risks. The first big risk is that the data collected is invalid because people are fearful of telling the truth. I have learned that the sicker the culture is, the more distorted and less valid the survey data is. The second and even bigger risk is that once the data is collected, the organization fails to act on the information, which sends a negative message to people and undermines enthusiasm to participate in any further cultural surveys. The most accurate measure of how engaged employees are is customer satisfaction – because the frontline employees can't wait to give to the customer what they been getting from the organization. Other indicators of how engaged or disengaged people are could be excessive turnover and absenteeism, low productivity and how eagerly people show up to the organization's social events. One of the most quantifiable methods of measuring employee engagement is by tracking the number of employee suggestions that are proactively coming up from the frontline employees. Truly engaged frontline employees who are thinking and acting like owners will naturally come up with ideas, big and small, on "how to make things better around here."

This admittedly arbitrary continuum below is my attempt to make the concept of engagement more concrete to better allow you to assess how motivated or engaged your people currently are.

Collaborative Engagement

Dedicated Devotion

Creative Commitment

Discretionary Effort

Cheerful Compliance

Willing Compliance

Dutiful Compliance

Cynical Compliance

Careless Compliance

Malicious Compliance

Open Rebellion

The **underpinning principle** of creating a high-performance culture is to create an environment that supports growth of people's self-esteem. Remember that motivation is a function of the subconscious emotional brain, which operates on the basis of meaning. To make my point about the governing principle of engagement, I kindly request that you participate in a guided visualization exercise with me. Picture someone who reports to you, or if you are not a manager then picture a coworker in your mind. The scenario follows that it is after dinner on a Sunday evening and this particular employee is in the kitchen doing dishes alone. For the very first time in forty-eight hours, as the weekend draws to a close, the thought of going to work for you at your organization enters their mind. The key question now becomes, upon this thought piercing their consciousness, does a slight smile come over their face or a slight frown? Do they start to think about all the exciting projects they're working on and the people they want to get there early to have coffee with? Or do they start to think about calling in sick, faking a dentist appointment or how to stretch their lunch break. This example is so simple and yet it's not simplistic, as it is based in neuroscience complexity, which we discussed in Chapter 8.

Engagement is determined by what it means to people or how people feel about working in the organization. The key engagement question becomes, does the organization provide the opportunity for and support people in growing their self-esteem? If working in the organization makes people feel valued and important, it will inevitably unleash employee energy, talent, creativity and commitment. However, if working in the organization lowers people's self-esteem, making people feel less valued and less important, then once again, I highly recommend you open the fridge door and get out the marmalade because the organization is soon to be toast.

Seven Essential Principles or Pillars of Engagement

Here are the seven key principles or pillars of engagement and the best practices to actualize them.

1] Leadership

- Trusting the organization and team leader has "your best interests at heart." This is why family-run businesses tend to have a natural engagement advantage, as they do truly care about their employees as opposed to short-term quarterly profits.

- Clarity of mission, vision, values and providing clear direction with well-defined roles and goals. Confusion and organizational dysfunction erode employee engagement. It is essential that all employees believe that the organization is in good hands.

- Highly effective leaders help people believe that they can and do make a difference by helping employees understand how their individual efforts contribute to the big picture. The story goes that a man walking down the street in Europe comes across a person who is breaking rocks with a sledgehammer, and he asked the person what he's doing. The person snaps back, "I'm breaking rocks, can't you see?" A few yards down the street he encounters another person breaking rocks and asks what he's doing, and the person says, "I'm breaking these rocks to build a beautiful granite wall." Once again, a short time later he sees a third man breaking rocks and asks, "What are you doing?" and the person gleefully says, "I'm breaking these rocks to build a magnificent cathedral." Of the three workers, who do you think the most productive might be? This explains why it is more challenging to drive engagement in large organizations, because people are more likely to feel like a number, and what they do day to day doesn't really matter.

2) Empowerment

- Trying to separate engagement from empowerment is like trying to separate the sun from sunshine. Because building engagement is really about building people's self-esteem, we must recognize that achievement is one of the most powerful and potent fuels in the furnace of self-esteem. The greater the degree of control the manager can give an employee on any task or project, the greater the sense of accomplishment and thus self-esteem growth upon completion.

- To further create a sense of achievement, try to give people responsibility for complete work units or the entire job or project, if possible, as opposed to a little piece of this project and a little piece of that project.

- Great leaders create a "bias towards action" in their people by creating a culture where people feel safe to take prudent risks in pursuit of their goals – which is the breeding ground of innovation! Mistakes should be seen primarily as an opportunity for learning and not something people should be punished for.

- To have empowerment work, it is essential that people be properly supplied with information, resources, tools and equipment to do an effective job. If employees are given inadequate resources or second-rate equipment to work with, the message to them is what they do is not very important.

3] Accountability

- As soon as I mention the word "accountability," people assume I'm talking about dealing with poor performers and being heavy-handed. Holding poor performers accountable is important, but it is equally important to hold the best and mediocre performers accountable. If you fail to hold people to account, the unintended message is that what they do doesn't count and is not very important. And as we discussed in Chapter 18, the ideal outcome is to help people establish such crystal-clear performance expectations that they can hold themselves accountable.

- In high-performance organizations, poor performers are dealt with swiftly and fairly. Tolerating poor performance is an astonishingly widespread problem and is immeasurably destructive. It is corrosive to the culture, results in workload imbalances, and in time the best performers get frustrated and leave.

4) Involvement

- The basic principle at play is "no involvement, no commitment." As stated previously, adults don't argue with their own ideas and conclusions. Employees today demand real involvement in planning or decision making.

- Very open and honest communication where people feel well informed and "in on things" is vital. Communication must be open, honest and fast. It is essential to create an environment where information flows smoothly and is shared with everyone.

- The best way to involve people is simply to ask for their opinion and then take what they have to say seriously by listening closely. Every time you really listen and value someone's opinion, you can almost see their self-esteem going up.

5) Positive Relationships and Work Environment

- Gallup research reports that one of the single most important engagement factors is the relationship the employee has with their direct boss. The research suggests that for people who work in a healthy organization, if they have a poor relationship with their direct boss, engagement drops off dramatically. The opposite also held true, in that even in a sick organizational culture, if the relationship the employees have with their direct boss is good, they will still be engaged to a degree.

- Politics, backbiting and game-playing are particularly destructive, as they are both the cause and effect of low trust, which kills open, honest communication and undermines performance in significant ways.

- Success and winning at all levels – organizational, team, department and individual – creates positive energy. People want to work for and be part of winning organizations.

- Camaraderie, a sense of community and meaningful collaboration. Having fun from time to time. Gallup further reported that many people find it very important to have a best friend at work.

- Being trusted. Not having to complete a requisition form to acquire a pad of paper or pen.

6) Recognition and Appreciation

- Providing recognition and appreciation for contributions is the most obvious method of building a person's self-esteem. It amazes me that this is the easiest, least expensive and fastest way to build self-esteem, and yet many people report that they do not feel recognized or appreciated for their efforts and accomplishments. Not being given proper credit for your ideas or contributions is a sure-fire engagement killer.

- Compensation is a form of appreciation. This chapter would not be complete if we failed to attempt to answer the frequently debated question: is money a motivator? Frederick Herzberg conducted pioneering research in the 1950s and '60s and attempted to answer this question. He concluded that money is not a motivator but is what he referred to as a "hygiene factor." What this meant was that more money did not sustain higher levels of employee satisfaction and performance in the long run. However, the perceived lack of money will create employee dissatisfaction and demotivated people. More recent research is indicating that the younger generations are now putting a much greater emphasis on money, so it may be becoming a more important motivational variable into the future.

7) Personal and Professional Growth and Development

- As previously expressed, if you want to grow your organization, you must first invest in growing your people. It is the classic win–win in that the organization wins through improved employee performance and productivity, and the employee wins big because growth is a huge self-esteem builder for people.

- Peter Senge, in his book *The Fifth Discipline*, helps us understand that a critically important competitive advantage in this century is becoming a "learning organization." He makes a convincing case that, in a turbulent, unpredictable world, the winners will be those who learn to learn faster than the competition. The Japanese call this same philosophy *kaizen*, which means "continuous improvement," and is best nurtured by ongoing, never-ending learning, which is the real key to organizational adaptability.

- An increasingly significant challenge for organizations to recruit and keep the best people is that young people demand a visible career path where they can see their progression; however, in a flattened organization where there are only two to three levels of management, it becomes very difficult, if not impossible, to promote people because there's no job to promote them up into. If people are stagnating in their current role and there is no place to move them, then if possible, it is important to do what is referred to as "job enrichment" by delegating new and challenging tasks outside their current job description.

- As covered in Chapter 18, taking time and making the effort to coach and provide feedback to people is a major indicator of how much you value them, which means these activities are key drivers of engagement.

- Young people coming to school are now more than ever looking for organizations (and they have the choice of whom to work for) that are willing to make a serious commitment and investment in their professional development in the form of ongoing training programs. A wise person once said the only thing worse than training your people and having them leave is not training your people and having them stay.

Overcoming Resistance to Change

The constant rate of change can cause a continual feeling of uncertainty, which can severely erode employee engagement. The following are some best practices for managing change and getting people to buy into change initiatives.

- ❑ Remember, people are not machines, and they have no quick fixes. Organizational or departmental initiatives cannot be "installed"; they can only be "grown." For strategic initiatives to take root and become effective, it must be a grassroots, bottom-up effort of involving people to gain buy-in and commitment to implementation.

- ❑ People don't mind change – they don't like being changed, and they fear not being in control. The key is to involve people to the greatest degree possible in strategizing how to deal with the change.

- ❑ People also fear the unknown, so remove the mystery by communicating as openly and consistently as possible to help people "feel in the know." People don't like surprises! Give information consistently, but be slow and easy. Beware of too much, too fast, and avoid "change shock."

- ❑ As clearly as possible, provide a vision of the future of an appealing and realistic state and what it will mean to them.

- ❑ Be realistic without making the past overly negative. People fear ridicule of past behaviour or performance. Avoid making them feel wrong or inadequate. The new managers who take over and proclaim that they have to "make a lot of changes around here" send a very destructive message. Instead, it is best to talk about future opportunities for improvement.

- ❑ People fear looking dumb when they don't know how to do something. Assure them that full and effective training will be provided to help them learn to make the change.

❑ People don't like the disruption of change. Engage the group in planning how to minimize disturbance.

❑ When communicating, apply the "3 Tell" technique. Tell your people what you know, then tell your team what you don't know, then tell your team when you think you will find out. Most leaders tend to miss the second "tell," which is an essential one because if you don't tell your people what you don't know, the risk is they think you're holding out on them and it activates the rumour mill.

Removing the fear of change and overcoming resistance to the implementation of change initiatives is becoming increasingly central to the job of the leader. The only antidotes are constant communication and involvement.

Effective leaders motivate people, but highly effective leaders go further and unleash people's potential, creativity, talent, commitment and growth!

CONCLUSION

Here it comes, get ready to catch! The ball is in your court now. We covered a lot of ground, and hopefully you have been provoked to think in deep, meaningful ways and arrive at some significant conclusions about yourself, your career and your life.

I don't believe you become a leader by reading books or attending seminars on leadership any more then you become a car by standing in the garage. Leadership is about becoming the person you need to become. Obviously, I place great value on leadership books and seminars, as they can be catalytic; however, real leadership development is a lifelong journey that involves hard work, taking wise risks, suffering failures, and persisting through and learning from setbacks and difficulties.

It's not what you know that counts, but rather what you do with what you know. A wise person once said to learn something and not change your behaviour probably means you never really learned it in the first place. So now, the challenge to implement what you have learned is yours, and I wish you all the best in your leadership development journey.

INDEX

Emotional Intelligence Inventory

The validity of the inventory is a direct function of the degree of honesty with which the following questions are answered.
Please remember that it is for your use and benefit only.

Always True		**Sometimes True**		**Seldom True**
5	4	3	2	1

1. I understand accurately what my natural strengths and my weaknesses are   ____

2. I am aware of my moods and I understand *why* I am feeling or behaving in a certain way   ____

3. When caught in a traffic jam or late for important meeting, I can control my anxiety and stay calm   ____

4. I do not procrastinate on important projects   ____

5. When I make a commitment to myself or to others, I keep it   ____

6. I am a self-starter   ____

7. My moods are predominantly positive and I am generally happy   ____

8. I am a hard worker and I feel that the contributions I am making are significant ____

9. I am patient with other people (including family members) ____

10. I am capable of accepting critical feedback without getting defensive ____

11. I do not worry or get anxious about things I cannot control ____

12. I am not a perfectionist on things that don't really count ____

13. When I look back on my major life decisions, I feel good about them ____

14. I am more of a realist than a pessimist or an optimist ____

15. When I get angry, I am able to cool down quickly ____

16. I am genuinely happy when friends and family experience success ____

17. My friends and associates would consider me to be a good listener ____

18. I say what is on my mind at the appropriate time ____

19. When I do speak my mind, I do it in a firm yet diplomatic manner ____

20. I have demonstrated the ability to work well with others in the long term ____

Total ____

Scoring Guide
80+ – Excellent (or Delusional)
60+ – Above Average
40+ – Honest and OK
20+ – Need Help

ACKNOWLEDGEMENTS

I could have never accomplished what I have without my beautiful, wise, supportive and patient wife, Pamela. Passion is a great thing, and as my persevering wife said for the first few years of my new endeavour, "so is cash flow." She was using the expression "show me the money" long before the movie *Jerry Maguire* was ever released.

Raising my family and being a parent to my three wonderful children, Rebecca, Tim and Jeff, has been the greatest leadership challenge and thus developmental opportunity. I am incredibly proud of all three of them, and I will admit that most of the credit goes to their mother.

I want to thank my faithful and talented associates who supported me throughout the years – Susan Williams, Laurie Daschuck and now my daughter-in-law Stacy Campeau.

I owe a special thanks to the British Colombia Institute of Technology because becoming an instructor at BCIT in 1993 was a critical success step, as teaching at such a highly regarded educational institution provided me with instant credibility with my prospective clients. More importantly, I was provided with the opportunity to teach numerous different courses, which deepened my knowledge and sharpened my facilitation skills.

It quickly became evident early in my training career that, before I could add value to my students, I had to first add value to myself, for the simple reason that you can't pour water from empty glass. So, in 1991, I became a very serious student and remain one today. Many different authors have had a big impact on me. The most enlightening and influential were Stephen Covey, Peter Drucker, Abraham Maslow and Jim Rohn.

I am very grateful for two clients in particular, as I have facilitated professional-development programs for both the CPAs (certified professional accountants) and the professional engineers for well over twenty-five years now. My greatest fulfillment comes from teaching technically minded people leadership skills. A further benefit was that I always believed that, if my material could pass the logic test of accountants and engineers, it gave me confidence in its validity and practicality.

For More Information Regarding Our Services

Greg and his staff travel to deliver keynote speeches and workshops on the following topics:

- Leading from Everywhere
- Leading People to Peak Performance
- Leading a High-Performance Organization or Team
- Time Management for 21st Century Professionals
- Becoming a Highly Effective Negotiator
- Creating Constructive Critical Conversations
- Emotional Intelligence: The Myths and the Mastery

For more information and additional resources, please check our website at www.campeaulearning.com or call us at (604) 944-0642.

Book Purchases – We offer significant discounts on bulk book purchases of ten or more books. Contact us for the full discount schedule.